into what it means to fight for your children and for yourself, while powerfully validating experiences too often endured in silence."

—**Parijat Deshpande,**
author of *Pregnancy Brain* and founder of Ruvelle

"Mudrick's journey through conception, pregnancy, birth, loss, and beyond reads like tea with a friend. Those of us who know the same peril and longing will see echoes of their own experiences, and feel the encouragement women offer to one another to mend, love, and find light in whatever way we can."

—**Kate Inglis, author of *Notes for the Everlost***

I0418345

Praise for BLUE HOUR HOMECOMING

"I'm not being hyperbolic when I say that there is a passage in this memoir that changed my view of everything: life, its meaning, and how I think about love. Alle Mudrick has articulated emotions I've been unable to put words to for myself, and she's done it in a way that left me feeling bigger and more alive when I put the book down. This true story of unbearable loss brims with hope. I want to give it to every mother I know."

—**Mary Adkins, author of** ***You Might Feel a Little Pressure***

"The glory and rawness of this book shocked and held me. *Blue Hour Homecoming* is a gorgeous, technicolor, lyrical journey through loss, longing, and the hidden spaces of life. With tender yet unflinching prose, Mudrick explores the delicate balance between fertility and identity, finding meaning in the margins. This collection invites readers into the quiet, overlooked corners of the body and soul, offering a poignant meditation on how home can be found in the unexpected. This book is poetry in motion."

—**Mira Ptacin, author of** ***Poor Your Soul***

"In this chronicle of one woman's journey to motherhood outside the womb, Mudrick has gifted us with the spectrum of existence: this is a story of life, death, and the particular human condition that is surviving both at the same time. Raw, courageous, feminist, and feisty, this memoir is a must-read for everyone who mothers."

—**Courtney Maum, author of** ***The Year of the Horses***

"This book is a must-read for anyone who has been through loss. With the intimacy and candidness of a good friend, Alle Mudrick turns grief inside out and bares all of its truth: its enormity, its devastation, but also its capacity for light and growth. You will feel yourself right alongside Mudrick on her journey through life after loss—unwittingly caring for your own wounds along the way."

—**Annie Sklaver Orenstein, author of** ***Always a Sibling***

"*Blue Hour Homecoming* is a memoir that lays bare the realities of grief—the way it swells and recedes and swells. Mudrick invites the reader into her story with incredible vulnerability and masterful tenderness. In her own words, she shows us the infinitely complex experience of 'loving and hurting with abandon,' and through elegant prose illustrates the clarity of memory cemented by trauma and loss—how our most painful memories often live most vividly in our minds."

**—Brittany Means,
author of *Hell If We Don't Change Our Ways***

"A beautiful, breathless read. A wise and luminous meditation on womanhood, *Blue Hour Homecoming* offers up the surprising generosity of heartbreak—the way it carves space for transformation and resilience. A powerhouse-read for anyone who has faced the fragility of reproduction, wrestled with the ache of absence, or understood what it means to carry both life and grief in the same breath."

—Joselin Linder, author of *The Family Gene*

"'These conversations save lives,' Alle Mudrick writes when she finds the words to tell her story to a co-worker who shares a similar tale of loss and hardship. And so they do, in this brave, honest and generous memoir. *Blue Hour Homecoming* is the kind of book that helps you know you are not alone, and that any kind of loss and love you have ever felt as a woman or mother is one you have shared with a legion of others. Mudrick's essential gift is to hold your hand while she tells not only her story but yours. Her words will heal long after the reading is done."

—Vicki Forman, author of *This Lovely Life*

"A breathtaking, beautifully impressionistic narrative of the deepest love, and what it takes to birth yourself as a mother."

—Sarah DiGregorio, author of *Early*

"*Blue Hour Homecoming* is a gripping, realistic, and unflinchingly raw exploration of grief, life, trauma, and hope. Mudrick unveils the stark realities of living through loss, high-risk pregnancies, prematurity, and the complexities of preemie parenting—offering an honoring glimpse

Alle Mudrick

BLUE HOUR HOMECOMING

Finding Life on the Fringes of Reproduction

 THIRD RAIL PRESS

BLUE HOUR HOMECOMING: FINDING LIFE ON THE FRINGES OF
REPRODUCTION

Published by:
THIRD RAIL PRESS LLC
P.O. Box 20285
Albuquerque, NM 87154
www.thirdrailpress.org

Paperback ISBN: 979-8-9912123-0-4
Ebook ISBN: 979-8-9912123-1-1

Cover Design: Jessica Bell Design

Printed in the United States of America

For my three children, my greatest teachers—
I love you to the end of the stars.

Author's Note

This story contains the private and sensitive information of many people's lives; to protect their identities, all names have been changed, except for Sloane and Leo. In one instance, other identifying information that did not materially affect the story was also changed. Conversations with research participants have been altered to maintain the integrity of the personal impact of such exchanges without revealing any insights of the research.

I have also elected to break from standard number formatting when reporting gestational age by always using numerals (e.g., 6 weeks, 22 weeks 3 days, etc.), as this vernacular always seemed, to me at least, like its own particular language, worth breaking rules and being honored. And because, as my husband pointed out, it just hits harder.

Part One

1

ater, an attending physician would explain it this way: Respiratory distress is like drowning. As the body struggles for breath, it tires, and if it works too hard for too long, and too and too and too beyond ability or reason or strength of heart, it gets too tired to keep going. Then it just stops. Respiratory failure. Drowning. Like in the ocean, in a lake, but on land, in the middle of nothing but your very own life.

My daughter could talk without talking. In a dark room humming with automation—beeps, whirrs, drips, and from the ceiling corner, a single, buzzing light that threw her towhead into sharp relief—her blue-gray eyes called out to me through the plastic slats of her hospital crib. Lying still on her belly, one plump cheek smashed into the mattress, they called louder and louder, but my ears only pounded. She was not yet two. Black pressed in through the windows.

I tried, without vigor, to unhear everything. My body sat limp in a heavy armchair that could unfold into a bed of sorts, cushions thick and pleathery. If I could have lifted my arms, I would have wiped at my face, hot and muggy from my breath behind my mask; instead, I stared back at my daughter and caught the edges of other things: behind her crib, a blocky gray highchair; on the floor, my blue Vans; on the wall opposite me, a small square canvas, in shadow. It was a store-bought painting, like you see in every doctor's office, except this was the pediatric intensive care unit and our fifth night here and the painting was of a pink feather, with the word *dream* in italicized gold letters, all lowercase, off to the side.

I longed to hold her. To let her close those eyes against my chest and feel her soft legs, her small back, beneath my palms, the measured rush of breath through a tube into her nose close to my bent ear. Always, always longing to be in a hospital room, holding my daughter.

But my muscles were stiff and leaden. Sunken.

And really, I was nowhere to be found.

This was supposed to be over.

2

For a long time, I didn't realize how different the dark of night is from the dark of morning—that one depressed me and one electrified me, even though they looked the same. Sometimes I wonder, if I were dropped into darkness, would I know what time it was, just based on how my body felt?

Maybe now, but not back then.

Five years before that night in the hospital, the sun hung deep below the Sandia Mountains on the eastern edge of Albuquerque. The cerulean sky, thick as paint, cast everything blue—big white tent stalls, stretches of native grass, skin on cold cheeks. It was six a.m., that hour before dawn when the honest-to-God temperature of the atmosphere makes everything good seem so possible, makes me feel so alive that I question the need for the sun, and I stood on a dry field, my hands, chilled at the knuckles but warm in the palms, clasped around a foil-wrapped burrito. Mine with bacon and red chile, my husband, Dale's, with sausage and green; both with fluffy eggs and soft potatoes. We stood side by side, watching, and my heart swelled; whoever decided to do all of this—wrap up breakfast in a tortilla, lift hundreds of hot air balloons into the sky at dawn—was a goddamn genius.

It was October 2015 and our first time to the Albuquerque International Balloon Fiesta. We had awoken at four, dressed in hats and scarves, and stood in a long snaking line in the mall parking lot for a school bus to take us to the fiesta grounds. In the nine months we had lived in Albuquerque, we had heard all about the city's marquee event, but what we would soon learn was that it's nearly impossible to imagine the enormity of such an experience without being there yourself. The mass ascension, when hundreds of hot air balloons take to the sky at once, wouldn't happen for another hour, but the field was already crawling. In the dark blue air, a hundred thousand people young and old, home and visiting, were waking up, laying out falsa blankets, eating breakfast burritos, and drinking Piñon coffees, buzzing and forming and swallowing our state like it was energy, sustenance.

I bit the hell out of that morning magic.

"Let's walk around," I said, balling up my empty foil wrapper and pulling Dale's arm.

The field was open. That is, everything was right up against us: crews hopping out of truck beds, balloon envelopes unfurling over the grass, woven baskets, charming and larger-than-life, waiting patiently to be lifted into the sky by nothing but air and heat, as if it were the simplest thing in the world to be carried on breath alone. We walked and watched the fiesta grounds unfold, and it all seemed... not impossible, but almost. Not the physics of it, but the magic.

By seven, the sky had faded from sea to lemon, and we had slowed to a stop, a gawk. In front of us, a crew had lit their burner, a shock of flame blowing hot air into the mouth of a flat balloon; in five-second bursts of propane, our cheeks flushed with heat. And then slowly, all around us, massive shapes came alive. Fifty-foot stretches of curved nylon rose out of the ground, each balloon a world in and of itself; it was like parachute day in elementary school gym class times ten. And then rows of them together—half-inflated, they lay on their sides and bumped up against each other, the floor of a bounce house. I felt myself receding, shrinking, wonderfully, down to seven, six, five years old because when else do we enjoy such unwieldy forces beneath us— water beds, trampolines, wave pools—but when we are young and most alive.

Before I knew it, I was bouncing from one cluster of balloons to the next, Dale struggling to keep track of me. I had more inside me than I knew how to handle, my heart catching in my throat at the miracle of these balloons, the beauty of their growing bellies, close enough to touch. I snapped photo after photo, a dozen of the same view, and when I paused, I watched and envied those climbing into the baskets. The pilots, the passengers—how their stomachs would soon rise and sway with them over the Rio Grande valley, taking land and sky into their mouths together, at once, the whole world.

"Would you ever go up in one?" I asked Dale when we found each other again, breathless.

"Hell yeah," he said.

"I bet it's a lot scarier than it looks." I thought of shifts in the wind rocking the basket, but how not being strapped in also meant being free. I slid an arm around Dale's waist, his brown jacket thick and soft in the morning chill, and squeezed him close. "But also exhilarating."

A handful went up first, the crowd cheering. Then a dozen, with applause, and within minutes, hundreds, with whoops and whistles and fists punched into the air. The balloons took every shape, color, and pattern: some striped, some checkered, some ombre from top to bottom; others a full rainbow with panels in every gradient; and still others giant penguins, teddy bears, Darth Vader, and Yoda. They rose to varying altitudes, caught different currents, floating and spreading and covering the sky—a constantly shifting mosaic. I spun in 360-degree circles, face tilted upward, every angle, every second of shift, an entirely new view shattering something—everything—inside me.

"This is fucking incredible!" I shouted to Dale, spinning, laughing, glittering inside. "I've never seen anything like it."

It wasn't just for the eyes—this sky full of toys, above what was already a rich and layered cake of desert, river, forest, and mountain—but the ears, too: music and laughter, cheers and hollers. And then something more, for the soul, the unmistakable energy of a feeling long forgotten: that this was the stuff that dreams were made of.

Not grown-up dreams, but kid dreams—real dreams.

Made of joy, love, wonder, amazement.

I had had kid dreams once. *Be an author and live in Paris with my boyfriend*, I had said when I was six, sitting at the kitchen table over a plate of tuna casserole, and my parents had asked what I wanted to do with my life, as if I actually had a choice. What a cruel joke that was. I don't know where Paris came from, or the boyfriend either; I think I just meant somewhere far from there with someone who loved me. But writing was the dream I knew. And soon after, I knew I wanted to be a mom, too.

I didn't know it was possible to return there, to that original magic of life. And yet, there I was, arriving right inside of it, on an open field in central New Mexico, a hunger for life tugging in my belly, pulling from the haunting feeling that I hadn't really lived yet.

Dale and I had just decided that we would start trying for a baby after another year. We had always talked about having a big family—four kids, at least, and a dog—but I wanted more pure wedded bliss first: evenings riding our bikes to breweries downtown, weekends backpacking into the wilderness. I had all but stopped writing by that point in my life, feeling confused and conflicted about how something so necessary but so solitary felt like stealing from our time together. But it was okay, I had told myself. I was in love; I was doing love. And besides, it had always been harder for me to write when I was happy.

Later, Dale said that if he had known everything we would have to go through to have a family, he would have wanted to start earlier. I maintain that I wouldn't, that we needed that time, just us as a couple.

Or maybe it was just me who needed it. Because that entire next year seemed to take something with it from that balloon-filled sky—some lingering scent of unfettered joy, of everything good seeming so possible. I read somewhere that something like 90% of happiness is anticipation, and in that year between our first Balloon Fiesta and when we started trying for a family, I felt that hope surging in my veins.

There is a trope in the healing world that we're always thinking we have arrived. That we have finally reached the place—the revelation, the release—where the hurt ends and we can begin anew. I hadn't realized it at Balloon Fiesta, but I had known that dark morning hour before, and the otherworldliness it can bring, from the first time I felt I had arrived in life.

When I had turned sixteen, I had driven around Orange County, California with my mom, collecting paper applications from anyone who was hiring, and within a week, I had two part-time jobs—one at a grocery store, one at Chuck E. Cheese's—and a two-year-long habit of lying to my high school guidance counselor about how much I was working at each in order to get my work permits. Every time, she glared at me over her small rectangular glasses, her lips set in a thin line, but I wouldn't have even known how to articulate the real answer: *I work as much as I can, so that I have to be home as little as possible.*

What I knew instead was that a perfect Saturday was bagging groceries from six a.m. to three p.m., and then ringing up pizzas from four p.m. to closing. And on Sunday, hosting a string of birthday parties, sweat caking my back under my red polo uniform as I lit candles for kids to make wishes on their own arrivals, their own dreams. Because at work, I was *doing* things. I was productive, engaged, a part of something. Even when I fell asleep in calculus and skipped my AP English assignments, even when I only saw my parents in passing, I pressed on; work was where I came alive.

Walking around the fiesta grounds in the blue morning had awakened something in my body. The feel of driving to the grocery store for those morning shifts, only me and Death Cab for Cutie coursing through the empty streets, only me and one checker opening up to conversations more intimate than usual. A time that I constantly longed for: half of my daydreams with me in black Dickies and an olive green button-down, driving in the dark, and free.

Because the truth is, there is no arrival.

Only beginning again and again.

Being pregnant for the first time felt like an arrival, even though that arrival was quiet, simple, sweet. For the first few months in the fall of 2016, every little dream within the bigger dream was sacred to me: the two pink lines, the cravings of bagels and cream cheese. The ultrasound printouts that I used as bookmarks.

That innocence still stabs at me.

Even our announcements were subtle. Dale and I—and by that time, we had gotten a dog, Leo—took a photo in the *bosque* along the Rio Grande, sitting in crunchy leaves, with the caption, *Excited to be a family of four!* On a trip to my old office in Los Angeles, I slid a flat pink box onto the kitchen counter and sent out a company-wide email: *Because the baby is craving donuts!* I wasn't one to cause a scene—and besides, everyone who was anyone already knew how much this meant to me. Whenever a co-worker had announced her news in the past, I was always the loudest squealer, the puppy with paws perched on her lap. Mama, mama, let me be near you; let me be a part of this miracle.

When that drive—wanting a little version of me to love—began thrumming when I was eight, nine, ten, I had already picked out her name, already saw her with my thin, blonde hair and big blue eyes, already knew she would be made of sugar and spice and everything love. I already wanted to give her the world—already knew I would.

Most everyone else knew, too. A year earlier, my co-worker Taj and I were in Philadelphia for work when he finally decided to get his first tattoo. I already had seven or eight by that time and for years had been telling Taj I would be there for his first. In a small shop downtown, he got a compass on the inside of his forearm, dotted with three sets of coordinates for where he adopted his children from, and I got a quote from a Postal Service song, in typewriter font, across my lower back. Buzzing with adrenaline at eleven o'clock at night, we ate cheesesteaks bigger than our faces, and then back at the hotel, things quieted and tenderized, as middle-of-the-night caretaking often does. I held his arm in my hand and bathed it in warm, soapy water, gently pressed a towel into his brown skin, leaving it moist. Soft dabs of thick, clear ointment, smoothed out to the edges.

"You're going to be such a good mom," he said.

Only my parents couldn't see it. They were happy for me, but that wasn't the same as loving me; I had learned that much.

"I can't imagine you with a girl—another little girl just as intense as you," my mom said.

And my dad: "I can't wait until she's older and gives you hell."

We didn't even know if the baby was a girl and already people had ideas about her. Already she was being told to be quiet, simple, sweet.

But Dale and I had our own ideas, like we had our own life here in New Mexico. I had bought a stack of patterns to sew the baby animal-print bibs and fluffy sleep sacks. We liked gender-neutral onesies and backpack-style diaper bags. We would cloth diaper—absolutely. And we would start looking for a four-bedroom house in the neighborhoods with the best schools.

The life we had dreamed of together was happening. Day by day, the pieces lined up—items added to the registry, appointments set up with the realtor—until there were no more days on the calendar before my 20-week anatomy scan in early January 2017 and I woke up with the sun shining inside my chest.

The dream, the dream—it was a living thing.

Four hours later, I sat on the end of an exam table, not knowing what to think, or what had even just happened. It seemed I had just been lying down on the ultrasound exam chair, holding Dale's hand, fizzing inside from the news that our baby was, indeed, a girl, and having the briefest moment of living a dream—my belly pulled out to sail, smooth, riding on the wind—when the ultrasound tech, a nice woman, said she would be right back, and we were shuffled to this exam room, where my midwife flew in, saying, "You only have five millimeters of cervix left," and flew back out. Everything seemed like a whisper of something larger.

I realized I didn't understand what she had said. I was twenty-eight and pregnant for the first time and didn't know what a cervix was, much less how long it was supposed to be. A familiar but vaguely-formed question flickered through me—something about whether this made me more or less of a woman. Was I supposed to know this about my body, or was this how much I trusted it to function as it should? Or maybe the truest answer, which was that no one had really ever educated me about my body, and what I knew I had discovered myself. In middle school, I had spent afternoons on the toilet, paper diagrams unfolded on the tile floor before me, poking a tampon around to see where it fit. In high school, my dad had sat with me in the doctor's office to get a prescription for birth control; my mother was so disappointed in me losing my virginity that she had removed herself from the situation entirely. And now, even with two older sisters who had seven kids between them, me and my body were still on our own.

I was already learning how much I didn't know. Months earlier, after my first ultrasound, my midwife had asked me if I had ever been told anything about my uterus. Other than consistently abnormal pap smears that both my parents and our family doctor brushed off in my teens, no, I didn't know anything about my insides down there. With a pen, she had drawn seven or eight little pictures on her notepad, all vaguely resembling a Texas longhorn.

"There are all different shapes of uteruses," she said. "Some are like this, some are more like that. Some women have two uteruses. Some have two vaginas. You have what's called a septate uterus."

She explained that I had a septum running down the middle of my longhorn, nearly cutting it in half. She went on to say that this normally isn't a problem—that the septum sort of just moves out of the way as the baby grows—and we would monitor it.

Now there was the cervix.

The midwife flew back in. "I got you an appointment at High Desert Perinatal for this afternoon. Can you make that?"

I said yes, and she paused, eyes on mine. She tilted her head. Her gaze felt expectant—of what I didn't know. I was suddenly aware that I still looked like I was fifteen—a grey crewneck sweatshirt, torn skinny jeans, my blue Vans; a messy bun and strange ear piercings. I had actually taken a photo of myself in the mirror that morning, to show a friend that I was wearing the sweatshirt she gave me, with *Mommy* lettered across the front, and I almost didn't believe the photo when I saw it; I couldn't actually be that beautiful. My skin, my smile, all the way to my ears: I had vigor and shine. *A mother's glow*, I had thought.

It was more than happiness; it was meaning, purpose.

"Ok, I'll go let them know," she said and left.

I looked at Dale, his clean-shaven face, head of shaggy blond hair. I thought about how he had already been telling dad jokes, like *Watch out, there are snakes here!* when we drove through the mountains and saw winding road signs. I thought about how he would be such a good girl-dad—how he would make her laugh, teach her how to bat left-handed—and it dawned on me: Something was really wrong here. Hot tears sprung to my eyes; my face felt flush.

When the midwife came back in, she said, "Ah, there it is," and rubbed my thigh.

My belly, where my daughter swam, flooded with acid. I felt naked and pathetic.

"I don't understand what's going on here," I heard myself say.

"It looks like you have what we call an incompetent cervix," she said, "where your cervix starts to weaken, or open—starts to give birth—earlier than it's supposed to."

As we drove home, I retreated. Quiet on the outside and loud on the inside, I ran back and forth in my body—up to the attic, down to the basement—desperately grabbing my belongings as the whole house burned down, all the while through the windshield appearing absolutely deadpan. As Dale turned into the driveway of the townhouse we were renting, I burst.

"What if I can't have kids!" I shouted. The question went off like a gunshot in the silence, the recoil leaving me panting. In my head, I followed the wisp of gun smoke:

What would that do to Dale... to us...

To me.

The car slowed to a stop. Time slid backward. We were seven years younger, he and I, driving to campus from his apartment on a winter morning. The ground was covered in snow, throwing the darkened buildings and trees into icy blue relief, and as we drove down Douglas, an empty two-lane road on the northern edge of campus, the wheels of his old Honda began to drift toward the right shoulder. Even at the dumb age of twenty-one, with all the other dumb things we did, Dale always drove with two hands on the wheel; me, only my left, with my right elbow leaning on the center console. He also grew up in Maryland—me in California—so he knew how to do this kind of stuff. But we were sliding—slowly, gracefully, almost imperceptibly, and yet, sliding all the same, sideways and around and back through time and space and other planes. The beats had been long but quiet. Everything weightless.

"Whoa," Dale had breathed when we stopped, backed up against a snowbank on the left shoulder. I knew in that moment that I trusted him like I had never trusted anything before.

In our driveway in Albuquerque, he said something reassuring—I don't remember what. But he had the same look on his face as that winter morning long ago, staring out across the slippery road: *I don't know what the hell just happened, but we're ok; we will be ok.*

The air inside our townhouse seemed stale, the light cold. Everything was still right where we left it that morning—in what I would come to think of as the *before* times. My home office, quiet and unalive; my oatmeal pot soaking alone in the sink. It seemed that maybe if we did nothing at all—didn't make a sound or move a muscle—then none of this would be real. If we slid our feet over to the living room, let our thighs sink into the couch cushions, and passed the hours in silence, we could avoid slipping further into the grip of whatever this was; we could keep ourselves intact while we were still, seemingly, alive. It seemed worth a shot.

When we sat down, I pulled the front half of Leo, our black-and-white cattle dog, onto my lap and buried my face in the thick fur of his neck. We had adopted him a year before—the only dog not barking in the whole shelter. I had never had a dog before, but the love was instant and deep. On the couch, tears burned beneath my eyelids.

It seemed like this might be the time when other people would draw on something bigger than themselves. I had tried to believe in God when I was younger, tried to be good, tried to pray, lying in bed at night, eyes closed, my head on a flat pillow before an open window. Sometimes my mom had dragged me with her to the Catholic church across town; sometimes I had willingly tagged along to my best friend's Lutheran Sunday school. I liked the sound of it all—the booming sermons, the chorus of voices in the hymns—but it was the optics that disturbed me: how I was supposed to believe in something I couldn't see, just trust that the love was there when at every turn, God just felt like another parent to obey, fear, disappoint.

One time, on the phone with that friend—the Lutheran girl—I had told her I was scared to ask my parents if she could come over.

"The worst they can say is no," she had said.

I got quiet, the line humming. We clearly lived different lives.

At age twelve, I had marched into my parents' room while they watched TV and declared myself an atheist. On my own in this world. Solitude, and the cool night breeze, my only salvation. I didn't have something bigger.

Dale grabbed my phone to take a photo: Leo and mama. I started to protest that this was not the time but stopped. I recognized a quiet but urgent need to document every moment I could; not knowing where we were headed or how we would get there, I wanted a record of the journey. I hugged Leo to my chest, pressed my lips into the back of his neck, and looked up.

I only recall fragments of our first visit to High Desert Perinatal, the high-risk pregnancy doctors, that afternoon, but Dr. Jeffrey I can see with perfect clarity. He looked like a younger, rawer Santa Claus—full face, beard, and thick, wiry eyebrows, all reddish brown—and although his demeanor was frank and detached, I felt a kindness underneath. Over the years, that inner light would push outward, causing cracks in the shell of his scrubs where it would pierce through and warm me. Dr. Jeffrey was a gift himself.

Dale and I sat in an ultrasound room, lights on. Dr. Jeffrey watched the screen as the technician moved the wand over my belly that had only begun to round a few weeks before. The exam was brief. I didn't know then that what Dr. Jeffrey did next was his signature look; all I saw when he finally turned toward me were wide eyes and raised eyebrows.

"Well," he said, "the prognosis is terrible."

He kept talking while I stayed stuck on that first sentence. The bluntness of it—swift, hard, but nothing if not honest—and something about that word *terrible*: that he was assigning judgment to this whole thing, and I knew where he stood; he, the expert, the objective third-party, agreed this was *terrible*. Humanity wrapped in candor was this awful, awful statement—a quality I would cling to on this journey.

"I'm going to do a digital exam," he said. With his fingers, he meant.

And afterward: "Your cervix is still closed, for now. I won't do a cerclage—too risky. Let's get you started on progesterone and take it easy with activity. We'll see you back here in two weeks."

3

I don't think I ever knew how much we play a role in our own lives until I had to start making life-or-death decisions. It wouldn't have looked like that from the outside—that previously, and even for a long time after, I felt like I was just whipped about by life—but sitting with Dale on our living room couch the day after our lives ruptured, it was clear that I was going to have to get intentional.

"Dr. Jeffrey just said, 'take it easy,'" I said. "But everyone I've come across has talked about bedrest. Like, twenty-four-seven sitting or lying down. Some women won't even sit."

I was talking about the women in the incompetent cervix forums that I had been scouring for the past twenty-four hours, doing my own version of not moving. They all seemed to be on some form of bedrest—using a common language of *strict, moderate, light*—even though, from the rest of the internet, the research on it was split; some academics and practitioners supported the idea that bedrest relieved pressure put on the cervix by gravity, while others said it was ineffective and could cause more harm, like blood clots and depression. And then there were the ethics of it.

"What if by being on bedrest," I posed to Dale, "I'm just prolonging the pregnancy to the point of survival, but then she ends up sick? What if I'm giving her life, but a horrible one? A *terrible* one?"

I worked in research. I was skilled at gathering information to make informed, if not inspired, decisions, so I had sought the kind of information that made sense to me: data, to understand the parameters of the situation, and stories, for color.

Turns out the cervix is the passageway that connects the uterus to the vagina—part of the birth canal. The data said that 1 out of 100 women has cervical insufficiency, also called a weak cervix or an incompetent cervix, and it's typically addressed with a cerclage (sir-klah-soft g), or a stitch sewn into the cervix to hold it closed. A baby was considered viable—able to survive outside the womb—at 24 weeks' gestation; birth from 24 to 28 weeks held a high likelihood of long-term complications, from cerebral palsy to chronic lung disease.

The stories said that a woman could learn she has an incompetent cervix, be dilated to three centimeters, lay in bed for eighteen weeks, and deliver a full-term baby. They said that a woman could have bulging membranes, get an emergency cerclage, lay in bed for four weeks, and deliver a viable baby. Both the data and the stories said that positive outcomes were possible. But they also said that, for most women with cervical insufficiency, the typical path was to lose their first child and then go on to have a successful pregnancy with a planned cerclage.

In my work, data and stories gave me insights. Now, in my personal life, all of this information felt almost useless. The only insight was that absolutely anything could happen.

And if anything, I think that's what was most overwhelming: that the spectrum of possibilities was nearly infinite, and it felt like each slice of that continuum needed its own consideration. I was only 20 weeks 3 days along at my anatomy scan; that meant nearly another four full weeks before we even reached viability, and after that another four weeks of who the fuck knows what.

"I don't know, babe," said Dale. "I just don't know."

He was an engineer. And an atheist.

"The only thing I keep coming back to," I said, a weight dropping into my belly, just above where my daughter lay, "is knowing that we will have to live with whatever decision we make. Forever, regardless of outcome. And for me, that means moving as little as possible."

Dale stared at the floor. Then he exhaled, clutched my knee in his hand, and said, "Yeah—yeah, I'm with you."

•

Bedrest was hard. But what strikes me now is that it was also nothing, although I would never say that had our journey not unfolded the way it did—perspective is a minx—because in that soft beginning, I had hope. I had optimism. I didn't fully know fear yet, hadn't felt its hot breath on my neck, its talons on my heels. Even though my life from this point forward hinged completely on my faulty cervix, I was still, at this time, tipped back toward innocence.

What I knew during this time was the couch. Thin-ribbed corduroy in royal purple, we had gotten it reupholstered from the faded red and blue plaid that it was when Dale had it in grad school; we had made it ours, and now it was mine. It felt like my boat, sitting in the middle of the living room, my floating vessel, carrying me through each day: breakfast, work, lunch, work, dinner, work, until I crawled up the stairs and into bed. The couch was comfortable; the couch was livable. I could do this. I would do this.

That's more or less the only way I knew how to go about life: a bullheaded pursuit up the mountain. No rabbit trails, no rest—just the march. It started when I was a kid, always wanting to be older than I really was. I was the eight-year-old watching *Beverly Hills 90210*, the twelve-year-old reading Leon Uris's *QBVII*. Through a constant refrain, my dad had convinced me that whatever age I was wasn't enough— "You're only six; you don't know anything"—so I thought if I could just keep my nose to the ground and spin the earth faster, one day I would get there, to *enough*. But by the end of sixth grade, I hungered for high school; halfway through, I was ready for college. And once I was there—at the University of Notre Dame, halfway across the country from everything—that was where I wanted to be.

Free.

A Catholic university is a strange choice for an atheist, I know. But by that point, I had softened to being agnostic, unable to say with certainty what was anything, and anyway, I had grown up in Notre Dame sweatsuits, shouting *Go Irish* at the TV. My dad was an alum, but when he took me there for a visit and my feet stepped onto its grounds, it became wholly mine. That campus had a magic growing beneath it—

a sense of belonging that I had never felt, an embrace I didn't know I needed, and that I wouldn't feel again until we moved to New Mexico.

I was a hungry college student. I ate up the lectures, the textbooks, the professors; the dorms, the parties, the football. That place loved me, and I loved it back, running miles around its lakes, combing the fourteen floors of its library, talking to the yellow bricks of its buildings. They were of this land, too—dug up from the dirt at the bottom of the lakes. Me and them: We were the same.

By senior year, as a business major—because "an English major was going to get me waiting tables," my dad had advised, or threatened, or shamed—the fall career fair was not a goalpost I was interested in. Still, I had worn a brown pantsuit with short, stupid ruffled sleeves, and my dyed black hair, fading to blonde at the roots, pulled into a pomp at the front. I hugged a black pleather portfolio to my chest, the copies of my resume inside still living in high school, highlighting my SAT score (1480) and my part-time jobs (the grocery store and Chuck E.'s, then eventually Vans, too) and no clear aim.

What had I actually done in college? I had lived in Austria for a year. I had studied philosophy and economics and statistics. I had written a ten-page paper in German on the financial crisis of 2008, as it was unfolding; I had given an oral analysis of my favorite painting, Edvard Munch's *The Scream*, my heart pounding in my ears; I had learned how to like beer and roll my own cigarettes. I had done drugs. I had fallen in love. I had had the time of my life. And yet somehow, the guidance was that none of this actually mattered for what was supposed to come next: the real world.

Because the *real world*, it seemed, was breakfast cereal. And toilet paper. And yogurt that you squeeze out of a tube. All the consumer packaged goods behemoths had a folding table set up at the career fair—rows and rows and rows of them filling up the basketball arena—with poster boards of brand logos propped up on easels in front of them, each one leading to a long line of college seniors in business formal attire and shit-eating grin demeanor, resumes in hand.

I stepped into one line. My stomach lurched. I stepped out, walked down a long row of tables, and left the arena. Me and them: We were not the same.

It's not that I wasn't ready to leave; it's just that my dogged pursuit of achievement was nearing an intersection, and I had been on my own for far too long to ask for directions. What I knew at the time was that I didn't give a shit about helping companies make more money. I didn't care about brands; I cared about people. I was only a business major because I didn't have any balls. I didn't know enough about the world to know that my dreams were worth caring about, and I didn't know enough to know that I was worth caring about.

The following semester, the last one of my undergrad, one of my professors would rub up against this idea with a brazenness that caught me. He taught a marketing course that emphasized the academic path; twenty or so of us seniors had been hand-picked by the faculty to be in it. We sat in a semicircle of desks around the lecture podium, where he sat and doodled while he taught, looking down through his rimless glasses. Said it helped him think.

One day he sat quietly, looking at us. Then, he said, "There's something peculiar about Notre Dame students. Everyone sits in his or her seat during class, not raising their hand, not saying much at all. And then they turn in their papers, and they're brilliant. You are all wearing masks."

No one said a word. He smiled. I don't think any of us really knew it until that moment, but I suspect—maybe for the first time that day, and maybe only somewhere deep, deep inside—we eventually all came to know what he said as the truth. A hundred times I had sat in my seat—in the back row, if I could, so that I could see everyone—thinking I had something insightful to say, rehearsing it in my head, only to let the moment pass for fear my voice might shake and catch and everyone would hear it. The problem, at least for me, was that we thought this was just *who we were*: perfectionists, in fear of falter, of failure. Better to keep your hand unraised, your mouth shut, your head down. Play it safe. The business degree. General Mills. Cheerios.

"Take off your masks," he had said.

My dad has this saying whenever I'm taking too long to do something: "What are ya waitin' for?" he says. "An invitation?"

When my professor implored us that day, I had never heard such a sincere invitation to be vulnerable, to be human, to let go. Had never heard such an invitation at all. So often, I think, that's what we're waiting for: permission. Many of us, all our lives.

Instead of heading out into the *real world*, I applied to the MBA program at Notre Dame and got in; in a year, I had another business degree, this time a master's in finance. What I thought I was pursuing is beyond me. Still that relentless mountain, I guess, of trying to get somewhere, trying to be someone. Old enough, smart enough, accomplished enough to matter.

But then I actually *did* start to get somewhere, and it quietly began to terrify me.

After finally—sadly, reluctantly—leaving Notre Dame, I got a job in consumer market research in Los Angeles and fell in love with it instantly. I had the same hunger I had in college: I ate up the data tables, the interviews, the business problems; the analytics, the stories, the reports. And the people—oh, the people! Thrift store shoppers and small pet owners; basketball fans and boxed meal cooks; sneakerheads and foodies. That's really what the job was all about—studying people, their needs, their values—and then delivering those insights to our clients, those same Fortune 500 companies that I had walked away from at the career fair, not to help them sell more crap, but to—hopefully—help them give people what they really want. I was in it for the people, and I was in it hard: clamoring for more work, putting in long hours, advancing quickly.

Thriving at work so that I didn't have to be anywhere else.

At the same time, Dale was nearing the end of his PhD in materials science down in Florida. The plan was that we would get married and move to wherever he got a job as an engineer; I was stable enough in my job that I could transition to working from home wherever that was. And as the pieces fell into place—we got married on a perfectly temperate Saturday in September and the following January moved to New Mexico—I saw all of these lines—our careers, our marriage, our savings account—rushing forward ahead of us with no sign of stopping but only accelerating into a house, children, advancement, wealth, success, happiness—life, life, capital-L *Life*. It was wonderful and exhilarating and terrifying. Because behind all of those dreams, a fear lay dormant: that one errant turn, one false move, and the whole thing would come crashing down. To remain the bull, pushing ever forward, was the way of life. The only way.

Soon after we moved to Albuquerque, I had woven all of those lines together into a timeline. Across a spread in my notebook, I had written a series of dates over several years—mile-markers—and beneath those, the estimated size of our bank account, as we saved. I had circled the number that I thought would give us enough for a down payment and drawn a little house next to it, and on the next line, at each of the mile-markers, I had written what age we would be, and below that, how long each of us would have been at our jobs. Below that, I noted when we would conceive each of our four children, when they would be born nine months later, and how old each of the living kids would be at that time.

There. I had needed to see it all laid out in front of me, in one picture. It was all right there, and if I could just build the right scaffolding—if I could place each element just *so*—this perfect life could be ours. I could get somewhere; I could be somebody.

One morning, I heard the doorknob click open in the latch on our bedroom door. I was still in bed, eyes closed, but awake. Only a few days into bedrest and I had already turned from an early bird into the slug that gets eaten.

I heard Dale before I saw him. Face red and wet, he crawled into bed, and I folded him into my arms.

"I'm just so scared for her," he said, his voice muffled on my chest.

"I know," I said, pressing my cheek into his hair, staring at the wall behind our bed. "Me too."

As we held each other, it felt as if we had been holding each other this way for years—tightly, without end, him leaning in, me steadfast. When we first met my freshman year at Notre Dame—his sophomore year—he was sort of dating one of my roommates. I say sort of because they had a thing, but it wasn't really going anywhere. So, we were friends for a while, and I never thought twice about it. But then suddenly, overnight, we were a thing, and that thing was the most genuinely, blissfully, deliriously in-love that I had ever been, or could ever hope to be. I'm not exaggerating. Dale awoke something inside me that I didn't know was asleep. Only we had to keep the whole thing a secret, because of my roommate. It was only for the last month of the school year, but to this day, I can't believe we actually did that.

We were young and dumb and in love.

In those early days, everything we did together was special. We holed up in the back of the stacks on the ninth or tenth floors of the library, studying over cans of Coke and taking breaks to make out in the empty stairwells. We drove to McDonald's and ate cheeseburgers in his car in the parking lot, swapping stories from our childhoods. He couldn't believe I had worked two jobs in high school and loved every minute; I, in turn, found it hilarious that he had enjoyed high school.

And then, as we got older, and no longer had to hide, we dreamt. We dreamt of being in the same place, not having to fly across the country just to see each other for a weekend, of getting married and having a family. We dreamt of doing anything together. Seeing the world. Picking out furniture. Buying pencils.

Anything, anything together. Even this.

Years later, on a drive through northern Arizona, Dale said he always loved the fields of saguaros because it looked like they were all waving him a friendly hello. I laughed harder than I had in a long time, and said, "I think they all look like middle fingers."

Dale had always been the more optimistic one between us—me more jaded, more cynical. Him patient and flexible; me anxious and unyielding. I pulled him together; he let me fall apart. But stress had been known to warp our tendencies. When we first moved to New Mexico, we had gotten lost on a hike in the San Mateo Wilderness; some key trail signage had gotten battered and scattered in a recent storm. Dale had panicked while I remained calm, finding a known landmark and moving toward it. *One bite at a time*, Dale always said, as his dad had coached him on how to eat an elephant.

But this time in our lives was maybe less about worldview and more about love. The fullness of it, the depth. There is something enviable about this time. Looking back on it, it feels precious, pure, like its own little gestational period—for the birth of what, I don't know.

The life that came after, I suppose.

•

One evening I laid on the couch in a weird state. To be fair, every minute of the prior ten days had been weird, but this was different—otherworldly, out-of-body, as if part of me had approached the edge of something and a fainter part of me had already stepped off it.

My head was unbearably heavy, lying on a thin pillow, my achy legs draped over Dale's lap. My dad sat in a tattered butterfly chair next to the couch, his hair as thin and faded as the chair's sun-dried fabric. He wore a bright green sweatshirt, *Notre Dame* embroidered across the chest in gold lettering. He had flown in from California to help out while I was on bedrest; my mom, the owner of her own small business, had to stay and work. *I can ship your dad out*, she always said, then and in the years that followed; she wanted to be asked, to be needed, and I wanted her there but didn't want to be rejected. So, my dad it was, and we were watching TV, or a movie—some strange form of togetherness, the three of us, just waiting. A tear rolled down each of my temples.

Dale looked over at me. He looked tired. He was tired. But with those tired eyes—and their creases that always crushed my stomach into glitter—he saw me in a way I didn't know I needed, and my entire world narrowed to only what was on that couch: me, my husband, and our unborn daughter.

"I don't know why I'm crying," I whispered. I didn't want my dad to hear. "I think I'm just scared for her."

I smoothed my hands over my belly.

Dale did the same. His hands—strong, masculine, clean—had always been my favorite. In college, when we would sneak away from our friends—down to dark, empty basements or through holes in fences—he would slide his hands up the length of my back, and I would melt in his soft grip, folding into his body. I thought about those hands holding his daughter, how safe he would seem to her.

Quickly, I drained. I was done. In the bathroom, I wiped before inserting my nightly progesterone suppository. The tissue was streaked with slimy light brown matter. I stared at it. Squinted. Brought it closer. Turned it to different angles. Threw it in the toilet and pushed a small, egg-shaped pill up toward my cervix.

●

The next morning, my dad ran out for donuts—a trademark errand of his. I ate two chocolate Long Johns and tried to enjoy them, tried to taste the love in their light, yeasty middles, but I was exhausted. To the bone. I buried myself in blankets.

When I awoke hours later, it was like the donuts never happened and the night never passed; I was back in the bathroom, the tissue now streaked in pink.

"Just get checked out," the nurse said when I called. "It might be nothing, but this way you can have peace of mind."

Advice that would become a way of life, advice that I would give to future pregnant women. They would protest: *But what if it's nothing, but what if this is normal, but I don't want to seem…*

"If you can't do it for yourself," I would say, "do it for your child. It's always worth it."

Dale and I left for the hospital.

We brought nothing.

We were just getting checked out.

4

I t's funny now to think of that drive to the hospital. Of all the time we would spend there over the next few years, that was the only time that we came to it from that direction, going north up I-25 from our townhouse near downtown, exit at Montaño/Montgomery. Every other time, we would just drive due west down Montgomery from our house in the foothills. Of all the things that I love about Albuquerque, that is one of my favorites: that it's built on a grid, with the same roads running east-west and north-south all the way through. No matter where you are, you can instantly orient yourself to everything else, and with the Sandias holding up the eastern edge of the city, it's almost impossible to get lost.

I'll never forget the first moment I saw her, heard her voice: Dr. Page. I was in triage, lying propped up in a bed, paper drape covering my legs, Dale in a chair beside me. When the door opened, she peeked her head in first, calling out in her sing-song voice.

"Helloooo," she said, first raising the *o* and then lowering it. She was full and sweet, in face and body, her brown hair pulled back in a loose, low bun. She closed the door behind her and bathed her hands and forearms in sanitizer. "I'm Dr. Page, the OB on call today. I hear you came in because of some discharge."

"Yeah, last night and this morning," I said and paused. Her voice— I wanted to hear it again. "At my anatomy scan, they found I only had five millimeters of cervix left. That was eleven days ago."

"Ok, let's get you checked out." She pulled up a rolling stool and ducked behind my raised knees, lifting the paper drape. "You might feel a little pressure."

After she closed my knees, she pulled off her blue gloves and told us she would be back soon.

Angelic, that was the word that kept coming to mind. Not like *sent from above*, but the sound, the appearance of the word: the soft *g* and its descended loop, then soaring up to the top of the lilting *l*, ending in the open curve of the *c*. The musicality of Dr. Page's voice held me, comforted me.

"Ok," she said, coming back into the room. "Do you guys kind of know what's going on here?"

"Sort of," I said, although I couldn't have explained it.

"You're dilated two and a half centimeters. I can see membranes."

I suddenly wondered why this room was so large. One whole wall had a built-in counter, three feet deep, with drawers and cabinets above and below it. Mellow sunlight filtered in through the half-closed blinds. The room felt blue-gray but not unbeautiful.

"22 weeks is pretty early," Dr. Page went on. "The risk of infection—to you and the baby—is very high." She paused. "We should induce you."

Dale and I both nodded. "We understand."

Whether or not we knew it, we had already prepared for this. Already had these conversations. Maybe not out loud but somehow.

"There are a few things you should know," she continued. "We can't do anything for the baby. We won't try to save her."

It sounds wild, now—all this knowing. All this understanding of what was really being said, what was really going on—that this was the only option, and it was out of everyone's control, and nobody wanted it to be this way, but it simply was. Years later, after *Roe v. Wade* is overturned and doctors begin refusing healthcare to women in premature labor for fear of violating anti-abortion laws, women in my position will develop that infection, become septic, and die right alongside their unborn children. Some of their stories will make the news; most will never be known. All of them could have been prevented.

"It's natural to still see muscles twitch... or her heart beating... but they don't mean that she is still alive. It takes a little while for that to stop. I just want you to be prepared for it." She moved toward the door. "I'm sorry—I know this isn't easy. We'll get you started on some Pitocin soon. In the meantime, if you haven't already, you might want to think about a name."

She left, and the room was still.

Heavy.

Full of every single thing in the universe.

Like in a pool, when you hold your body suspended, surrounded by water and nothingness. Not unbeautiful.

Dale and I spoke slowly, in reverence, for the situation, for each other. We each decided, independently, that we did not want to see her after she was born. I couldn't fathom what she would look like, only half-baked; instead, I kept seeing myself middle-aged, twenty years from now, huddled in a dark attic, unable to escape the mental images of my dead daughter. Things no mother should ever see.

I didn't know anything about motherhood.

The name—the name I knew, but it tore me apart. Staring straight ahead at the wall, I blurted out, because I didn't know a better way to say it, "I can only think of her as Sloane. That's her name to me."

I couldn't look at Dale. Violet had been the name I always wanted to give my first daughter—my favorite name, my middle name. As an eight-year-old, I had dreamt of Violet, my daughter; as an eighteen-year-old, I had gotten it tattooed on my back. As a couple, *we* had visions of Violet. This was the dream, in six letters. But months ago, even before we found out about the sex and the incompetent cervix, it just wasn't sounding right: *Violet Mudrick, Violet Mudrick*. I couldn't do it. I didn't know why. I just knew that this baby was not Violet; she was Sloane. And even though I knew that, not giving her the name I had longed for felt like I was taking something away from Sloane. Some connection, some intimacy.

Like I said, I didn't know jack shit about motherhood—not even the love part.

"Ok," said Dale. "Sloane."

Maybe it was that I expected him to fight it, and I would have to beg—*Please, please don't do this to me; please don't take away that part of the dream, too*—but that was when the dam finally broke, and I laid in torrents, now knowing we had a deadline with Sloane.

A dream is an image; that image is a feeling. For decades, I dreamt of the loose drape of a hospital gown, the heat of birth and love pulsing beneath its caress. Every photograph I had ever seen of a mother who had just given birth looked the same: tousled hair framing her breathless, sweaty, glowing face; the fresh, plump babe curled upon her bare chest; a thin, blue-patterned hospital gown draped over them both, collarbone exposed. The whole image is luscious, edible—so many births at once. One of a thousand smaller dreams within the big dream; one of a thousand secondary griefs within the lost dream.

Me—I was wearing a T-shirt. Forest green, Notre Dame. I won it in a trivia contest at an alumni event the year before. *Onward to Victory*, it said across the chest, in block letters.

I don't know why they didn't change me into a hospital gown. Maybe because the labor moved fast—too fast to dress, too fast to get an epidural after they gave me a green chile cheeseburger for lunch—or maybe because they knew she wouldn't need my skin, my breast. Maybe I could have just asked for one.

But I still got full-blown labor, and I celebrated it quietly, a keepsake just for me. Water breaking, thick and dense, like primordial soup, contractions ripping me apart from the inside. Vomiting. Oxygen. Dale letting me squeeze his hand, his gaze occasionally turning toward the football game on the TV hanging in the corner of the room. It was January 15th—divisional weekend. Cowboys versus Packers.

It is hard for me to imagine what it was like to be him in those moments, watching his wife writhe in pain, to birth his daughter who would die. *Let him watch football*, I thought. Hell, if I could have focused on anything, I would have been watching, too.

But awareness was hazy, only the pain sharp, and at one moment, one clear thought. I turned toward Dale.

"I want to see her," I said. "I decided I want to see her."

And now I think, if I hadn't, my entire life might be different. I might not even be here.

And then everything inside me dropped.

"Oh *fuck*," I said to Dale. "*Fuuuuuck*. I need to push *now*."

The room was empty except for us. I had no idea what the fuck I was doing. My hold on reality tumbling sideways, I caught a glimpse of the phone and heard myself cry out, "Call the nurse, call the nurse, call the nurse."

Bodies filled the room.

The front of the bed dropped down before me.

Dr. Page. Her face, her voice, her hands.

And I screamed.

The part of me that was outside my body couldn't believe that I was screaming. The rest of me couldn't stop.

Someone said something about calming down. I screamed louder.

This scream was important.

It was primal, from somewhere I didn't know yet.

It was not physical pain.

It was not fear.

It was the final moments of my daughter being alive.

It was everything in me splitting open, holding on.

Loving and hurting with abandon.

In the coming years, I will sometimes wish that I had held Sloane right away. Especially when we learned she lived for ten minutes. But most of the time, I maintain that I would have been too weak to actually do it, my arms useless, my body frazzled.

At half past seven, twenty minutes after she was born and eight hours after we had arrived at the hospital, I said, "I'm ready for her."

And when she was placed on my lap, half-bundled in a white cotton blanket, all breath left me.

"Oh, oh, oh," was all I could say, over and over. "Oh, of course, this is her—of course, of course."

Whatever I had been imagining earlier, she was not that. She was a baby. A beautiful, perfect, tiny baby.

I was overcome with love.

I didn't even know life could be this wonderful.

This was my daughter—of course, this was her.

One pound and one ounce but bigger than the universe. She looked ruddy and alive, her heart still thumping softly, pushing up on her chest, her tongue poking through between her lips. She had her dad's perfectly carved calves. One arm was swollen purple.

My heart, my heart, my heart.

I wanted nothing more than to just stare at her, just be with her. Propped up on my thighs, facing me, as if we were having a conversation, only she was doing all the giving, me all the receiving.

Being in her presence was the most immense joy, the sweetest peace I had ever felt, and have ever felt to this day. I could have stayed there forever. With every fiber in my being, I wanted to, in this mammoth hospital bed, a fold-out chair in the corner for Dale, cabinets, a sink, a big round table, and on the rolling tray by my bedside, a baloney sandwich on white bread—the kind that you get from a vending machine, cut diagonally and wedged into a triangular plastic container, cellophane over top. The cafeteria was closed; restaurants were closed. It was a holiday weekend—MLK day.

I didn't understand it, but I didn't question it either, this blissful experience with my dead daughter. It felt like the most natural thing in the world. It wasn't the dream but fuck if it didn't blow the dream out of the water. This was truth. *Real life*. Along with Pop-Tarts and shampoo was *this*.

Maybe I didn't know anything about anything, but I knew this, and in those moments, I wasn't sure that I really needed to know anything else, ever.

Dale and I took turns holding her. My only regret is that we don't have a picture of the three of us; instead, we passed our daughter back and forth, sliding our hands beneath her in sync so as not to jostle her tiny body, her tiny head. I had no concept of time except that it was finite when I wanted it to be infinite.

At some point later, a nurse asked if she could take Sloane for a few moments to take photos of her for us to take home, even though we had already taken our own. When she returned, she laid our daughter in the clear, plastic bassinet behind my hospital bed, and I didn't know if I could bear to hold her again.

Maybe it was because it was all just so much. Or maybe it was because the time I already had with her was perfect, and I wanted it to stay untouchable. Maybe it was because I didn't want to have to keep letting her go, again and again.

There is so little that our small human selves can understand at times like this. Why we feel the way we do, why we do what we do, what we will wish we had done. How infinitesimally fleeting these opportunities are. How we will never stop wanting them to be bigger, longer, fuller, despite their being more than enough, just as they are.

A while later, I stood over her bassinet. Dale took photos; I was finally in a hospital gown. It fell forward as I leaned over her, hands clasped behind my back. It is an odd stance—distant but brave, like I wanted more but was denying myself, protecting, already, because what you can't see in the photos, is that her tiny face poking out over the blankets was already taking on a waxy quality. She already looked different. Half-dead, even though she was fully dead. That was too much for me to bear.

I don't know what else I could have done in my time with her. Or maybe I did all I could, all I needed, all she needed, which was to love her and let her go.

The next time the nurse came in, she asked if we were ready for our daughter to be taken from us, and there was really nothing to say but yes.

5

The morning light was soft, a washed-out photograph. I had slept long, maybe because I knew it would be like this when I woke. I mean, not *exactly* like this, because these are not things that people can know ahead of time, but I knew nothing would make sense. Like the phantom baby in my belly, the sudden lack of direction.

The questions.

A nurse I had never met brought in a packet of papers—some for her to fill out, some for us. The normality of her voice struck me.

"These first forms are for the birth certificate and death certificate," she said. "You can decide whether or not you want those."

"Ok," I said, scanning the fields on the forms: *Baby's name, Mother's name, Father's name*. I was still sitting in the white whale of a hospital bed where, hours earlier, when the morning was still black, a different nurse had shaken me awake, saying, *I couldn't find your pulse; I thought you were dead.* I had mumbled, *it's always that slow*, and sunk back into sleep, but now awake, everything seemed unnaturally slow. I questioned my ability to hold a pen.

"Do you want a social security number for her?"

Dale and I looked at each other. I thought of rows of cubicles, stacks of paperwork. For what?

What is it all for?

"No," I said.

"What would you like to do with her body?"

"We were hoping we could donate her…," I said, not really knowing the right words, "to science?"

"Oh… no—I'm sorry. We can't do that. She wasn't full-term."

I couldn't find a single word, not even wrong ones.

"French's offers free cremation for the loss of a child," the nurse went on, referring to a local funeral home.

Again, Dale and I looked at each other. Suddenly I was fifteen, in the sunny living room of an old woman's house—my sewing teacher. For all of my teenage years, I had spent every Wednesday afternoon with her, eating her homemade butterscotch cookies and bringing weird ideas to life: funky A-line skirts, exposed-seam tank tops, and once, an impractically heavy black robe with my last name embroidered on the back like a prizefighter.

One afternoon, when I had finished a project and didn't have another one to start yet, my teacher had said, "You can get some community service hours by making funeral gowns for preemies."

The only part I had understood was that I needed community service hours for school. But preemies? Funeral gowns?

As if she had heard me, she added, "No one makes funeral gowns small enough for these babies. We donate them to local hospitals. Then they have something nice to be buried in."

Bent over and with a hand on one knee, she rummaged through a cabinet and then hefted a big plastic bag onto the cutting table; in it were folds of pastel satin in yellow, purple, white, spools of matching thread, and wheels of ribbon, quarter-inch with eyelets.

Nearly all the community service hours that I would later note on my college applications would come from making these funeral gowns for preemies. Cutting, pinning, sewing dozens.

In my mid-twenties, I was gifted a plastic bag of fabric, leftovers from a friend's flopped business venture. Inside were piles of solid satin, wheels of wide ribbon. I set up my sewing machine on a card table in the middle of my studio apartment and searched the internet for a pattern: *preemie funeral gown.*

And yet, those dresses always felt like *other people's lives*; the clearest vision I ever had for their use was down some blurry hospital corridor. Now here we were—said hospital.

I wondered where Sloane was at that moment. Thought about how she had never been outside these walls, never touched the earth. I thought of a wooden box, and inside it, wide angel sleeves in lavender.

And then I wondered where everyone else was right then. It was a Monday, eight o'clock in the morning, Mountain time. I had forgotten it was a holiday—I imagined my sisters stuck in the school drop-off maze; my parents in their home offices on opposite ends of the house; my co-workers rolling out of bed and toward the coffeepot. Everyone in their own little boxes, doing their own little life. I saw the boxes multiplying and covering the earth—cars, rooms, houses, cars, rooms, houses. Walls separating, confining, interring. I thought about how we all die in these boxes every day, even if just for a moment—a moment when we are too quiet, too hurt, too alone.

When I nodded to Dale, he nodded back.

I turned to the nurse. "We'll do that," I said. "The cremation."

And that was when a sheen of impossibility began to wrap itself around my life. I filled out the forms with her name, our names as her parents, and the only thing in the room that moved was my hand across the page, the only sound the shush of the side of my palm.

This process.

These papers.

This was the end of my daughter's life.

I put back on the only clothes I had—the same ones I had worn in. Black joggers. The green T-shirt she was born in. The same pair of black and white Chucks I've had since I was fifteen.

I couldn't believe I was going to have to go back out into the world. To pick products off of shelves, to obey traffic laws. To see people. I had the thought that I might never eat again—that I might never feel the pang of hunger, because it seemed like that was for everyone else, still living in this world, but not me.

I was somewhere else, something else.

It took a while to catch up with grief. With this new life, this new way of being. Because everything was different, but I was still a bull, not knowing any other way but forward.

Others seemed to know something that I didn't. When we left the hospital, we picked up sandwiches and beer, because what else does one do in this situation, and meandering in small slow circles outside Total Wine, I called my oldest sister and told her what happened.

"Why do you sound so ok right now?" she asked. I didn't know how to answer, didn't know how I was supposed to sound. I made one or two more phone calls like that, and that was enough.

My dad hung around for a few days. On one, mid-morning, he and I sat on the purple couch, angled toward each other. He wore a jungle green sweater he'd had for thirty years. And yet, he was entirely new to me in that moment: his shoulders shaking violently, his wet face pulling into parts of life that he didn't know but was allowing himself to go.

These were gifts I wouldn't open until much later.

Dale and I both went back to work the following week. *What else was there to do,* we said to ourselves. *This happened; nothing is going to change that. It will always and forever have happened.*

We thought that was acceptance. But what I found instead was myself constantly butting up against life, without knowing why. I had good days and bad days, and I didn't understand the difference between them. I didn't understand why some days I felt like I was going to vomit the emptiness inside me and other days I felt on the cusp of some beautiful wave; on some, exhaustion sat on my chest like seventeen bricks, and still others, my heart seemed to be growing wings, lifting. I didn't understand why I felt so fucking tired all the time—why just being awake felt increasingly hard.

I was hyper-focused on *managing* this—whatever *this* was. Life now, I guess. It needed to be managed, controlled, as if lots of *doing* could make it all un-hard—I could manage the hardness into oblivion. Because isn't that what I had always done? My daughter died, and it was awful, but wasn't it also just a part of life, and who was I if not a grown-ass adult capable of managing my own life?

But when my sternum would crack at random, and I would double over, clawing my way through my ribs because I wasn't sure my heart could still hold itself together, what exactly was there to manage?

That summer, I finally realized I was broken. It felt like a release—in my shoulders, in my skull, but also back into life; I finally arrived in grief. *Grief is healing*, I heard one day—suddenly, clearly, from somewhere inside me, while walking across the sunbeams streaming onto my wood floor. *And when you fight grief, you fight healing.*

In the fall, I was asked to describe my life in a six-word sentence. It was a work assignment—an internal cultural initiative. On a blank PowerPoint slide, I drew a line up and down, to varying heights and depths, then down and around and back and forth at differing widths, and occasionally drawing over itself furiously in little rat's nests. I added tiny circles to the line and labeled them with text boxes:

Bone-crushing despair.
Yellow, sparkly joy.
One thousand tears.
Tuesday.

And on the next slide, my life sentence: *Grief doesn't end; it just changes.* Day to day, hour to hour, dark to light and back again. All these months that I had my eyes closed to the truth of grief, it had been shaping my body; the raw, aching mass that I had become was absorbing every experience it found itself in, becoming more expansive. Swelling with love as Dale and I cried together at a sushi restaurant in LA. Sobbing on the bare floor where her toys should have been. Looking at the photos I took of her whenever I hadn't smiled in a while. Every moment a world in and of itself; every experience pushing outward on the confines of what I had known life to be.

Other sentences I could have written:

Grief is emptiness; grief is fullness.
Grief is all life—a door.
I know nothing and yet, everything.

It's this paradox, these extremes, this spanning between that is at the heart of grief. Because, I learned, grief is a cracking open. For life to flood in. And that is fucking beautiful all on its own. But if that had been enough, I wouldn't have ended up where I did in the Jemez, or Durango, or Georgia, or at a dead-end in my own neighborhood.

No.

A dull ache persisted in that chasm that grief had created: the pain of feeling incomplete with no way to ever make myself whole again.

She was gone.

Part Two

6

It was dark when we arrived in Atlanta. Driving in a rental car from the airport to our Airbnb, the black windows, occasionally flashing with an amber streetlight, made it feel like we could have been anywhere, or nowhere, and while I normally hate that—being unable to see the shape of things—I was too tired to really care.

It was May 2018, sixteen months after Sloane died. Dale and I had planned a trip to Georgia around his brother's PhD graduation: We would spend a few days in Atlanta, drive up to Athens for graduation weekend, and then swoop down to Covington for a special night of lovemaking—read: conception—bed-and-breakfast-style. I wanted this trip to be everything like Charleston, South Carolina was the August before, when we were grieving but blissfully in love, roaming the cobblestone streets and eating seafood by the handful. But I didn't understand that it couldn't be—that I was a different person. That every new loss, every new trial, had pulled me further and further from being anything that I understood. That there wasn't much of me left anyway, now that my life had narrowed to a singular point of interest: to be pregnant again.

I felt wild and desperate, feral.

At our Airbnb, we laid on the bed on our bellies and flipped through the laminated pages of the guest information binder.

"This city seems kind of intense," I said.

I showed Dale some remarks the host made about the city: how it was aware of its prejudices and yet seemed to succumb to them, organize itself around them. Atlanta suddenly felt massive and dangerous. Swallowing. Not because of its composition but because of its division. That feeling seemed to be alive out there and seeping in through the black windows of our room.

They say that your outer world reflects your inner world. I don't know if that's true, but it doesn't seem inaccurate to say that, at that time, I could have been Atlanta.

I like to get to know places on foot. It means something to me that the soles of my feet have met with a city's pavement and sidewalks, its stones and grasses, its very bottom layer, and by May, in Atlanta, that ground was seething with heat. So, the next morning I threw on a thin, blue cotton sheath of a dress and my blue Vans; we parked the rental car in an all-day lot and set out on foot. I had been to Atlanta before for work—once for Levi's, and once for UnitedHealthcare—but the only thing I really knew about the city was that every third or fourth street seemed to be named Peachtree. I wanted to do the touristy things. I wanted to not give a fuck.

Morning was easy enough. We roamed the Coca-Cola factory, where Dale drank too many samples, and I yearned for simpler times. He talked me out of the College Football Hall of Fame, and I talked him into the puppet museum with a Jim Henson exhibit—again, a simpler time. A time, I knew, when having a baby was still a distant and certain dream.

But by late afternoon, it was clear that our time in Atlanta would not be like our time in Charleston. There would be no trees dripping with Spanish moss and no gardens with leaves bigger than our faces, no rainbow buildings charming us from a rollercoaster of heights. In Charleston, the blend of brick walls and colored doors and peeling facades felt like my jumbled soul—raw and messy but still beautiful. In Atlanta, the hot gray sidewalk and cutting sun glare felt like what my insides had become since then—angry and done.

I was ready for a drink.

I had read somewhere that more than six drinks a week could affect fertility, so Dale and I had both been trying our best. Although conception wasn't really our issue; it was keeping the pregnancy that was the problem. Since Sloane died, I had had two miscarriages; after the second, Dr. Page had suggested a work-up for recurrent loss.

"I'm going to reclassify your first born as a pregnancy loss," she had said, moving her pen across the paper on her clipboard. "We both know she wasn't, but insurance requires three pregnancy losses to qualify as recurrent loss. That's the only way they will pay for the hysteroscopy."

I loved her fiercely for what she did but mostly for what she said. And now in Atlanta, we were in our first season of trying to conceive since the three hysteroscopies it took earlier that year to cut out the septum in my uterus, my fertility specialist having to stop each time when he could no longer see through all the blood. Now its absence was supposed to mean successful pregnancies. Here we were— arriving—but on the way there, I had gotten so lost that it didn't feel like the grand re-entrance to the world of trying to conceive that it should have been.

Maybe partly because that's a miserable little world to begin with. It was a fairytale the first time; we got pregnant on the first try and found out on our second wedding anniversary. That became my clever way of telling the first few people: We *gave each other the best anniversary gift… but it won't be here for nine months! Haha!* But then she died right after she was born and we were ripped apart at the seams and our next two pregnancies ended in miscarriage and the whole endeavor had begun to feel like a nightmare that we were willingly stepping back into every month. Monitoring my cycle became a compulsion, sex became a chore, anticipating my period became a vigil. Every negative test pushed the knife in further; every positive one only turned the dial from misery to anxiety. And yet, we kept on. We wanted a child, alive.

"This is cute," I said as we passed a bar with an outdoor courtyard. Big leafy trees edged the patio, giving some tables relief from the sun. A few people were scattered throughout, each alone and working on a laptop. For a brief moment, I saw myself writing there, at a table in the corner, breezy shadows blowing across my notebook. I wasn't yet consistent or prolific, but grief had given me reason to return to the page after years of negligence. "Let's get a beer here."

We sat down and settled into easy conversation, into us—the us that always shines when we can let the rest of the world fall away. I didn't feel like Atlanta inside or outside.

"We should do it outside," Dale said, on his second beer.

"What—where?" I asked, giggling.

"I don't know yet. But doesn't it sound fun?"

"It is broad daylight outside."

I laughed. It felt good. It wasn't like us to do something like that, but it made sense, in the way that two people who have gone through the same intense grief together can not be themselves but still be completely in sync, in the way that we had both gotten to the point of *fuck it* in every area of our lives except each other, in the way that holding onto each other fiercely was what always brought us back from that edge. *What the fuck does it even matter*, one of us would say, *how much I drink or how much I weigh or how much I get done today. My daughter is still dead. What the fuck does it even matter.* And the other would say *I know, I know*, and pull them back to shore again.

"Ok, I'm in," I said, smiling. "But where?"

"I don't know. Let's just see if we see somewhere."

We were giddy by the time we left the courtyard. I can't even say what we thought was going to happen. I had no idea at all. But it didn't really matter. What mattered was that this was exciting again.

"That gas station?" I asked, as we came upon a sparse lot.

"What?" Dale said. "That's not outside."

I didn't know he literally meant *outside*.

Instead, we found another bar, big and empty. We slid into a two-top as far as we could get from the bartender and giggled about our prospective plan, which, like everything in trying to conceive, was less a plan and more a hope.

By the time we finished our beers—and still no one else had walked in—we were drunk enough to actually do this. We walked towards a neighborhood, and soon we were on a paved footpath through a large park, the slopes of grass verdant, the canopy lush. Far from the hot gray of the city center. People were out walking their dogs—a

Doberman loping down the path, a Bichon Frise toddling in the grass. It was a Wednesday afternoon.

I said to Dale, "Here."

"Here?" He laughed, incredulous.

"Over there," I said, pointing off to the right, where dense rows of trees backed up to a quiet row of houses. It looked like there might be a chain-link fence separating the park from the backyards, which does nothing for roaming eyes but means someone could only come upon us from one direction. "I think that's as much coverage as we're going to get."

"Are you serious…" Dale said, as he followed me off the path and up the slight slope to the trees. The flicker in his voice made me laugh, like he was nervous now that his idea was happening and maybe even being one-upped. Sometimes, even in the oddest moments, it hits me that Dale and I will love each other forever.

The trees worked. The backyards were all empty; the park fell away. Someone might see us out of a window, but truthfully, if we got caught and hauled away for whatever crime this was, fuck it. All we had was each other, anyway; we might as well have each other with grass in our hair and dirt under our nails. That's how we were; we loved with our whole selves. *My whole heart for my whole life*, we had gotten engraved on the mason jars we drank out of at our wedding. It was a singular intensity that defined our relationship from the beginning—which, incidentally, was also in the grass, but eleven years earlier.

"You guys should wrestle," one of our friends had said one night my freshman year in college—also a Wednesday. We had been sitting outside the house where Dale rented the basement from an older couple we never saw. I was the only girl hanging out with four or five guys, and we had all had a couple of Keystone Lights—that was beer back then. I don't remember exactly how we went about "wrestling," but Dale and I were friends, and it was funny.

"You guys should make out," the same friend said, smiling at himself. I had never once thought of Dale as anything more than a friend, but as soon as he leaned over me, lying on my back in the grass, and slowly took my mouth into his, I was forever changed. I don't think either of us knew that would happen, but afterward, it seemed almost impossible that it wouldn't have.

In the park in Atlanta, we got down and dirty upright and fast. The instant I hiked up my dress, Dale was inside me. Sure, I kept watch in all the directions I could see, but goddamnit if I didn't also want to enjoy this. And I did. And I wanted to do it again, in other parks in other cities, and when he finished, I didn't really want to be finished. We held hands as we walked out of the trees, me leaning into Dale, my wet thighs trembling. The sun had begun to sink below the treetops. The coolness in the air was nostalgic.

"Mmmm," I moaned into this man I called mine. Delicious. Maybe Atlanta and I could be friends.

But when we reached the paved path, my step didn't land right.

"Ahhhh," I said when I looked down. "Ahhh fuck. My shoes are covered in dog shit."

I must have stepped in it when we were in the trees. It was clumped onto the underside of both shoes and all along the outer edge of one. I dragged my feet over the grass, trying to scrape it off and only making it worse. And now the stench had seeped into the air.

"My shoes are ruined," I said. All I could do was stare at all the brown wedged into all the white.

Poor Dale. I don't remember what he said—something about it not being a big deal or laughing it off—but it was the *wrong* thing, and I began to boil inside.

"Don't you even fucking *care*?" I said. I heard my mother's cutting tone. "This was *your* idea. I did this for *you*. And now my fucking shoes are ruined."

And just like that, whatever had been seething in Atlanta was back, licking my insides with its forked tongue and riling me up. I walked with my eyes on the ground and a fury in my shitty, uneven step, silence between us when before there had been only skin. I didn't know my anger back then—didn't know all the things it had to tell me. All I knew was that I was explosive and devastated and alone. Not because of my shoes, but because of what my life had become. The end of me always seemed just beneath the surface.

Before long, it was dark. When we walked into a restaurant smelling like dog shit and probably sex, I walked straight to the restroom and ran my shoes under the stream from the faucet, wadding up soapy paper towels and scrubbing until the muscles in my hands cramped. It was no use. The shit was embedded in the cross-hatched rubber around the edges. The soles I could live with; it was the edges that got me.

In my socks, I walked through the patio of the restaurant, out to the sidewalk, and chucked my shoes into a trashcan chained to a signpost. It was one of those old school silver ones, like the grouch lived in. A simpler time.

The next morning, we did all things Martin Luther King Jr.—his house, his church, his memorial—and I felt like I might burst, walking up and down the length of that bright blue pool with the sediment in my heart severely disturbed. Anger—all the anger, at all the injustice, all the suffering—stirred with deep reverence. Clouding, muddying.

We got to Athens that afternoon for graduation weekend, and I can't explain it other than: Everything started to hurt. There were too many people around all the time—loud, rowdy, full of life. Every meal was out at a restaurant; every time, I left half my plate and still felt disgusting. The drinking was constant—rounds at the breweries, margaritas at lunch, beer pong in the backyard. Laughter. Music. And my fucking shoes: I only had one pair with me now—shiny black Vans—and I was fucking pissed every time I had to put them on with clothes that didn't match. I wanted all of it to go away; I wanted all of me to go away.

I don't belong here, I kept thinking. *Someone give me a goddamn baby already.*

When we arrived in Covington, and it was just me and Dale again, I finally took a breath. We parked in an all-day lot and found ourselves on Floyd Street, a quaint district of historic homes. The air was moist but cool in the shade of massive oaks. As we walked, I was reminded of my feet touching the earth, and I began to loosen.

"These homes are beautiful," I said. I liked gazing at the houses on the other side of the street more than the side we were on; with just a little more distance, the whole property came into view: the shape of the roof, the outline of the trees, every species of flower. I suddenly felt as if I were showering in paint; the richness in the air was palpable. "Not my style, but gorgeous anyway."

We walked and walked, and I let go of my grip. I forgot about Atlanta, about Athens. Saw only the purity of white columns and vibrant gardens and wide brick porches. I should have stayed in that reverie longer—should have seen how good it was for me. Should not have ventured back to the main square.

Covington is considered, by itself at least, the Hollywood of the South. The message is all around the square—the backdrop for such-and-such film, the restaurant in such-and-such show. The town's history was also significantly marked by the Civil War—this building was damaged, this home survived. I hate Hollywood, and I hate war. There have been many other times in my life when I've been able to set those feelings aside—like my love for all things *Breaking Bad* in Albuquerque, and my study of World War II for my German major in college—but at that time in my life, in Covington, Georgia, it all became too much. Everything began to warp. The loosening that had begun on Floyd Street now left me spinning outward, danger at every turn. War, vanity, alcohol, food; grief, heartache, loneliness, despair.

I don't belong anywhere. I don't belong anywhere.

My breath became just out of reach. Earlier we had passed a boutique, and through the window, I had seen things that looked familiar: books, pillows, starfish.

"I'm going to check out that shop," I said aloud, somewhere toward Dale, and floated toward it while he found a bench in the middle of the square, stretching out his arms along the back.

But inside, the shop felt alien. All pastels, on blankets, on candles, and out of ceramic, seashells and sailboats and cats curled up on couches. My chest felt vacuous around my heart. Swallowing hard, I shuffled my feet.

I stopped at an aluminum bucket of upside-down umbrellas. Their curved wooden handles looked smooth and hollow; wrinkled white price tags stuck to their metal shafts at an angle.

Nothing had any real character to it. It was all just shit to buy.

The bookshelves in the back corner of the shop pulled me back, if only for a moment. I picked up a pocket-sized book that said *Mindfulness* on the cover in gold, all caps. From top to bottom, the book was an ombre green and made of fabric; I ran my finger down its spine, across its front. I opened it to a random page, scanned a few sentences, and thought, *I need this*. That, and apparently a small, conical vase in jade green.

Back out on the square, I said to Dale, "Let's get a beer. I don't care where—anywhere."

But the beers we threw back on a rooftop bar didn't get through to me that evening; nothing did. And I didn't get better back home.

Instead, I thought about guns. Or rather, guns forced themselves upon me, raped my mind, strangled my breath—all day and most forcefully at night. I laid awake in bed, eyes squeezed shut, an image of a black handgun pulsing rhythmically in the darkness.

It wasn't the first time something like this had happened, but it lasted the longest.

I spiraled. Down, down, down.

It seemed as if I was moving forward and backward and nowhere all at the same time—as if something had been set in motion sixteen months before and needed to play itself out. When or how that would end, I didn't know—and maybe that was what terrified me most.

7

Goodness knows I need the wilderness like birds need the sky. Three weeks after we got back from Georgia, Dale, our dog Leo, and I headed down to the Gila for the long Memorial Day weekend. The Gila National Forest is over three million acres of rugged mountain land in southwest New Mexico and home to the Gila Wilderness, the first designated wilderness area in the United States. For reasons I'm not entirely sure of, it holds a special significance for us. Maybe because it's the first place we camped in New Mexico after we moved here; maybe because it's where we broke in our long-distance hiking chops. Maybe because we had been pronouncing it *GEE-luh* until the first time we went down there and talked with a park ranger who had long gray hair tied into a low ponytail and weathered fingers that swept deftly across an equally weathered map as he educated us on the *HEE-luh*. Maybe because it's where we really became New Mexicans.

That May after Georgia, we had planned to hike out from Whitewater Canyon, along the western edge of the forest. The trailhead was about five hours south of Albuquerque, and the route to get there passed Cosmic Campground, the first International Dark Sky Sanctuary on the continent—and one of only fourteen in the world. The nearest artificial light is over forty miles away, across the border to Arizona. Nothing and everything as far as the eye can see. We planned to camp there on the way.

When we got to the sanctuary, it was completely empty. Silent. The ground was the signature yellow-tan of the New Mexican desert, hardly distinguishable between road and campsite, and round juniper bushes dotted the earth for miles before rising up into blue mountains. The only evidence of human intervention was a sign, a pit toilet, and large paved circles for setting up telescopes. Even in the daytime, the dome of sky overhead was intense.

The opposite of desolate, it felt like Death Valley. At the end of 2016, two weeks before we found ourselves in a real death valley, the four of us—me, Dale, Leo, and Sloane, in my belly—had camped in Death Valley National Park. On Christmas Day, we had taken a singular road out to the middle of nowhere, driving and driving until we could no longer see anything but yellow brush and purple mountains, where we pulled onto the gravel shoulder and got out.

The midday air was brisk, the mellow sun like a baby's breath. Cotton clouds stretched across the sky. It was all too beautiful to be real—Sloane tapping on the inside of my belly, the utter peace of silence. The air was both dense and weightless.

Still, if I ever need to take a deep breath, that's where I go.

Or I go to the nighttime sky in Death Valley, when my pregnant bladder forced me from my warm sleeping bag at midnight, and I crawled out of our tent and directly into brilliance. I had stood there for I don't know how long, frozen hands stuffed into my pockets, head fallen completely back, gaping at the universe. Millions of white dots stretching back and back. Life felt both immediate and infinite, I both full and inconsequential.

The vastness.

"I need this," I said to Dale at Cosmic Campground, as we raised the hatchback of the car. I stretched my arms out wide, felt the middle of my upper back pop.

"Yeah, me too," he said, as I gave him a kiss, a thank you.

We knew our jobs; Dale unpacked the car while I let Leo out and filled up his plastic water bowl. He ignored it, nose to the ground, sniffing out the new digs. And then, like a dance, we set up home: tent, with footprint and rainfly; sleeping pads, bags, and pillows; stove for dinner, and finally, chairs.

We sat and rotated brats in a foil pan. Neither of us mind silence, especially in the wilderness.

Another couple drove up. They seemed like us, only an hour behind—late twenties, freshly married, no kids. Doing their own thing. In love.

Is that what we look like? I wondered. *Would anyone have any idea of the places we've been, the things we've seen? What have they seen that we can't see?* Having lived for so long in a land of innocence myself, I often wondered about the depths to which other people had traveled. Not as a measure of judgment, but so that I may hear the stories they have to tell. Because, at some point, don't we all have one?

And if we don't, what are we even doing here?

"I can't believe there aren't more people here," I said to Dale, as the sun sank into the horizon and the sky turned dusty purple.

"I know—this is awesome," he said. He was so sweet, such a boy at times. I envied his youthful excitement for life. He brought it out in me, but I was more cautious, more guarded. Dale was… free.

I didn't know back then how possible freedom was for me, but I had just learned that I was on some forward path. A few days after we got back from Georgia, I had found myself sitting cross-legged on the couch in my living room, laptop on my lap, head in a vise. It was the middle of a weekday, and I couldn't focus on anything. I tried and failed, tried and failed, and eventually just closed all of my work files on my computer.

In their wake, I opened my internet browser. As though I was moving through water, each letter appearing one by one in the search bar, I typed in *s-u-i-c-i-d-a-l i-d-e-a-t-i-o-n*. I had no idea what I was looking for or what I needed or what the hell was going on inside of me; all I knew was that it was a perfectly normal day—birds chirping in the trees, trucks delivering the mail, earth revolving around the sun—and I needed all of it to stop.

I scrolled past the national hotline number. *I don't need that*, I thought. *I'm not, like, going to do anything. Right now. Right? What would I even say?* I started this conversation with myself.

"Hi. I think I'm having suicidal thoughts. But I don't think I want to kill myself. Or… I don't know."

"Ok. How can I help you?"

"I don't know. I don't think I'm in danger...?"

"Ok. Hope you feel better."

I kept scrolling. I could feel my blood in my eardrums, my breath slowly leaving my chest. *This is not what I need, this is not what I need, I don't even know what the fuck I need.*

"I am ok, I am ok," I said aloud to the empty room. But what I needed to—and couldn't seem to—articulate to myself was that I was, in fact, *not* ok. Somehow I both knew and didn't know that.

Link after link, I wasn't finding anything useful, and when I thought about facing the rest of the day—days, weeks, months—being hit over the head with the blunt image of a gun, I began to panic.

Should I call? How are they going to help? Am I in danger?

To have lost my internal compass for answering such questions was jarring in a whole different way—that beyond the threat of the thoughts themselves was only a blankness, without comfort, without assurance, without anything at all, was utterly terrifying. I had become glass. My chest hot, my arms cold, and yet, I had no sensation at all.

I was gone.

I clicked absently, here and then there. Nothing got through—just hit glass. And then I knew I wasn't going to make it very far. I was sliding, sliding—rain down a windowpane.

Suicide: read this first, read a search result.

I clicked.

A webpage straight out of 1998: big blocks of text, weird fonts, homemade graphics. And at the top: *If you are feeling suicidal right now, please stop long enough to read this.*

That felt on my level. *Ok,* I thought, *I can do that.*

The author of the site explained he was not a mental health professional—just someone who cared. And then:

Suicide happens when pain exceeds resources for coping with pain.

It doesn't even mean that you really want to die, he went on. *It only means that you have more pain than you can cope with right now.*

A beat for it to register.

And then another, and another—the drum back, awake.

I slid my laptop onto the couch and let my head fall into my hands. Waves crashed through me.

That's it. That's exactly it.

My pain is just too big.

I need more resources to handle it.

I don't actually want to die.

I just want the pain to not hurt so bad.

It doesn't sound revolutionary. In fact, it sounds obvious. But when you have been blown open by unfathomable loss—after loss after loss—and people are too chicken-shit to be there for you, and time goes on and the world moves on and scars start to form and every fifth day is actually a really great day, you stop knowing what is true anymore.

You stop knowing.

But now I knew something: resources. I needed resources.

My relief was immediate; everything inside quieted down. So that two weeks later I could sit there in my camping chair, leaning back and gazing up at the darkening sky, at ease.

Safe. Alive.

"Ah geez," said Dale, sitting next to me in his own chair. "I get now why there's nobody here."

I followed his gaze. Just above the eastern horizon, the moon was rising—perfectly round and full. In a couple of hours, it would bathe the campground in light and wash out the night sky.

"I didn't even think of that," he said, shaking his head and dropping it into his hands. He laughed at himself. "Geez."

I burst out laughing, leaning over in my chair to crash into his shoulder. We were so dumb and in love.

As we set out for Whitewater Canyon the next morning, we were equally dumb and equally in love, but more reckless and, thankfully, more resourceful. The trail began on a popular catwalk, which made for an odd start to a backpacking trip: informative signage, casual strollers, a sidewalk path. We parked in an actual parking lot, with painted white lines between the spaces. Maybe that should have been our first clue. But it had been almost two months since we were out with our packs, so we were ready to go, and that was that.

Our route was a twenty-mile loop, starting in the canyon and then rising above the river and deep into the forest. We planned to stop for the night at around twelve miles, but two hours in, we had barely gone a mile on a trail that had all but disappeared, stone-stepping across shallow pools of river, scaling near-vertical rock faces, and seemingly trapped inside the enormous gray walls of the canyon.

"Maybe we should have stopped by the ranger's station beforehand," I said. "This is not maintained *at all*."

Finally, impossibly, after a dozen course-corrections, we popped through a gap in the rocks and dropped onto a trail. Things normalized. We settled into the forest, the pallor of the overcast sky.

"Ahhh," I said. "This feels good."

"Yeah, that was wild back there," said Dale. "I didn't know if this trip was actually going to happen. We might have had to go up to Mogollon or something instead."

I inhaled deeply. It felt good to know this place. The Gila. New Mexico. When Dale first got a job here, there was no question that we would move, even though we knew nothing about it. Everything was strange at first—the pueblo-style homes with red chile ristras hanging near doorways, the enchiladas flat instead of rolled. Zia tattoos on shoulders, forearms, backs, and calves. I had grown up under a lot of non-White influence in Southern California, but this was different. This was history, this was character—an ancient and alive sense of identity. New Mexico knows who it is. Is unapologetic about its open space, its vibrant skies, its willingness to live for the day that is here. "The Land of Enchantment" its real nickname; "The Land of Mañana" its colloquial one. Dale and I both fell hard and fast. This was our place. I had never felt so at home.

The trail had become our home within a home. Neither of us had hiked much before we moved here, but that was more about opportunity than interest; he had spent the past five years in the flatlands of central Florida while in grad school, and I had been working in LA where people thought walking to high places and overlooking miles of city blocks was getting outdoors. From Albuquerque, you can drive forty minutes and be in the middle of nowhere, see no one, surrounded only by land and sky. Red mesas, yellow cliffs, pine forests, and ten-thousand-foot peaks. We grabbed New Mexico with a fervor.

Even when the trail from Whitewater Canyon began to disintegrate, I still wanted to walk it. It had always been narrow—in some places barely wider than my two feet, side by side—and it had always been steep, dropping off at maybe a sixty-degree angle down a long descent to the river, but eventually it also started to just fall away in parts. A hop here, a small leap there—I barely even missed a beat. Hiking becomes a meditative state before too long.

"Oh shit," said Dale, stopping abruptly. We had been walking single-file: him before me, Leo before him. I gently placed my hand on his pack to peer around him without either of us losing our balance.

Five feet in front of him, the trail was a broken edge. A huge swath of mountainside had been washed out to ten feet below, like a skateboarder's half-pipe. The other end of the trail picked up five or six yards ahead, across a chasm of nothing. In all our backcountry hiking—in New Mexico, Montana, Tennessee—we had never seen anything like it. At that point, it was more incredible than anything else.

"Wow," I said, scanning the area, the rawness. "It looks like we can cross pretty easily up into those trees. It sort of flattens out a bit."

It wasn't the easiest thing, but we made it across and settled back into our reverie. Or I did, at least—the rhythmic crunch of my boots on the hard, dry dirt becoming my own white noise. Before we moved here, I didn't know cities like Albuquerque existed. Cities of a solid size—half a million people—with everything you needed, but then: a limit, a place where the buildings stop and the empty land begins. In Southern California, both Orange County and LA, the cities piled on top of each other, and the homes and the shops and the people and the freeways went on forever. It was relentless, suffocating. In Albuquerque, we spread out.

In Whitewater Canyon, we crossed two more washouts in the next couple of miles. It was an adventure now.

"I feel like we're kind of getting good at this," I said, as we came upon another one. I felt like a kid again, scrambling up trees with a book and a blanket. My adult hands had the unmistakable scrapes of tree bark and twigs.

"This is the steepest one so far," Dale said, holding the straps of his pack in a resting stance—the hiking equivalent of hands on hips.

"I think you're right," I said. But I felt confident. "I'll go first."

Fifteen or twenty feet up the side of the hill, the earth came together again at a sharp angle. Up there, low-lying trees ran along most of the seam to the other side; their leaves had scattered, leaving their branches exposed for support, and then covered a wide slope down to the trail. Its broken edge barely jutted out from the hillside.

I scaled up the side we were on with ease; I had done that before. When I got to the top, I grabbed a branch and started pulling myself across. With every step, the fallen leaves beneath my feet slid down the hillside. It was so steep that I could only walk on the knife edges of my feet—my outer left foot, inner right foot. I suddenly became very aware that I was carrying a twenty-five-pound pack on my back.

Before I even made it to the open slope, it became clear that the leaves ran so deep that I would not be in contact with solid ground. Clinging to the branches was useless; they would only keep me in a cascade of dry, slippery leaves. I was going to have to cross the remaining twenty or so feet in freefall.

I looked down. We were so high up in the canyon that we could no longer hear the river. All I saw below was brush. Still holding on to the last branch I could, I turned slightly from side to side, gauging the force of my pack—how much leeway I had to either side before its weight would pull me down. It was clear: I was going to have to run as fast as I could, straight ahead, until I was above the other side of the trail. Then, on all fours, I would let the sliding leaves carry me down.

I don't know if clarity gives you courage, or if it just gives you the security of having a path forward. With no more options to consider or decisions to make, all you have is *go*.

I set my eyes on a patch of slope and bolted.

As I ran, swaths of leaves poured down the hillside. The rush of their flat, dried bodies, slipping over and down each other, chased me across. I had the distinct sensation that I was running across a waterfall as it poured over the edge. But my eyes didn't waver, and when I finally reached the patch I had chosen, I threw myself onto hands and knees and let my heart pound.

"Holy fucking shit," I said aloud, chest heaving. If I had fallen, I could have easily broken an arm or a leg or worse. And I would have been somewhere down a canyon, in the middle of nowhere. "That was fucking stupid."

Sometimes it's hard to see the situation we're in when it's all around us. Even only a few weeks removed, I couldn't believe the places I had gotten to in Athens, in Covington. On my couch at home. How could I have let it get so bad? I thought I had been dealing with my grief—the crying, the writing, the loving. I had even started counseling in October, after months of folding and unfolding, down into sixteen even squares, the list of phone numbers from Dr. Page, and rehearsing aloud the initial call to book an appointment, until I could finally say the words "infant loss" without breaking down. But I did it, and was still doing it, and as much as the idea of resources was a relief, I didn't really know what more I could do, and no one was going to figure it out for me.

Grief is the loneliest of all places. That's the end of every day—everyone else goes home, and it's still just you in your own body, your own mind, your own heart. Just you.

Once I was on the trail, solid ground, I coached Dale on how to get across. It looked a lot easier when he did it. Leo skipped along.

The next washout was so big that we had to drop into it, fifteen feet. Roots as big around as my forearm jutted out along the bottom and sides; the dirt was fresh and rich. We walked up and down it, up and down it, looking for a way back up the other side. We even dropped our packs to lighten the load. I was exhausted; I didn't even want to try climbing out without having a snack first.

When we finally got back on the trail, it went on and on like this. Up, down, up, down. After six miles, we were spent. My footing was starting to slack; my pack felt heavier. Even Leo was worn out.

When we came upon the next washout, it suddenly felt impossible.

"I can't do the whole twelve miles like this, babe," I said.

"Yeah," said Dale. "Let's look at the map."

He pulled the map out of his pack's side pocket, letting the outer folds fall open and then pulling apart the inner folds with his fingers.

I swallowed hard. I don't know why our synchronization struck me so hard in that moment. Maybe because every time I really needed him, he was there, unwavering. Maybe because I realized I wasn't the only one beaten down by the journey. Maybe because it wasn't even half-over, and the rest was still so unknown.

Shoulder to shoulder, we pored over the green squares. We cobbled together the kind of plan we had become accustomed to in grief: some combination of directional awareness, in-the-moment way-finding, and... faith. In us.

It is a spectacular thing, to be in the middle of the wilderness with another person, tall grasses slapping at your legs, and to be simultaneously thirty-thousand feet overhead, looking down on the two of you, your tiny bodies crawling over the earth. Its vastness swallows your smallness, and yet, you are so fully alive in this body, this moment, this connection, that you contain everything.

And it all seems so possible still.

8

With a name like Eggslut, I expected this breakfast sandwich to be better than it was. I had imagined egg yolk—the rich, orange kind from free-range chickens—dripping down my chin, my bite releasing the juices from thick, salty bacon. Instead, it was pretty basic, pretty clean—not at all slutty. Probably for the best.

Six weeks and two heavy periods after the Gila, I was in Los Angeles for work, my client a major health insurance carrier. We were there to interview people about their views on health and wellness—what those concepts meant to them, what they looked like in their daily lives. Over the past three years that I had been working with this company, its projects had easily become some of my favorite work; while health insurance itself is impersonal, if not hostile, the topics beneath it are deep and intimate. I lived for conversations like those.

This was my first time working with this specific client, Julia. Sitting at a metal table in the back corner of the breakfast shop, our trays stacked together and topped with wadded-up napkins, we covered the most obvious topic: work history.

"I've been in marketing here for three years now," she said, "in a few different departments. They're like separate companies—all working on their own thing."

"I guess that's why this masterbrand-level marketing is so important," I said, "to bring it all together."

Despite my disdain for consumer culture, the problems of big corporations fascinate me endlessly.

She nodded. "We need it. We have no idea who we are."

"You're not alone. I feel like that's so true of most of my clients."

We both laughed politely. Oh, corporate talk—it's like the business-world equivalent of the weather. It takes some relationship-building—but not much, honestly—to get to more interesting things: who is really just trying to put their stamp on some initiative, who is subverting it, and how at the end of the day, no one really gives a shit about the work they're doing.

"Before this," Julia said, "I worked for a couple of agencies. And before that, a nonprofit that worked with children's hospitals. It was amazing. But after a while, I couldn't do it. I was right out of college. I didn't know how to handle stuff that heavy, day after day."

Now we were getting somewhere.

"Wow," I said. "I can imagine. Sounds like a lot."

"It really was. I had to go on medication. Had to stay on it for a while, even after I left."

She took a sip of her to-go coffee, ran her hand along the strap of her crossbody purse. She had been wearing it the entire time we ate. I suddenly felt like there was a whole world beyond her short brown hair and big mouth—a life that no one knew about.

As we left the restaurant, it was more of that life that I wanted to hear about and less about what actually came out next: her kids. A boy and a girl, five and three, with some cute, modern names like Harper or Forest or Finley. Driving down the streets of West Hollywood, Julia and I in the backseat as my colleague drove, palm trees rose up along endless rows of red-tile roofs on white buildings, and Julia sang kids' songs. Aloud and loud and not even the classics.

"I just can't get this one out of my head," she said, bopping along to the tune. "My kids are *obsessed*."

The whole world is painful enough after losing a child without being reminded, within the confines of a moving car, of the songs they will never hear—the songs you don't have stuck in your own head because you're a different sort of mom.

"It's driving me crazy!" Julia said, still singing, and now laughing at herself. *What a silly mom I am!*

Nobody else in the car had kids; nobody said a word. I took a deep breath and looked out the window.

The last time I had been in LA for work—a month earlier—I had had dinner with my friend and co-worker Taj. Artisanal thin crust pizzas and counter-height seating at a joint down the street from our offices on Ventura Boulevard.

"How are you telling your story?" he had asked when we sat down.

Taj was always one to push into the harder things—to ask the questions that were difficult to answer, to turn people's faces toward the things that were hard to look at. Seven or eight years older and a foot taller than me, I stood in his shadow when I was first learning to moderate interviews; I mimicked his body language, his tone, his pace, until I realized how naturally it came to me. I had been listening intently, caring deeply, my whole life—for better or worse.

"It's really hard," I said. "I feel like I have to wait for the opportunity to be handed to me. An invitation—I need an invitation. Like, do you have kids, or are you planning to have kids."

Taj gave me his customary silence: a moderating technique, the invitation to continue. We had worked together for seven years, been friends for six. When I first met him, he had a buzz cut—young, fresh, and studious in his wire-rim glasses and plaid button-downs. Always Levi's. Last year, he took a year away from our company to work at a non-profit for teen reproductive health. It wasn't supposed to be just a year, but it ended up that way, and now, he had a mohawk, the front a shock of gray, the back tied up in a bun, and he wore T-shirts that said things like *The Future is Female*. Levi's always, still. I took the invitation, even though I was craving his wisdom.

"Otherwise, it feels too forward—like I'm putting my story on them when maybe they don't want it. I don't want people to get the wrong idea—that I want attention, or sympathy."

"What do you want?"

I paused. Oh, what did I want.

"If I'm talking to someone who doesn't know what I've been through—what I'm going through—I feel like they can't really understand me. Like, they would only be getting a small piece of the picture, and then what's the point? The whole thing would be meaningless. I guess I want real connection. Authenticity. Depth. And for me, right now, that means knowing where I'm coming from."

I didn't know then that that was only half the truth. Connection and authenticity and depth—yes, I wanted those. But also, something I couldn't articulate at the time because it was something I had only rarely experienced: a kind of holding.

"People don't want to hear this stuff," I continued. "They get uncomfortable. They don't know what to say. It's not their fault—we're just so bad at talking about these things as a society. No one teaches us about grief, or how to be there for people who are grieving. What to say, what not to say. People just freeze, not wanting to offend. And some not wanting to be a part of it at all."

"If it's that important to you, why can't you just tell them?"

I was suddenly aware that I had a full pizza in front of me.

"I don't know," I said. "Maybe I could."

In the car, I looked over at Julia. "Tell me about your kids," I said.

She grinned and gushed out all the things that I will say in future years: how she loves their little personalities, how they play and fight together, how she misses them when she is at work. When the car turned direction and the morning sun swept inside, I could see her heart, alive, beneath her blouse. She deserved it.

"I had a daughter once," I said. Not directly toward her, but more to the air, in general. "But she passed away."

I don't remember what Julia said, or if she said anything. It didn't matter. But I didn't realize then how complicated that was—how not feeling hurt or held by another could mean many different things. How they could all be the truth, but taken together, were not very clarifying.

That afternoon, Julia, her colleague, Sarah, and I found ourselves sitting on the covered porch of a man in his early twenties, talking about health and wellness. The sun was already low in the sky, filtering in below a drawn shade. A quality of warm haze set in.

Interviewing people for market research is a bizarre job. In essence, it is a mostly one-sided conversation between two strangers, in which the moderator swiftly and artfully gets to the other person's insides without them fully realizing what has happened. And then the magic unfolds: The interviewee is now discovering things about themselves in real-time. And you, the interviewer, become acutely aware that you are—gently, lovingly, *freely* because it is your job—exploring another human's existence. And sometimes, there comes this existential moment, when you rise above the scene and suddenly find it absolutely hysterical that we are all individual bodies roaming this planet and doing this thing called life. It is exhilarating.

Other times, that out-of-body experience is spun out of a kind of delirium, and you do whatever you have to do to keep from laughing— clench your jaw, draw your lips between your teeth, turn away. Because it's all just funny. Not the person you're interviewing, but the whole situation. That it is your job to ask them questions they've probably never asked of themselves. That, after this is over, they'll go on with the rest of their day, and you'll be combing through the conversation for weeks to come. Sometimes years. Sometimes you don't ever forget the people you meet, the stories you hear. The way they changed you.

That guy, that afternoon—he was a gift in some form. He had flat black hair and a long face, even longer legs in tight black skinny jeans, and he may or may not have actually lived in the house with the covered porch. He talked about the gym and Chipotle, and it seemed pretty likely from the moment we showed up that he was high on something. But the warmth of the sun and the absurdity of his stories filled us all with the kind of lightness that makes a subpar interview infinitely valuable on a more subtle, cellular level.

"Your health is, like, your body," he said at one point, staring off. "Wellness is… your whole being."

You gotta be able to hear an insight anytime, anywhere.

When the interview was over, the three of us shuffled out the front gate and down the sidewalk, not saying a word. Turning a corner behind a brick wall overgrown with leafy vines, we doubled over.

"I can't believe you were able to keep that going for that long," Julia said, one hand on my shoulder and the other over her chest. "Oh my God, what was that…"

"He was on something, right?" said Sarah, grinning.

"Oh yeah," Julia and I said together.

"Oh my God, and the sun—I would have fallen asleep if he hadn't kept saying such ridiculous things."

"I saw you close your eyes for a minute there," I said. The ache in my belly from laughing so hard felt good, raw, nostalgic.

"Never—never in my life have I heard an interview quite like that," said Julia.

As we walked and they quoted the conversation, laughter spilling up into the five o'clock sky, I thought: *resources*. Wouldn't be the first time work had saved me.

9

In my work, I am especially skilled at finding patterns. Not that every pattern has meaning behind it—I know that. Nonetheless, you note it, track it, keep it on the table, just in case. So, on the last day of July 2018, when I found out I was—finally, *finally*—pregnant, the patterns were immediately apparent: In our first pregnancy, we got pregnant on the first try; the second on the second try; the third on the third; and this fourth one on the fourth. One dead child, two miscarriages, three uterine surgeries, four pregnancies.

Sometimes, if a pattern ensnares your thinking too early, so that you start ignoring things outside of it—even when their value is obvious—you have to set it aside.

A beginner's mind, I had told my grief counselor I wanted to have for this pregnancy, as I mentally prepared for it. Especially because the beginning, I knew, was the best part; every pregnancy, that first day was pure magic.

I took the test the day before Dale and I were to leave for Redwood National Park. Determined to have at least this one day of unfettered joy, I zipped around the house, laying out all of our backpacking gear, packing a suitcase of street clothes for an interlude in San Francisco, and tying up loose ends on my research projects, a trail of glitter following me everywhere.

I kept it all to myself—that one whole magical day, all mine—except for my fertility specialist. I called their offices that morning, knowing that I would be in their care first before seeing Dr. Page and Dr. Jeffrey, the perinatologist we had seen with Sloane. This being my first pregnancy since the hysteroscopies, I was still under the umbrella of *getting pregnant*. That's how the fertility specialist had explained it to me—they were in service of *getting* me pregnant, while the perinates were in service of *keeping* me pregnant.

They asked if I could come in for a pregnancy test and blood sample that afternoon. Jump right onto this road? *Hell fucking yes*, I thought—it's the only place I wanted to be, other than on the other side of it with a living baby. I was beside myself.

When I arrived at their offices, a nurse took me back to a small lab area behind the reception counter. She tied off my arm with a neon green elastic strap and told me to make a fist. I did and looked away. I could handle seeing my own blood, but one time, a nurse had me hold my own full vials, and it was their warmth that got to me.

"All set," she said, filing a few vials into a plastic tray. "Danielle will be out in a moment."

Danielle was the physician's assistant who had been handling my case. I hadn't seen her since December, when I had my last pre-op tests and she put a balloon in my uterus and pumped ink into my fallopian tubes. These places test for everything.

Danielle walked around the corner, a full belly sticking out in front of her.

"Congratulations," she said, smiling. "Your test came back positive."

"You too," I said, suddenly sheepish. I had liked her, a lot. She was far more personable than the doctor. I don't think he knew me or my case from the women who came before me, but Danielle had told me how she grew up in the neighborhood where Dale and I lived, how she used to ride her bike to the McDonald's on the corner.

"40 weeks tomorrow," she said. "I don't know when this guy is gonna come."

I smiled and looked out at the reception area. The entire front wall of the office was glass. A granite countertop ran the length of it, decked out with two Keurig machines, two trees of K-cups, and a pyramid of mugs; below the counter sat a glass-doored mini-fridge, stocked with cans in a dozen different colors. Around the corner was the waiting area, set up cozy living-room style: plush seats, magazine racks, flatscreen TV. A burning fireplace.

I didn't know her story. And I was happy for her. But 40-week bellies hurt.

When I got home, I surveyed the piles on the floor, running through a mental checklist. Just the daily essentials left: wallet, book, notebook, and pencil. As I grabbed them all from the top of my dresser, my eye caught the corner of a light grey, hardback book beneath a pile of papers. I slid it out and ran my finger down its woven front. It still had a two-inch band of thin cardboard packaging wrapped around the front cover.

A Keepsake Pregnancy Journal, it said. *Guided prompts for 40 weeks.*

A dear friend had given it to me a month after Sloane died. I had treasured it, craved it, hated it. Every pregnancy, I had opened it—like I did now—and flipped through its pages, reading prompts like *How I'm feeling this week* and *What I learned at this week's appointment*, and every time, I felt an ocean well up inside me. Three times now, I couldn't bear the thought of filling out the early pages with my heart and dreams in neat, tiny print, and maybe even getting halfway through, maybe even to 22 weeks, but then having to stop because the baby was gone.

I slid the journal back beneath the papers.

Even when you set the pattern aside, it is still there, on the table, holding potential.

Every time, becoming pregnant changed my entire orientation toward the world. Or maybe just toward myself. My body became a temple, housing a miracle. The new life inside me became a constant part of my consciousness, and settling my attention on it—whether the size of a poppyseed or a mango—drowned out the rest of the world. I was never alone; I had purpose.

That connection was so pure; for me, it was life itself.

As Dale and I wound our way into the heart of Redwoods National Park, tree after tree after tree sliding by the windows, my head was on loop: *I'm pregnant, I'm pregnant, I'm pregnant.* I was shiny and new; I was the furthest thing from loss.

"I'm pregnant!" I shouted into the car, falling into giggles.

Dale was just as excited, but he didn't know this experience the same way. He couldn't feel the fresh magic in his muscles, the new way his body breathed. When we took a turnoff to get out, stretch our legs, and see Big Tree, I felt as though I was it: fifteen-hundred years old but nearly three-hundred feet tall. Unshaken and fully alive.

When we set out on our overnight an hour later, I felt Lilliputian. The park is a fairytale land, the ground blanketed in emerald clovers, stacks of mushrooms fanning out like forest mussels, living giants lifting the sky. I turned in circles as the trail wound through dense groves, layers and layers of thriving life to take in, as if my eyes could drink, their thirst be satiated.

"What are those trees called in *Lord of the Rings*?" I asked Dale, gazing up the endless trunks.

"Ents!" he said, beaming. Dale loved movies; I didn't care much for them. There were few things more disconcerting to me than walking out of a dark movie theatre and into the bright afternoon sun. It always felt like a whole chunk of my life had just disappeared.

"What are they like?"

"Very old. Very strong."

"What's that whole land called?"

"You mean Middle-earth?"

"Yeah," I breathed. The air beneath the redwoods felt ancient, mystical. Its wisdom moved everything inside me.

I had always wanted to be a tree: strong, solid, rooted to the earth. The years of my growth easily measured in rings; my seasons predictable and rich, each worthy in their own right.

"Take a picture of me," I said, leaning up against a massive fallen trunk overgrown with moss and clover. In our entire nine years together, I had only done that—asked Dale to take a photo of me—twice before. The last time was the year before, when I was 6 weeks into my third pregnancy. We were in Denver, the Colorado Railroad Museum. Hands in my jean pockets, I leaned against a black railcar that said Rio Grande in a white, italicized sans serif. The first time was two days after I found out I was pregnant with Sloane. Dale and I had gone to Notre Dame for a football weekend, and I stood in front of the golden dome, hands on my hips, grinning. I didn't think of any of those photos as just me; they were always me and the baby. I wanted them to know we were there.

But this time, in the Redwoods, I also just wanted to know that *I* was there. That there was something left, after all we had been through, of just me. Something that had survived. Something that would go on to find these last beautiful places on earth and feel at home in them. I took hundreds of pictures that trip, trying in vain to capture the scale of the trees, the texture of their bark. The one thousand shades of green from bud to canopy.

And as I walked, thick boots on soft soil, for one of the few times in my life, I felt like I was really there. Not ten steps down the road; not ten steps back. Just there. Right there. Taking a deep breath. Smelling the spiced bark. The sweet chlorophyll.

It would still be years before I really learned the value of presence, but I was trying. Even if I couldn't bring myself to keep a pregnancy journal, I wanted to enjoy what I had while I had it. Dale and I lived it up in San Francisco, devouring bowls of clam chowder on the street and raiding Levi's Plaza for jeans and crewneck sweatshirts. Then, back at my old office in LA for a week, I brought in another pink box of donuts for my co-workers Despite our losses, it was never too early for me to bring this baby into my life.

It was still years, too, before I knew what a trigger was and how it could drop the floor right out from under presence.

At home, in early September, I got a call from my fertility specialist.

"I'm sorry," he said. "You've tested positive for an antiphospholipid antibody."

I stood in the middle of my office, holding the phone to my ear, staring at the ground. Blinking. The mid-afternoon sun fell through the windows and onto the wood floor.

"What?" I said. Of the one thousand questions that had raced through my head, it was the only one that seemed to cover them all.

He explained: The antibodies can lead to clotting, inhibiting the baby's ability to get nutrients and causing miscarriage. In all the bloodwork they had done, I had tested positive for one of the five antibodies.

The treatment: blood thinner injections for my entire pregnancy.

The prognosis: with treatment, 70-80% likelihood of success, a viable pregnancy.

I sunk fast, hard. Sitting on the couch with Dale that night, I held my head in my hands.

"I can't go through another loss," I said. "I can't. I just can't."

My last pregnancy, a year before, I had been so sure. *This won't happen again; this couldn't happen again*, I had thought. *It's so rare*. I had looked it up: Only 2% of women had two miscarriages in a row. *How unlikely*.

Even when I had found blood. Seven weeks into that third pregnancy, I had woken up with a crimson stain in my underwear and told myself, *It's ok, this is normal*. In a motel bathroom, I had stuck on a panty liner and pulled up my leggings. Dale, Leo, and I had driven up to Española the night before to see the turning of the aspens—a savored event in northern New Mexico. It was early October 2017, nine months after Sloane died and five months after my first miscarriage. Still seven months before Georgia.

When we got to the Aspen Vista trailhead in Santa Fe later that morning, everything felt sharp and rich and alive. Stands of aspens dripped in egg yolk, the solid blue sky the only break in yellow, and people young and old were making their way up a wide dirt trail. The air, at ten thousand feet, had bite to it.

Fall is my time of year. It's when life seems to deepen and come together. Maybe it was the season, or maybe the new pregnancy, but that day, I had felt certain of something. What, I didn't know, but something at my center felt solid, unwavering. A springboard for progress. I knew the statistics, and I was holding onto them, but that wasn't exactly it.

On a steep, rocky stretch about two miles in, where the crowd thinned out to only us, I said to Dale, "I went through a really rough period earlier this year. I was kind of suicidal."

I had never said it aloud. But with the vastness of the mountains around me, the word didn't slice at my ears like it usually did in my head. It just sort of floated on by—a puff, a breath, a weightless dissolution. Maybe that's why I hadn't shared any of it with Dale yet, how I had struggled at the top of the cliffs in the Jemez, in Durango, felt unsteady on my feet; I was afraid it would be too heavy. That I would be asking more of him than was fair.

But what is love then, if not a place we can always seek refuge?

My heart trembled, only realizing in that moment how scared I had actually been. "I didn't say anything at the time because I didn't want to scare you."

I don't remember Dale's words. His sweet, tender being held open like a cave for the small animal of me. What I remember is feeling whole and torn all at once.

As we climbed, I told him about the cliffs. I wiped my dripping face with the ends of my sleeves, and he let me be utterly human, the mess of my insides laid bare, small and ugly on that mountaintop. Loving me quietly, steadfastly.

At the top, the trail sprawled into a broad overlook. The entire world to ourselves—still and quiet but for the occasional sweep of wind. Most people didn't make it up this high. Below, the mountain was a slope of burnt yellow, dark green rolling hills behind it, and the steel blue Jemez rising in the distance. I hung back as Dale and Leo roamed to the outer edges, not out of fear but to hold them in my view of this land of enchantment, this life of enchantment.

Dale stood on a boulder, taking in the view. Leo sniffed, trotted, paused, gazed. None of this was mine, and yet, I had claimed it all as my own: the mountains, the trees, the desert, the sky; the colors, the wind, this man, this dog. This was my life; this was where and how and why I lived.

Of this, I was certain.

And I thought: *Whatever has happened, I have this now.*

After lunch on a grassy hill, we made our way back down. At one point, still no one in sight, I shuffled downslope and squatted with my leggings pulled down to my thighs. A hot stream of urine steamed in the cold air. I checked my panty liner: a thimble of blood. *Good—that's manageable*, I thought. I shook myself off and shimmied my pants back on, climbing back up to the trail.

"Good?" Dale asked.

I smiled. "All good."

Having shared with Dale the worst of me, there was a new ease between us, a deepening that we could touch with our fingertips. As crops of two or three people, and occasionally a small family, made their way up, we exchanged waves, head nods, hellos.

And then a mile from the trailhead, a sensation. One I knew intimately, one that haunted my body, my pelvic walls, my inner thighs. A sensation that can only be described by one word: *gush*.

My breath caught in my chest. I paused mid-stride when a small moan—a foreign sound, from a cave inside that I didn't know existed—escaped me and then fled. I kept walking.

"You ok?" Dale asked, falling in step with me.

Another gush, this one spreading a thick warmth down my thighs. I paused again, caught my breath again. It was hard to notice that I kept holding it—that I was holding every part of me together.

I looked up at Dale, and we locked eyes.

"I'm having a miscarriage," I said. We stood there for a moment, looking at each other, surrounded by walls of yellow trees. Forever the two of us in this world. Then I nodded, and we kept walking.

"Is it bad?" he asked. His voice told me that he didn't know what to do, or how I was doing.

"Yeah," I said, eyes straight ahead. "It's running all down my legs."

"Oh, man." I could hear his face cringing.

"It's ok. Nothing I can do about it now."

We walked in silence—my legs close together, my steps light, as if trying to keep everything left from falling out. But the effort was known only to us; to everyone else on the trail, we were just a regular young couple out for a hike. With our dog. On a beautiful fall day.

That entire last mile back to the car, I noticed every single person we passed. Every other regular human being. And I wondered what was invisible about them. Those two older women in deep conversation, their track suits swishing with every step—did one of them just go through chemo? That family with two teenage kids, spitting images of their parents—was there a third kid, and was he addicted to opiates? That elderly gentleman with the soft brown cap— did he lose his wife in a car accident? Was he driving?

Who else was dying inside?

The day after we learned about the antiphospholipid antibodies, I went to the fertility offices to get the tools to deal with it. Boxes and boxes of alcohol wipes, syringes, and little glass bottles of Heparin—the drug. A nurse taught me all the motions: rolling the bottles between my palms to mix up the drug, sucking it out with the needle, flicking the syringe like a junkie to work out any air bubbles. And then stabbing my belly with a swift rush of force.

"Be intentional," she said. "Do it fast."

Twice a day. Six a.m. and six p.m.

The whole thing made me sick—sick of jumping through hoops, sick of worrying, sick of the constant threat of more loss, loss, loss.

I needed certainty in the form of a stitch around my cervix: the cerclage. I counted down to the procedure in half-day increments. First shot. Second shot.

Another day down.

10

I sat on the edge of an exam table, fully clothed. I was back at High Desert to talk about my options for this pregnancy, and despite the fact that the one and only time I had been there before, *the prognosis was terrible*, something about being there again felt comforting.

This time, I was seeing Dr. Kwan. I don't know where Dr. Jeffrey was, and I didn't have the balls to ask. Instead, I sat in the exam room while Dr. Kwan gave me his expert opinion.

"I don't think you need a cerclage," he said. "I'm not convinced of incompetent cervix for you"

I clenched my jaw. Slid my hands under my thighs, focused on my ears; tried to listen. I had just seen the baby—at 11 weeks 2 days, lying on its back in its own little room in my belly. While I had waited for Dr. Kwan to come in, I had traced my finger back and forth along its outline on the sonogram printout. Nose, chin, round belly. Leg bent at the knee. The cerclage was supposed to be placed around 13 or 14 weeks, once the threat of first-trimester miscarriage was gone.

"I think your first pregnancy was spontaneous premature labor," he went on. Dr. Kwan was fit and trim in mauve-colored scrubs one shade darker than the cushions of the exam table, his smooth skin the exact tone of the wooden frame around a painting of wildflowers hanging on the wall.

My chest caved. In my head: *This shit is so fucking unfair.*

That's not a term I ever used to describe our situation; to me, life was unfair, and we were just part of it. That's what I had written when we announced Sloane's birth and death: *Life isn't easy, life isn't fair, but it's what you make of it.* But this—this felt like cruelty: to be such an advanced society—scientifically, medically—and still not know why our daughter was born too early to live or how to keep that from happening again. Cruelty from whom or what, I didn't know—but it cut deep.

"A cerclage comes with risks," Dr. Kwan said. "Mainly infection. It's unlikely, but it's still a risk I don't think you need to take."

I stared at the floor. I saw my heart lying in the middle of the freeway, trammeled by every passing day of this pregnancy. *Whoosh, whoosh.* No cerclage felt like the real risk. But what the fuck did I know—I was just a broken doll on the floor of an empty playroom.

And yet, a bull sneered inside me. A rage I had felt the summer before, seven months after Sloane died, at a friend's baby shower. The friend and the baby, for once, weren't the problem; it was another guest, Krystal, who had gotten to me.

Krystal was the only other woman I personally knew with an incompetent cervix. As I understood the story, her cervical insufficiency was discovered during her first pregnancy the year before, but she was able to get an emergency cerclage and deliver her daughter full-term. At one point during the baby shower, I found myself standing outside a circle of women—how stingingly, enduringly true that is—and the story of Krystal's cerclage came up.

I had known her for a few years, and she had always been one for animated storytelling. She used her hands to show how, for the procedure, she was inverted, her legs sticking up in the air at sixty degrees, wide eyes to convey that she was fully awake but numb down there. She laughed and laughed, her full cheeks shining and hugging her small mouth, as if this story were an afternoon at the park with her living, breathing daughter—glee and fun and *oh, isn't that silly.* I was wearing the same blue sheath dress I would later wear in Atlanta. It stuck to my summer sweat in the same way.

And then she said: "I don't even know if I'll get a cerclage again. I might not."

It was so hot at that party. Everyone packed into the house, the bodies, the sweat… I wanted to back away from the heat, step by step, my blue Vans on the wooden floor so that I could remember that I had feet. But I was burning from the inside out. Her ignorance, her arrogance stunned me. I couldn't walk far enough backward to un-know what I knew. What can happen without that thread holding everything together. How it all falls apart.

How cavalier we can be when we haven't lost everything.

I looked Dr. Kwan in the eye and said, "I'm not going through this pregnancy without a cerclage."

"Ok," he said. "You can certainly make that choice."

Two days before my cerclage was to be placed, Dale and I walked into a new seafood joint across town. It's fast casual—order at the counter, pick up your food on a big metal tray when your number is called. I ordered a lobster roll, him a shrimp roll. Maybe we were trying to recreate the magic in Charleston; maybe we were just hoping to actually get good seafood in New Mexico. But it's not like the state had moved any closer to the ocean. We found a booth and slid in.

"I can't believe the cerclage is almost here," I said.

"I know," said Dale. "It's gonna be great."

He sucked water through a straw. All of our hope, literally, was hanging on this thread that would be tied around my cervix like purse strings—that's how Dr. Page had explained it to me.

"Are you really ready for it?" I asked. "For no sex?"

That was part of the deal—no intercourse until the cerclage was to be taken out at 37 weeks. That's six months.

My arms hung down by my sides, still inside my coat. Dark sky filled the floor-to-ceiling windows. The interior décor was so modern, so manufactured. The food was probably bland. Suddenly, I felt guilty for bringing us here, guilty for having a cervix that didn't work right.

"Yeah, it's fine. Not a big deal."

When our number was called, Dale picked up the tray. But when he set it down on the table, it was awkward: too big to take our red baskets off of and set aside, but too small to keep our baskets on without our food being too far away from us. We shimmied it around, took the first bites of our rolls, shimmied it some more. Finally, before I sent the whole thing flying out the fucking window, I picked up the tray and walked it over to the trash can, stacking it on top of the others.

"Are you sure?" I asked when I sat back down. I wanted to talk about other things, but my stomach felt swollen with saltwater, lobster sunken on the bottom. My sandwich had too much bread.

"Totally," he said. "Totally worth it."

I felt ridiculous. Like a child, a monkey, a clown—something that flails its arms about wildly. Anything other than a grown-ass woman. It suddenly seemed irresponsible to bring a child into my orbit. It was hard to tell what was hormones, what was anxiety, what was grief—but it didn't really matter either. I would berate myself for all of it.

To feel both absurd and powerless is a precarious place to be. But life itself had become a bit absurd in the last two years and I was having to do a lot of mental gymnastics to get through each day and I was fucking exhausted. I didn't know that what I needed was for someone to hand me a free pass, to write on it: *This is all hard, but you're doing the best you can and that is enough.* Maybe emboss it. Stamp it with a seal.

Someone, anyone.

This is all so motherfucking lonely, a voice in my head yelled. I looked up to see a couple getting up from their seats at a high-top across the aisle. They balled up their paper napkins and stacked their baskets. I watched them as if they might look over and lock eyes with me and see that I needed to be saved.

They moved toward the door. Pushed their trash into the swinging door of the can and left. I looked down at the bite marks in my bread. A half-eaten cup of wet coleslaw.

The day of the procedure, all I could taste was the delicious anticipation of nothingness. Of the anesthesia slipping into my veins and my head silencing, ceasing. In the bright white operating room, so wonderfully warm lying beneath the stack of hospital blankets, I counted ninety-nine, ninety-eight, ninety-seven. And then: nirvana.

11

The cerclage settled something inside me. I stood taller, walked with a new swagger. So far, this baby was really happening.

Fully into my second trimester and only barely showing, I was in Austin for work, talking with women about clothes and accessories—their style, where they shop, how they decide what to wear. A week earlier, I had been in LA for the same research and interviewed women who made me want to be more of a woman. One who got dressed up for date night with her husband and said, "Parenting isn't as hard as everyone makes it sound; you just do it." Another one who prided herself on her thrift store finds and had just written a book. One more who went to USC, then AA in her early twenties, and now was a professional dog walker. For two hours at a time, I sat on their couches and rifled through their closets and longed for them to welcome me into their club.

Dale and I also had a chance rendezvous in LA; he was there for a conference, and for one night in a secluded hotel, our trips overlapped.

"I found out the sex," I had said, grinning. He was sitting on the edge of the bed; I stood between his legs. His hands were spread over the backs of my thighs, mine tangled in his hair. The room was half-lit. "The ultrasound tech told me by accident at my appointment before I flew out here."

That was only sort of true. She knew we had done the genetic testing that would tell us the sex early, and I had told her we wanted to find out; I just didn't stop her when she thought I meant right then and there. I needed to know—needed to not be told at the 20-week anatomy scan.

"Tell me!" Dale had said, scratching his fingers wildly on my thighs. I loved him for not giving me one ounce of shit for finding out, for being a better person than I was. I looked into his eyes. Heard all the conversations we had ever had about wanting to have kids.

I smiled. "It's a girl."

We squealed and giggled and fell onto the bed in each other's arms. I rolled onto my back, Dale onto his side, propped up on an elbow. He pulled my sweater up to my chest and kissed my small belly, his lips covering the bruises—yellow from old injections, purple from more recent. As much as the threat was unsettling and the jab was nauseating, I had come to appreciate the twice-daily opportunity to actively care for the baby. Our second little girl. It reminded me of the nightly progesterone pill I had to push up against my cervix with Sloane—a sad but overt gesture of care, of love.

Dale lifted his head, pulled down my sweater.

"So," he said, smiling, meeting my eyes. "Violet?"

I took a deep breath. Another chance at the dream.

"Yeah," I said, my heart squeezing. "Yeah, yeah, yeah."

I buried my smiling face in his neck.

By the time I got to Austin, I was drained. Even in the energy high of the second trimester, the overstimulation of fieldwork—a constant performance of talking, listening, observing, analyzing, planning, wayfinding, and longing for solitude—had set in. Both the honey and the bee, my brain moved slowly while my body buzzed. And yet, I lived for these days. It's funny how what is most grueling is also often most rewarding. Most transforming.

Most exalting and most humbling.

The morning of the fifth day of research, in the stale light of my hotel bathroom, I opened my toiletry bag to see little silver bottles, orange-handled syringes, and no antiseptic wipes. I stared at the bag. No wipes. No. Wipes. *How could I have not packed enough?* I thought. *What—can I not even count?*

Fuck. Shit. *What am I gonna do?*

I looked at the bathroom counter. I thought of Taj, washing his fresh ink with mild soap and warm water. *No, no—that's not good enough.*

I looked at my watch. The first interview was in two hours. As I added up minutes for breakfast, driving, running into a store, poking myself, I could hear my heartbeat. It sounded too fast. *No, no, we don't have time for that*, I said to myself. Because what if they didn't have what I needed? I would have wasted everyone's time, dragging them along with me. My client, my co-worker, our videographer—all on a stupid errand for my stupid mistake for a stupid problem with this pregnancy.

I felt the light darken, felt something close in around me. I could not, for the life of me, figure out how to solve this problem. But I had a day to get on with, a team to lead.

Down in the hotel lobby, the four of us waited for the valet. Typical morning chit-chat that nobody really cares about—how you slept, what work emails you caught up on at night, what fixture wasn't working in your room. I mentioned my problem to my co-worker, Cosmo. He was new to the company; this was our first project together. But I liked the way he thought, the questions he asked, and he had been in LA with me the week before; he knew why I had to excuse myself with my black bag every night at dinner.

The three of them stood, hands in pockets, teetering on their heels. Me, I shuffled—here and there, like an idiot, completely indecisive about what to do. *Soap? Store? Skip?*

This is so stupid.

I caught Cosmo's face, his eyes on mine, the whites pristine around their brown centers. Everything about his face was round—full cheeks, a row of brown curls curving over his forehead, his soft, crescent-moon smile. He nodded at me and walked over to the hotel bar.

He and the bartender exchanged words, smiles. Even though I couldn't hear him from across the lobby, I knew Cosmo was being kind, genuine. He loved pizza and improv, wanted a "yes and" tattoo; he was the kind of person who there should be more of in this world.

The bartender pulled a small white square out from under the bar. Cosmo took it between two fingers and flicked his wrist toward the man—the subtle but tender thank-you for a small favor. Because sometimes life offers us moments, if we're paying attention, when we are drawn above our bodies, to look down and see the magnitude in the mundane. See that it's simple gestures that connect us all. The ability to not fully know a situation and still be kind in it. To not need a reason to recognize the humanity in one another.

"This was all he had," said Cosmo, holding out the wet nap, still between his two fingers. It wasn't what I needed, but the gesture was more than enough. How easy it had been for him to do what I could not do for myself.

"Thanks, Cosmo," I said. "Really—I appreciate it. I'll be back."

When I came back from the restroom, I said to my team, "Let's wait outside. The car's got to be here soon."

I held the lobby door open, the last to file out into the cool morning air. The sky was overcast, easy on my tired eyes. I turned to my client.

"We need to stop at Target on the way to the first interview," I said. "It'll be quick—we have time. I just have to take blood thinner injections for a pregnancy complication, and I ran out of antiseptic."

"I'm on Lovenox," she said. I knew that name; it was a drug similar to the Heparin I was on. I stared at her—Shannon. Trim dark jeans, beige sweater, statement necklace. Brown hair from a curling iron. She was straight out of a J. Crew catalog, only shorter and thicker. She was new to the project, too; I had just met her yesterday but already knew she was bold, intelligent, and only slightly discomforting. Kinda like me. "I'm not telling anyone yet," she went on, "but I'm 9 weeks pregnant."

The car pulled up, and we piled in. Thankfully, Cosmo drove; I rode shotgun, pulling up directions on my phone. I turned in my seat to face Shannon in the backseat.

"The shots suck, but they're worth it," I said. I thought of Taj, of Julia. "Last year, my first daughter was born too early and passed away."

Our videographer said something. Shannon said something. Cosmo's mouth made a sound and his round, boyish face, glancing back and forth between me and the road, was crestfallen. None of them had known. But all of them engaged—these twenty and thirty-somethings with more compassion than my own family, more bravery than people twice their age. I was humbled.

"We've gone through seven rounds of IVF," Shannon said. "I've never made it this far."

As we drove, we dove into it all—the losses, the tests, the hope, the despair. This was their last shot, she said; they couldn't afford any more. I didn't ask whether she meant money or her heart—knew that it was probably both. Our conversation was a dance; the guys swayed between horror and admiration. *These conversations save lives*, I thought.

Oh, to speak and to listen. To create something together.

This is why we have each other in this world.

That afternoon, we sat in the small living room of a woman named Cherie. We were each in a different color of wing-backed chair, her tawny Pomeranian burrowed in my lap. Cherie, in her early thirties, worked for a digital media company and lived for the local art scene. Her atmosphere was easy and alive; I let the interview wander to the most interesting places.

"The world wants me to hate myself," Cherie said, gesturing from her chest down to her knees. She was full-figured, her black maxi dress and yellow cardigan clinging tightly to her body, and wore her blonde hair curled and cropped into bangs. Black cat-eye glasses and red lipstick drew you into her face. "But I don't. I've learned to love this."

"How does that feel," I asked, "for the world to want you to feel badly about yourself?"

"Well, now I just say, 'fuck off.' I don't listen anymore."

"What about when you listened?"

"It hurt. I would agree with them. Yeah, yeah, I'm trying to be healthy, I would say, hating my arms. I would try every diet under the sun. Never wear a sleeveless shirt. And then one day, I just said, 'These are my arms! I'm gonna make you look at them!'"

My insides swelled. "What did that feel like?"

"It felt great!" She paused, looking at me. The rhinestones in the peaked corners of her glasses glistened. "You know how people always save their best stuff for special occasions? I thought, why do we do that? Why do we do that to ourselves? So, I started wearing my favorite clothes on regular-ass days. It feels fuckin' great."

When we followed Cherie down the hall to see her bedroom closet, Shannon caught my arm. She held up her phone, letting me know she needed to step out for a call. I nodded and waved her off.

In her room, Cherie stood in her walk-in closet and pulled hanger after hanger off the rack. Her walls were covered in local artwork, her dresser in handmade jewelry.

"I never used to wear sleeveless dresses like these," she said, holding out another maxi. "Or always with a sweater. I'm only wearing one today because it was cool out when I walked Triscuit."

She looked down at the brush of fur winding between her ankles. "She helps me get out."

When we left Cherie's apartment, Shannon caught my arm again.

"Hey," she said. "That was my mom on the phone. My dad is in the hospital, in Maryland."

"Oh, I'm so sorry," I said.

"He had been having some back issues, but I guess it's more serious than that."

The walk from Cherie's apartment across the parking lot wasn't long enough. I wanted more time in the open air, falling to dusk. Suddenly, I stopped, bringing my hand to the side of my belly. Violet's first kick. I smiled to myself.

"He's in his seventies," Shannon said. "It's not sounding good."

"Do you think you should go there?"

"My doctors don't want me in hospitals. The risk of infection..."

The next morning, Shannon got another phone call and left for the airport. During our last interview, with a Black female powerlifter who worked out in fully-coordinated neon and wanted her femininity to shine like a diamond, I thought about Shannon on that flight—a bundle of tightly-bound nerves, suspended and rushing all at once.

"I *am* a diamond," the powerlifter said. "I had to learn that."

Shannon saw her father that evening, in the hospital. He died the next day.

12

In the cozy winter of early 2019, I evolved a quarter-turn. We had made it to viability, and our fears had quieted. My cervix was still three centimeters, and Dr. Jeffrey took me off the Heparin shots. My growing belly became my sun, my moon, my center of gravity.

On my way into the shower every night, I paused in front of the wall-size mirrors in our bathroom. My lithe body, partially covered in tattoos, perfectly rounding at my breasts, my belly, my ass. I ran my hands over my curves, loving my own flesh like I never had before. My womanhood felt regal.

To carry her around with me everywhere was the most magnificent act my body had ever done.

I miss that belly with a goddamn ache.

Just as the term *self-care* was becoming popular, I felt like I was learning how to care for my body. Not just *be healthy*—I had always done that—but *care*, with tenderness. Daily walks, croissant and Swiss cheese sandwiches, vinyasa flows on my bedroom floor from an online prenatal yoga program. Yoga had always been too slow for me before—I was more of the running, weightlifting, circuit-training type—but now it soothed me. Made my body feel *good*. The sheer simplicity of *goodness*.

Life. Was *good*.

This was the dream.

Prenatal yoga, maternity clothes, childbirth classes—it was all another chance at becoming a mom.

On a cold but snowless evening in January, Dale and I left work an hour early to drive across town to a forgotten conference room somewhere deep inside a building, where ten couples gathered around a long table—or rather, several smaller tables pushed together. Dale and I sat at the head, just like I did in school, in work meetings, so that everyone was in my field of vision at all times. It's one reason I don't mind getting to the airport too early or waiting for a table at a restaurant; people-watching is a personal hobby. And I watched these women with interest: the size of their bellies, how put-together they looked, how happy they seemed. Not out of judgment, but curiosity: a club I still didn't feel like I fully belonged to. While soulful at times, this pregnancy still felt like a journey of one.

Our instructor, Meredith, gave us a preamble for the course. She was a mom of three, funny, off-beat. Laughed at her own quirkiness. I liked her.

Then she led us around the table through introductions. For most of the women, this was their first pregnancy, or at least that's how they told it. Two or three of them had a much older child and had forgotten all of this stuff in the years between. With every new name, every new voice, I tried to find some of myself in them, to don them like a costume. *Let me belong here*, I pleaded; *please, let me belong.*

As the introductions neared me, my heart pounded. *This is my truth, this is my truth*, I repeated in my head.

I took a breath. "I'm Alle, and this is my husband, Dale. This is my fourth pregnancy. One birth and loss at 22 weeks. Two years ago."

My arms fizzled, and my stomach sank. I was suddenly aware that many people were still wearing their winter coats; the fabric rustled as they shifted around in their seats. Dale squeezed my thigh under the table. I kept my eyes on Meredith, and she nodded respectfully.

"I'm so sorry," she said, and I felt like I could see who she was as a mom. "Welcome."

Why does there have to be such shame in sharing our own tragedies? Why is the pressure to make ourselves small so much greater than the truth? People can be such fucking assholes—not *these* people, but people at large. The people who can't tolerate their own discomfort, who make the whole world feel unsafe, unkind.

Meredith turned to pain management. With dimmed lights and PowerPoint slides, she laid out the various options, from all-natural to fully medicated. We went around the room again, this time giving ourselves a number—zero to ten, no drugs to everything you've got—and I wanted to bloody curse something for placing me on the outside once again: Every single woman chose 100% natural. No drugs; all pain. What the fuck.

I looked around the table. With everyone turned toward Meredith, I saw mostly side profiles and backs of heads. Washed and gelled curly hair. Pale scalps at the crowns. All of their own aches and memories somewhere in their bodies. Stories I didn't know.

On my turn, I laughed, tried to sound casual. I said, "Because I've been through it without an epidural, there is no way I'd choose that again. Give me all the drugs."

I didn't care. That was my truth.

When the class ended, Dale and I walked quietly out to our car. Neither of us had said anything, but I knew both of our heads were ballooning. Once the car doors were shut, we let the air out.

"Birth plan?" I said, giggling. "What birth plan?"

"Yeah, ok, people," Dale said. "Good luck with that."

It felt good to know things together—to know all the stupid shit to not get hung up on because it doesn't matter. Or maybe it was all just shit that I wouldn't allow myself to consider. Meredith had said, *Think about what kind of environment you want—music, scents, lighting.* I thought about how alive I wanted my child to be. How I wanted her to breathe, to look at me. How I wanted to hear her cry.

"They have no fuckin' idea," I said, looking straight ahead. Knowing that we were once them. Fighting the urge to wish we still were. A hardness edging into my voice nonetheless.

"I know," said Dale, and I felt the hardness in him, too.

That night, we laid in bed, staring up at the ceiling.

"We have to figure out her middle name," Dale said. "Have you thought of any?"

Every day for the past few weeks, I had stood in front of the four-by-five-foot map of New Mexico hanging in our entryway, scouring the squiggly lines of rivers, the shades of mountain ranges. It was a tradition we had started, by accident, with Sloane.

When we had left the hospital the morning after she died, the world had looked different. I saw things I had never seen before, appreciated details I had never given attention to. As we drove east down Montgomery, the Sandia Mountains rose up before us.

The Sandias are something everyone sees every day in Albuquerque. Massive and defining the eastern edge of town, they orient you, guide you. But that morning, it seemed as if they had sprung up overnight. Suddenly taking up all the newly empty space in my life, with depth and precision, it seemed I could see every tree, every ridge, every fissure on their western face, a deep mourning blue under soft winter clouds. And then I realized: It had snowed. The crowns of the mountains were dusted white. Powdered sugar. My breath caught in my chest, as if remembering something I didn't know I knew.

"We should have made Sloane's middle name Sandia," I heard myself say, my eyes unwavering, "after the mountains."

We had left that field on the forms blank. We just hadn't gotten that far yet.

"I love it," Dale said. "Let's do it."

"It's perfect," I breathed.

And as we drove toward the Sandias stretching into the gray sky, I gathered the mountains up in my arms and squeezed them tight. Something felt right. A million things were wrong, but something felt right with my daughter named after those mountains that would never leave me, that were big enough to contain me.

"I don't know," I said to Dale back in our room, my eyes tracing the outline of the ceiling fan like the contours of a landscape. "I have a handful of options but none that I'm super crazy about."

"Oh!" he said, clutching my forearm. "I have an idea."

"What is it?"

"You have to guess."

"Oooo ok." I like guessing games. "Zia?"

"No, but that's not a bad option."

"Rosa?"

"No. What? What is that from?"

"Santa Rosa. Nevermind. Luna?"

"Nope. Think, like, the most New Mexican name ever."

"Albuquerque…?" I laughed.

"Nope."

"New… Mexico…?"

Dale laughed. "No, and you are out of guesses. Picture this," he said, raising one arm out in front of him, as if panning across a sign. "VIOLET. CHILE. MUDRICK."

We burst into giggles and rolled around, in love.

"Violet Sopaipilla Mudrick!"

"Violet Balloon Fiesta Mudrick!"

In my mind, I saw blue-gloved hands placing her fresh, sticky body on my chest, her face—the cheeks we had seen in the ultrasounds—right up against mine. Her warmth, her weight; both of us safe. I propped up on one elbow. "What about Gila?"

"Violet Gila," he said. I could see a scene playing in his eyes—his daughter. I thought of his hands holding my belly that last night with Sloane. He grinned. "I like it."

Marie Kondo was right: Ticying was magical, and it did change my life. We are not thing-people, and yet the amount of stuff we got rid of that winter under the brilliant guidance of *The Life-changing Magic of Tidying Up* was impressive. I can't imagine still hanging on to any of that shit.

In February, I cleared out every space that lived behind a door. I perfected folding my clothes into little squares. I let my socks breathe. And it all made me feel better about my whole life. A blank slate—that was what I had said I wanted, when she asked in the beginning of the book why I wanted to tidy.

Why? the book asked, pushing me a level deeper, like I do with research participants in my job. I wrote down that, to me, a blank slate was freedom, peace from meaningless things, so that I had the space and energy needed to deal with my actual life.

A thought winked in the back of my mind—how people and memories weren't all that different from clothes and knickknacks.

Why? the book asked again. Because I don't want to slog through life, I wrote—to feel like I'm just getting through it rather than really living it.

Why? Because I want my heart to be open to the world. Broken as it is, it craves beauty and joy and love to move into those cracks.

I had started making a list in my journal: *Things That Help*. Writing my resources down instead of trying to hold them all in my head.

Writing. Which I was still doing very little of.

Fresh air. When I could find the time.

Hearing others' stories. Mostly through work, research, reading.

Sloane. Or really: grief.

Dale. Always.

Baby. Everything baby.

And for the moment: *Tidying.*

Over the long holiday weekend in February, I came to the last room in the house: Violet's. Dale had painted it peach and moved the white furniture into place: crib off the wall and in front of the window, changing table anchored to another wall. As I stood in the doorway, resting against the doorjamb, I tried to picture her in the room— sleeping, playing, growing, the sun streaming through the window in the morning, every day of her young life, a rectangle of sunlight falling onto the floor. And I finally felt something settle into place: that this wasn't Sloane's room. Even though we bought the house a week after she died, this room had always been marked to me, as the room of my first-born, my oldest. Who everyone would forever think is Violet. And what would I do—correct them and make Violet feel less-than, or let it stand and dishonor Sloane's existence? Neither felt right; the truth was bendier than that. Motherhood was bendier than that.

I unrolled an earth-toned shag rug in the center of the room, angled a rocking chair from the corner. On the three floating shelves, I spread out the classics, their covers facing the room: *The Very Hungry Caterpillar, The Snowy Day, Ferdinand*. On the shelf above the changing table, I sat an elephant, an empty picture frame, and an orangey stuffed triceratops I had bought for Sloane, months after she died. I hung a llama backpack from a clothespin hook.

On a poof—woven and marigold—in front of the changing table, I tightly folded all thirty-six cloth diapers and stood them up on their edges in the top drawer. Tiny clothes in the middle drawer; swaddles, blankets, and burp cloths in the bottom one.

When I was done, I stood back. I slid a book an inch, straightened the rug a degree. Smoothed the cover of the changing pad.

This room was for Violet. It was her home; from my body to this room, she would go. I wasn't due for two months, but it was ready for her. I was ready for her.

On the exam table at my 32-week appointment that Monday morning—President's Day—I sat exhausted to the bone. *Maybe I overdid it*, I thought. I pictured the piles of tidied things still strewn across the floor of our great room: to donate, to relocate, to toss. *Next weekend*, I assured myself. After hearing the thundering gallop of Violet's heartbeat through the Doppler, I drove home in a daze. Sleep—I would sleep as long as I needed to.

Which ended up being most of the day. By mid-afternoon, I hadn't moved from the couch for hours, my body mealy and chilled and buried under a heavy pile of blankets. What a waste of a day off.

Suddenly, limbs flailing, I threw the blankets off me, sprinted to the bathroom, and hurled everything inside me.

I think I have the flu, I texted Dale. *Can you bring home soup?*

By eight that evening, I leveled out a bit. Neither the chicken nor the noodles had stayed down very long, but there seemed to be a calm on the surface of my stomach as Dale and I sat on the couch, the TV on, the black night pressing in through all of our windows—ahead, behind, above. The darkness soothed my aching head.

Under the blankets, I spread my hands down my belly. Pushed my fingertips into the lower sides where I usually felt her kicks and punches, those most precious sensations—a conversation between us and only us. After a day spent on the fringe of my body, I longed to be brought back into its center. Instead, something else slowly emerged.

"Babe, she hasn't moved," I said, only realizing it was true as I was saying it, "in a long time."

"Ok," said Dale, turning towards me, a question in his voice. He didn't know what it was like to be with her like this—constantly, intimately—or to count kicks. He didn't know what I was saying.

"I want to say it's been like… three hours," I said. I had been distracted while my body was crumbling in on itself, so I could only guess, but the important thing was what I knew for sure: This was not like her. "Babe, I need to go get checked out. This… is not right."

13

When we parked at the hospital, the mid-February chill felt like cool water down my throat. I drank it in, feeling life come back to the body that had laid stiff and dry all day. *What is it about this hospital*, I wondered, *that makes me feel all the right things at all the wrong times.* I tilted my head up to the sky. Even in the middle of town, in the soft glow of the building lights, the stars were out.

Triage, on the third floor, seemed empty. Quiet. A slow shift. Two nurses sat behind the check-in counter, one typing at a computer, the other sipping tea from a white Styrofoam cup, her feet propped up on a chair. The one at the computer slid a clipboard across the counter.

"Sign in here, please," she said. "What brings you in tonight?"

"I think I might have the flu, or something," I said. "I've been exhausted all day—chills, aches, throwing up. I had called the nurse earlier today, and she ordered a prescription for Tamiflu, but I haven't taken that yet." I paused. "We came in because I haven't felt the baby move in a few hours."

"How do you feel now?"

"I actually feel ok. Not great, but better than earlier."

"How far along are you?"

I knew all the questions already; they were always the same, everywhere you went. How many weeks, number of pregnancies, number of living children, any complications. Years later, I would hear from many women who had lost children or pregnancies how triggering such questions were, on every form, every appointment, every new doctor. I seemed to be the only one who found them comforting. To me, they said that my history mattered—that my body came with a story and that story was worth knowing.

32 weeks. Fourth pregnancy. Zero living children. History of premature birth and incompetent cervix. Cerclage at 14 weeks.

These nurses, these doctors—unlike everyday people, they knew what to do with that story. But I hear I am lucky in that regard, too— that not every woman feels cared for by her medical team. Within minutes, I was lying on a bed propped to forty-five degrees, a strap around my belly, listening to Violet's heartbeat.

The room was small, dim, the back corner of something. It all felt so temporary. We hadn't brought anything. Dale kept his jacket on.

I couldn't understand every word from my nurse—Kaya, the one who had been drinking tea—but I didn't mind. Standard swabs and measurements weren't that complicated; plus, I liked her. She had a heart-shaped face of smooth, black skin and an accent I couldn't pinpoint. South African, maybe. A goddess in sky blue scrubs. Her sharp eyes said she knew what she was doing, like she had been waiting for me to walk in that night, like she was born to do this.

When she left, I texted my boss: *Think I have the flu. Getting checked out. Probably won't be in tomorrow.*

An email to a co-worker: *Hey, sorry for the last-minute notice, but I'm going to need to reschedule our meeting tomorrow. Came down with the flu; will probably be back Wednesday. I'll let you know.*

I hated doing that shit. The only sick days I had taken in the seven years I had been there were in the last two—when all I could do was stare at the wall.

A woman came in. She appeared in shadow from the backlit doorway and moved toward the bed as if through water, so smoothly that I wanted to cry.

"I'm Susan, a midwife here," she said and smiled. The monitor next to my bed lit up her face. Thick, dark eyebrows and a straight line of bangs cropped high on her forehead. She clicked on a slim silver flashlight, waving it toward my bare legs. "I'm going to do a light exam to check out your cerclage. Just a quick peek, to not disturb the area."

From under the paper sheet draped over my lower body, she called, "It's a little red. Are you feeling any pain?"

"In my lower abdomen," I said. "It started since I've been here."

"Braxton-Hicks?" she asked, standing up and gently closing my knees together.

"I don't know—I've never had them."

"The pain is in front, not in your back?"

"Yeah, in front. Not in back."

"Ok," she said. "Just rest for now and we'll keep an eye on you. Oh, and the flu swab was negative."

When Susan left, all sense of time seemed to go with her. In that dark room, in the dark of night, everything hung suspended. My belly felt tight, full. Magnetic. The pain had gotten worse, and the ache in my muscles from earlier in the day was back. I squirmed, rolled my head back and forth, let my eyes glaze over at the monitors: Violet's heart rate. Her movement.

Every conversation with Susan or Kaya was the same:

"Has anything changed?" they would ask.

"The pain is worse," I would say.

"Still in front?"

"Still in front."

"Let someone know if you start feeling it in your back."

"Ok."

Near midnight, I turned to Dale. His eyes were half closed. Jacket still on. "Let's go home," I said. "I am so uncomfortable. I would rather be uncomfortable in my own bed."

"Are you sure?" he asked.

"Yes," I said, clenching my jaw and suddenly near panic. All I could hear in my head was: *I need to get out of this bed, I need to get out of this room,* not knowing that what I really needed was to get out of that body. Both of us: me and Violet.

I told Kaya, "I want to go home."

She tilted her head slightly. Her eyes—dark brown on bright white—sliced through me. "Why don't you just stay here?" she asked.

Despite her intensity, the music of her accent made this a soft, pillowy suggestion.

"I'm just so uncomfortable lying on this bed," I said. "And the pain hasn't moved. I think I'd feel better at home."

She suggested, asked, implored me no less than seven more times to stay but eventually unhooked the monitors and swept graham cracker crumbs from the bedside table into her palm. I felt like a disappointing patient.

"Come back for anything at all," she said.

Once we had gotten down to the ground floor, I said to Dale, "I need to pee before we leave."

And in another corner of the hospital—the single-use restroom at the end of a long, white empty hallway—everything shifted. As I sat on the toilet, one set of muscles already going to work, nearby I felt another set kick into motion. I don't know if the body can ever forget the feeling of a contraction. Two forces, one gripping each side of my opening and pulling apart with all their might, despite the muscles and bones holding me together, and in the span of a few minutes, again. I clutched my knees, panting. The thin red emergency cord dangled in my periphery. My lower back throbbed.

When I walked out, I met Dale's eyes: "We need to go back up."

"I thought you would be back," Kaya said, standing behind the reception counter when we walked in. She smiled. I laughed softly, surrendering.

Back in the same dark room, I was hooked up again. Violet's heartbeat. Susan came in and smiled. "We're going to give you some things to try to stop the contractions."

"Is this real labor?" I asked.

"I think so," she nodded, slowly, firmly. "Let's see how these treatments go. They should help."

Nobody would explain to me the effect of a magnesium sulfate drip until much later, so when the mag began to fill my body with lava, I slid unprepared into thick, hot sludge. I managed to let my head fall to the side, toward Dale.

"I feel awful," I said, the words swollen in my mouth.

Then I seemed to topple backwards. Down a rabbit hole.

•

Everything either felt slow or sudden. Like how the hours dragged on, labor progressing. Or how my bed was suddenly under bright lights, me horizontal on top of it, the ceiling shifting overhead in white angular shapes as I was moved down hallways and around corners. The new room was neither dark like the previous nor bright like the journey—only that soft glow of predawn.

The time in that new room was mostly a blur of shapes and shadows. The mag was working hard, despite it not working at all. Everything was in hospital hues—white walls and sheets and lab coats, clear bags and tubes and tapes, dull blue scrubs and blankets—and personnel were in a constant flow around my bed, checking this, changing that, measuring this, injecting that. I swam in and out with every contraction: white hot rage ripping through my pelvic area, then head flopping back onto the bed, completely drained.

Dale seemed to float in and out, too. When he was there, I gripped his hand, imploring him to guide me through the breathing exercises we learned in our classes. I liked the one where he would pick a random number, one through five, a count for me to breathe to.

"It's helping, it's helping," I said, his face incredulous.

What got me the most was that I had been through labor before. And this was so very different. This was absolute fucking chaos, and I was half-alive, right in the center of it. It was the mag—the mag to slow down my body, the mag to protect Violet's brain, and the unasked question of why my body wasn't responding to it.

"What is happening," I moaned more than once, rolling my head back and forth. No one ever answered. No one seemed to understand that I really didn't know what the fuck was going on. What was the plan, and where were the goddamn drugs.

A doctor I vaguely remember meeting in the dark room appeared at the foot of my bed. She was soft, calm, if not all the way there. An illusion, maybe. Dr. Cabrera. She said, "If we're going to deliver this baby, you'll have to have a C-section. She's breech."

Maybe I was the illusion.

"Ok, ok, ok," I said. Another contraction took me in its jaws. When it let go, I disappeared into the bedsheets.

This whole time… this whole time, I didn't know this was where we were heading. Call it denial, call it ignorance, call it the same thing that separates the griever from the non-griever: that all of these experiences live fully in the body and only a fraction in the mind. We comprehend so little, yet we know so much. So, even with everything we had been through in the past two years, in those hours in the hospital, I didn't get the new story we were in: the emergency birth of a premature baby who was expected to live. And it would be years before I got the real story beneath that, the story my body knew: that if she wasn't born soon, she wouldn't.

Call it by its true name: fear.

Covered by shock, by shutdown, fear so paralyzing that it can't be felt; and yet, it is the same fear that protects you from knowing the bigger thing beneath it. So big that only a bull could carry it. Up the mountain, ever forward.

I came back to Dale's face leaning over me. Tear-streaked, pink; exhausted, wired.

"It's snowing," he said, a little laugh that seemed to bubble up straight from his heart. "Like when Sloane was born."

Over his shoulder, I saw a small, two-pane window, black as black, white flurries swirling just beyond it.

"32 weeks," he said, taking my hand. Fresh tears lined the brim of his eyelids.

"32 weeks is ok," I said. "She'll be ok."

His whole body broke over our clasped hands. Later, he told me he thought we were going to lose another daughter. The fear and sorrow that must have entered his heart still brings me to my knees. I held him, dry-eyed. *32 weeks*, I repeated to myself. *32 weeks is ok.*

She will live. She will live.

Now with direction, the snowstorm seemed to hang overhead.

Flashes of white here and there and everywhere.

Lab coats, IV bags, contractions pulsing in my eyes.

A handful of papers thrust into my face.

Hallway ceilings.

The operating room.

Its austerity, its spaciousness: all like a hush.

This is where it ends. It's ending, ending.

Adrenaline, falling.

Liquid plunged into my back.

"Tell me when it reaches your toes."

Through my pelvic area, down my legs, into my feet.

Slumped forward, eyes burning.

"It's in my toes, it's in my toes."

Laid out flat. Long, slow blinks.

Dale, at my head, in full medical dress.

I closed my eyes. The conversation was like music—him and the anesthesiologist talking about skiing, about New Mexico, about the world outside of this hospital that I had temporarily forgotten about.

I sunk, down, down.

Letting go.

Then my eyes flew open.

"You can cut the cord if you want," I said to Dale. We hadn't talked about any of that yet. We still had eight weeks.

How were we here, already.

I'm not caught up, I'm not caught up.

"I want to stay here with you," he said.

A muscle twisted in my chest—a hope that I wasn't taking a memory away from him. How were we here, already.

I'm not caught up.

And then the necessity that my body only knew as violence: heavy tugging in my abdomen, back and forth, back and forth.

A shout: "Seven oh-one!"

A high-pitched scream. my heart exploding.

"Is that her, is that her," I asked Dale, tears streaming down my temples and into my ears.

"That's her," he said. "They're getting her ready for the NICU. I'm going to see if I can take a picture."

"Go, go," I said.

I squeezed my eyes shut, fresh tears spilling out.

Violet. Her cry.

14

The impossibility of life first became visible when Sloane died, and then increasingly clearer and more vibrant in the months that followed. The moments of joy that would suddenly surge upward from the depths of grief were at first alarming, confusing, shame-inducing. But then that head-spinning eddy of good, bad, and ugly began to feel more real than any other version of life.

Oh, truth—so abundant and so elusive.

"Do you ever feel your heart," I had asked Dale, four months into grief, "like, when it's just beating normally?"

We had been hiking in the Bisti Badlands in northwestern New Mexico. Forty-five thousand acres of undirected wilderness—no trails, no signs, nothing between you and the land. It was late May and hot. The straps of my red daypack stuck to my shoulders.

"No," Dale had said. I had expected this, but it still saddened me, as I had been getting lonelier and madder by the day, and my heartbeat regularly reverberated throughout my body. Occasionally it stuttered.

That day, I tried to push the beat into the background as we explored the moon. That's what the Bisti is often compared to: a lunar or Martian landscape of unique rock formations, no water, and no direction. All the books and websites advised wearing a GPS tracker and charting your course because, in its vast openness, it was easy for even the most seasoned outdoorsman to become lost and disoriented.

Dale, Leo, and I roamed for hours. Over open expanses of gravelly sand, through clusters of hoodoos that formed rock palaces with columns and rooms and thrones, and around rocks that looked more like dinosaur eggs, potato chips, and split-open cabbages. The labyrinth went on for miles, years, and under that May sun, I spun in 360-degree circles, the white sand and stone breathtaking against the solid blue sky. How freeing to be the astronaut holding the whole of Earth in one view. So distant. So quiet. So possible.

I had begun to feel at peace in that strangeness. In that wild terrain where grief was immediate and calm, where the belief in a bigger world felt like surrender.

It was the same feeling those first few days in the NICU.

The neonatal intensive care unit is another world—an utterly sacred place. The first time Dale wheeled me in through its locked doors, six hours after Violet was born, I felt a reverence drop over me. The main unit was a womb: dim, warm, cozy. Twenty, thirty incubators lined the perimeter, each baby's room sectioned off by curtains, twins rooming together, each incubator a large and complex ship of gray machinery, streaming with wires and tubes, the clear box at its center covered with a thick fleece blanket—unicorns, puppies, planets in fuzzy brights. Screens flashed numbers, drew graphs, and beeped, all on loop. Tired moms and dads laid slack in rocking chairs, and nurses moved like water, spoke like liquid soap. I would come to learn that they were what held the whole place together in that delicate plane between life and death.

There was so much to learn. Most importantly how to override our instincts: to only hold Violet for a limited amount each day, to not rock her, to not rub her skin with our thumbs. To keep her covered, where we couldn't see her. To keep the lights off. And if she got upset, to unlatch the windows to her box, reach in, and place our hands firmly over her body, holding limbs to torso, to recreate the womb: a snug container whose walls had felt safe. To a premature baby, everything was overstimulating; her underdeveloped nervous system couldn't handle the world yet. In other words, it was imperative that I learn to keep my distance.

But that first day, she seemed closer than ever. When I folded back her bubblegum pink blanket, covered in llamas, and saw her for the very first time, lying on her back and surrounded on all sides by semi-firm padding, my breath caught in my chest. I hardly noticed the wires and stickers covering her body, the tube down her throat. All I saw was her reddish-pink skin, her fuzzy hair—*she had hair!*—and her tiny button nose. She was magnetic; I couldn't look at anything else. The color of her skin—she looked so alive. My heart swelled as everything told me that she would be okay. I knew it thoroughly and fiercely, softly and easily, like the handful of other truths I knew in this life.

Dale. New Mexico. Leo. Sloane. Now, Violet.

That evening, still sitting at her bedside in my hospital gown and wheelchair, memorizing the rounded hills and valleys of her profile, a nurse said that her bedding needed to be changed.

"Mom," the nurse said, turning to me. They called everyone Mom and Dad; it ripped me open every single time. On some days, in the weeks to come, I wanted to stay in the NICU all day, just to hear the word I had been craving for two years, for my whole life. "Do you want to lift her over her bed while everything gets swapped out?"

"Yes, of course," I said, even though part of me was terrified to hold this tiny, fragile being, to be solely responsible for keeping her safe and secure and not suddenly, accidentally slipping to the floor and shattering both of us.

I pushed myself up from my wheelchair and took a deep breath. I held out my arms, palms up, ready to receive whatever was going to happen in the next moment. And then she was there: resting on my hands, head cradled by my left thumb, bottom by my right. And *solid.* Sturdy. Three pounds and fourteen ounces of pure strength.

This is her, I thought. *This is her, this is her.*

She was so strong, so strong, so strong.

Tears streamed down my cheeks.

"Uh-oh," a male nurse said. "Are you ok, Mom?"

My nerves bristled, but I nodded. I couldn't stop these tears if I wanted to. And I didn't want to. Even though it was just with my two hands, this was the first time I got to hold my living daughter. If I wanted to, I would cry until salty waves crashed against the walls of this womb. She was alive.

When I think about those first few days with Violet, I get nostalgic. Her, this tiny angel, burrowing onto my bare chest. Dale, head over heels for her, also bare-chested. Her head cupped in his hand, them gazing at each other. She was such a force.

All that, even amidst the machines, the equipment. The jagged bright lines and flashing numbers on monitors, the constant beeping and occasional alarms. The CPAP, feeding tube, IVs, bili lights. The reality that she was under *intensive care.*

It was like Sloane—even death couldn't stand in the face of all that joy, all that peace, all that love.

My mistake was in my experience; it was in thinking *how lucky are we, she made it to 32 weeks, she is alive.* At the time, that perspective felt right; it felt *good.* Like sunshine and warmth and safety. Whenever I hobbled to the bathroom, in my own hospital room on the floor below Violet, I looked in the mirror, and what I saw was similar—only more subtle, more weathered—to what I saw the morning of Sloane's anatomy scan. I glowed. I was a mom. With a living baby.

As if her journey into this world hadn't completely turned me upside down. As if I wasn't still caught in that night, lost in the sheets.

But I didn't know any of that back then.

Six days after giving birth, I found myself lying on a slab of a bed, my whole body raging with heat. Only a thin curtain separated me from a throng of other raging, moaning bodies. That morning, after Dale and I had left the NICU and I had found the waistband of my grey sweatpants stained with yellow pus, Dr. Page had sent me to the emergency room. There they had jabbed a long cotton swab into the swollen seam below my waist, pulled out a dime-full of thick egg yolk, and confirmed: My C-section incision was infected.

"We never see this on someone your size," a doctor said, when the labs indicated that the infection was just from normal bacteria on the skin. "Your potassium is low, too."

"Am I going to be in here for a while?" I asked. I was already making a mental list of what I would need Dale to bring me. Wondering when I would be able to see Violet again.

"We'll see," he said. "We'll get you started on antibiotics first—here. Once you're in a room, we'll get the potassium going."

"Can I get a pump? My daughter is in the NICU here." I had been pumping for less than a week and I already had preferences; the hospital-grade pumps were far smoother and more efficient than my home setup.

"Sure," he said.

As afternoon dragged into evening into night, I learned that I would be in the ER until morning, at least. The hospital didn't have enough staff to move people to long-term care rooms. All night, this ground floor pit of bodies writhed along a spectrum—the high-pitched scream of the mentally ill caught in psychosis to the guttural groan of the old and weak—and every manner of bodily fluid hung in the air, poorly masked with antiseptic. An almost otherworldly contagion seemed to seep into everything.

My incision was infected. My cerclage had been infected. And what we learned when we saw Dr. Page that morning was that I had had a placental infection with Violet, leading to a partial abruption, or when the placenta begins to separate from the uterine wall, cutting the baby off from oxygen and nutrients.

That was why the mag didn't work, why the labor didn't stop.

She needed out, in order to live.

And yet, the conversation was fleeting; the information barely registered. Call it by its true name: the bodily memory of having been there before, of already having one dead daughter.

My mind was a trap, and now it was infected with cerebral palsy and blindness. I slept in two-hour stints, otherwise pumping milk and scrolling on my phone through pages and pages of scientific research on the outcomes of premature babies. It could be months, years before we knew any long-term effects of Violet's prematurity on her health.

But first: potassium. The room wasn't coming, and they couldn't wait any longer.

"When the bag is empty, it will burn," the ER nurse told me in the morning. "I'll try to time it and get back here before that happens."

I was pumped with bags and bags of this stuff, and she was late for every one of them. When the IV in the crook of my elbow felt like it had been doused in ethanol and lit with a match, I pounded on the call button and then sat on my hand so that I didn't just yank the motherfucker out of my arm. Six, seven, eight times.

"We're not used to caring for patients over such a long period of time like this," the nurse said.

I understood but fuck.

That afternoon, I finally got into a room. A corner on the fourth floor, it was quiet, with a window. My nurse was pregnant and due in April, when I was.

Days went by, the hospital still understaffed. Alarms went off in my room errantly, incessantly, and my calls to the nurses' station rang without answer, leaving me alone to pump and pump and pump until my breasts ached and I had a long line of two-ounce bottles of creamy white milk in the mini-fridge, waiting for Dale to pick up and bring to the NICU.

I was not allowed to see Violet—risk of infection. Again, again: infection. I survived on Dale's stories and pictures.

Days went by, my daughter two floors below me.

One day I opened a text from Dale and saw an IV stuck on top of her head. It came out of her scalp at an angle, propped up with folded white gauze and held down with a dozen pieces of clear tape in every direction. It looked like a tiara. I wasn't into princesses, but later I would call her something similar: angel. I wasn't into those either, but it came from somewhere and it fit too perfectly.

One day I opened a text from Dale and saw her bare face. For the first time, she had no tubes, no wires, no IV; they were changing everything out. My heart caught in my throat, and I sobbed. Her face—her beautiful face. Two floors away.

Another text: *She's pulling off her nasal cannula, lol.*

Another: *Got to give her her first bottle! She took about 25 milliliters. They'll do the rest by gavage.*

Growing already.

Days felt like weeks, and the antibiotics were not working.

"We need to reopen your incision," said the doctor on duty one day. Dr. Baca. She had also been the one on duty after my first miscarriage.

"I'm sorry we are meeting under these circumstances," she had said, two years before.

Now, under these circumstances, it was the middle of the afternoon, in my corner room, in the same bed I'd been living in for four days, and my only thought was, *right here? Right now?*

A nurse dropped a hit of fentanyl into my IV. Dr. Baca shoved stacks of quilted paper under my body, shuffling them around and spreading them out. Shocks of cold liquid landed on my abdomen.

"Ok," she said. "Here we go."

I laid my head back, closed my eyes. I felt it as numbly yet vividly as the tugging when I was first cut open, this time my insides flushed, scraped, flushed, scraped, scraped, scraped, scraped, and then left open, gaping, feeling both violated and relieved, both inhuman and hopelessly in this body, both further down the rabbit hole and somehow coming out the other side. *De-breeding*, I will later learn the process is called.

Home—home was delicious after nearly two weeks in the hospital. I ate like I did when I was pregnant: whole grain English muffins, split and covered with peanut butter and sliced bananas; hunks of white cheddar cheese and roasted almonds; platefuls of homemade dinners from Dale's co-workers. The holes in my stomach felt endless: my hunger, my wound, my empty womb.

Dale couldn't stomach my open stomach. It was, respectfully, a view of his wife he didn't need to see—although he would later tell me that all these new angles were shaping me into a warrior in his mind—

so a home health nurse, Carmen, an angel in scrubs with a raspy, motherly voice, taught me how to change my dressings myself.

My changing times became burned into my mind. Every day, they required an intensity of presence that I wasn't used to. One day, like every other day, I laid on my back on my bed with a towel beneath me and shimmied my shirt up and my pants down. With only my head lifted and my chin tucked to see what I was doing, I peeled the bandage off of my re-opened C-section incision and pulled out the long stretch of packing material, a quarter-inch wide strip of thin paper, carefully folded into the two-inch wide hole in my abdomen. It gave the whole thing form and strength—rebar for wounds.

I piled the stained, crumpled material onto the used bandage like wipes on a dirty diaper, pulled on blue surgical gloves, and bathed the whole area in a watery antiseptic until it dripped down the sides of my hips. This was the only time this four-by-six-inch plot of land on my body got to breathe, and even the stale room air felt refreshing.

I laid my head back for a moment. What a strange, strange moment it was—this odd ripple of relief running from my heavy head to the wet, chilly skin surrounding the canyon in my body like a mesa.

Inhale, exhale. Fully, deeply.

I hated this fucking moment, but I also loved it dearly. I didn't understand it at the time, but something fierce ran through me. Something like pride, something like strength—the things I had come to loathe in the loneliness of grief. All the people who sent me messages after Sloane died:

"You are amazing."

"Your strength is incredible."

And one evening, out to dinner with an old friend, when I had told her that my sister hadn't once asked how I was doing in the six months since my daughter died, and how that crushed me, and she had said, crestfallen, "I always thought you were so strong."

Nobody thought I needed a goddamn thing.

Because I was taught. To be a bull.

"What's the problem?" my dad would ask, whenever I cried at two, three, four years old. I can still hear the inflection in his voice, emphasis on *problem*. What's the *problem*, what's the *problem*.

I heard it so often it became my catchphrase. I would walk around restaurants, stopping at each table: "Problem? Problem?" At three, I seemed so caring, so empathic. So focused on others.

I tucked my chin once again and gave myself three small squares of gauze: two to wipe the skin clean, one to lightly brush at my insides, where I was both marveled by and repulsed at the undulations of red and pink tissue, its density as it pushed back on my fingertips, the thin layer of skin separating me from all of this all the time. *I know nothing*, I thought. *I know absolutely nothing.*

Oh, how I would have loved to just lay there, breathing.

Something deep within me bristled at the idea that the wound needed to be stuffed, suffocated, and for what, so that I could thrust myself back into the *real world*, to work, cook, shop for groceries while my body only cared about fusing, healing where it was broken. Breakfast cereal and responsibility went hand-in-hand.

I snipped off a long strip of packing material. Accordioning it across my abdomen and gently setting it inside my body, it filled the space flush, valley floor to clifftops. Thin, padded bandage over top, tape on all four edges.

Sometimes I wonder if life is cruel, or if we are just cruel to each other. To ourselves.

Or all of the above.

15

When I look back on photos from the five weeks that Violet was in the NICU, my stomach hollows out into a pit. There are photos of me learning how to nurse, Violet stretched out on my chest, looking up at me, and the first time I wore real clothes, nineteen days after she was born: black jeans, black Vans, a gray sweatshirt that said *Elmo loves books*. I smiled these moments. But I wasn't fully there. And I didn't even know it.

I had developed a miserable little schedule. Wake, pump, eat. Work a half-day; pump while typing, seethe inside. Pump, eat, nap. Change my bandage. Pump, pump, pump. Spend the afternoon at the NICU; deaden everything. Pump, eat, watch *The Sopranos* with Dale. Pump, sleep, pump, sleep.

Label milk.

Sterilize parts.

Massage breasts.

Hinge my entire existence as a mother on my ability to produce milk. Master my process, finesse my strategy, chart my output, because it felt like the only tangible way I could mother my daughter who lived in a box, six miles down Montgomery. I had tried nursing, untangling all of her tubes and wires and holding her tiny head to my breast, but it lit my insides on fire, too wonderful and too terrifying, impossibly intimate for the distance I was trying to keep, and I needed something safer, colder. I became an exclusive pumper, managing my motherhood in my own way: pushing and pulling until I was empty, nipples chapped and bleeding, overproducing by twice as much, fifty ounces a day.

Because I could not—*could not*—spend all day at the NICU.

Violet was doing well. She was growing, learning to coordinate breathing and sucking, and gradually lowering the amount of oxygen support she needed.

"At least she's a girl," one of the NICU nurses said one day with a smirk. "We call the boys around here 'wimpy, white boys.' They have a much harder time than girls."

She may have been a girl, but she was my daughter, and I didn't know how to keep my heart from shattering when I sat by her bedside, in the soft, dim womb that was not mine.

I tried. I really fucking tried.

I didn't know that this was grief, too—that I could, once again, find release by seeing how broken I was. I mean, Violet was alive. And yet, I somehow forgot how to breathe for the four, five hours I spent with her every day.

Who was living?

What… was living?

Not me; not this. And not because it was hard—I fucking knew hard.

But because I wasn't there.

Not in the NICU, not with my daughter.

Not anywhere.

Weeks went by—that's all time was, something to pass—and my wound had only healed marginally. I was not resting enough, not sleeping enough, all of my calories going to my milk. I got scraped out again—this time in a doctor's office, under only a topical anesthetic, my teeth grinding as she nearly tunneled right back into my uterus with just her scalpel.

It didn't help.

So, Carmen brought in the big guns. He was a tall, lanky man in glasses who looked me over and approved me for a "wound vac," a portable vacuum of sorts, the size of a hardcover book, that I would carry around with me 24/7 as it whirred and sucked and magically healed me. We had talked about this option in the beginning and decided that I didn't need it—that I was young and healthy, and my body should be able to repair itself. Turns out we were wrong.

The day I received the wound vac, I got a break from nurse duty. I laid back as Carmen undressed my wound and cleaned it. But instead of packing it with what I had—oddly, affectionately—come to think of as the tapeworm, she pulled out a dense black foam. She hovered it over my wound, taking mental measurements, and then cut it, tilting her head to the right, and then the left, getting the size and shape just right and holding it up when she was done, squinting. It looked like a giant comma, two times the size of my wound. Then she stuffed it into my abdomen, and my eyes could not believe that shit. As she began to seal me shut with a sheet of sticky plastic wrap, Leo whined from his bed on the floor.

"In a minute, buddy," I called out, still lying on the bed. I turned my head to Carmen. "I forgot to give him lunch before you got here."

"You give your dog lunch?" she said, looking up at me, hands paused mid-seal.

I laughed. "I do. Three meals a day."

She smiled. "You're going to be such a good mom."

The wound vac quickly became a wretched thing that I wanted to throw out the fucking window. But, buzzing and chugging constantly, and half the time, plugging me into a wall, it worked; my incision was closed, done, turning to scar in a matter of days. The black foam was now condensed but still attached to the seam of my body, so when Carmen came back to remove it, and she had to really yank it, I told her to do it all at once, and fast—I was done with this thing. The whole damn thing: wound, work, NICU, milk, schedule, exhaustion. Feeling like utter and total shit all the time. I was just done.

When the fuck could anything—one thing—just be normal and easy and doable. I didn't even need good; I just needed simple, straightforward, uncomplicated.

When.

•

The tail-end of a NICU stay is like a re-birth in some ways. By this time, you're humming along in your routine, knowing the end is nearing as your baby continues to grow and meet the criteria for life outside the NICU, and then one day, the doctor says: *tomorrow*. Your water breaks all over again, and your baby is going home tomorrow.

When I heard that word for Violet, my entire world shook. My bubble of self-protection burst into a cloud of glittery pink dust, and I ran around the hospital in circles, beside myself with joy. *Tomorrow, tomorrow, TOMORROW!* The dream, the dream—my daughter was coming home.

It was only a week earlier that I had kissed her for the first time. For four weeks, I had been so afraid to overstep my bounds as NICU Mom and venture into Normal Mom. Nothing seemed to be going right, and I was the central feature of all of it: I couldn't get a cerclage right; couldn't have a baby right; couldn't breastfeed right; couldn't heal right. I didn't want to do the NICU wrong, too. So, I only touched Violet with scrubbed hands and a clean chest, and never more than necessary.

Oh, if only I could do the NICU all over again.

"There's Mom," one of the nurses said when I walked in one morning. Once my wound had healed, I had changed my NICU schedule to mornings instead of afternoons; I wanted to be more awake when I was there. "Nine a.m. exactly—I could set my watch to you."

I beamed and handed her my milk. Violet was on the growers-and-feeders side of the NICU now—in an open-air crib, on low oxygen support, and just needing to eat more before she could come home. This side was brighter, more stimulating: walls in lime green and bright orange. Fewer babies, fewer alarms. Quieter, homier.

Violet slept on her back with her head turned to the side. She was only loosely swaddled, her short arms raised up to her face. She wore a onesie borrowed from the NICU—pink with cupcakes. They had just started to dress her—one of the many little joys I couldn't bring myself to participate in.

Like the milestone cards. Dale's brother and our soon-to-be sister-in-law—we were going to miss their East Coast wedding in a week—had sent us a pack of cards when Violet was born. They were square and painted with pastel graphics of NICU milestones—*Kangaroo care! Off CPAP! Open-air crib!*—along with cards for every pound gained and every gestational week reached. I kept them in a purple mesh bag, drawstring ribbon, in the front pocket of my diaper-backpack-turned-NICU-backpack. They were the pregnancy journal: I loved them, craved them, but I just couldn't.

I watched Violet snooze. I find few things more precious, and it doesn't matter who it is; watching someone sleep is a gift. Their wholeness, their goodness, their absolute peace, and, best of all, their quirks: the positions and sounds and small comforts to their skin, their muscles. I give Dale endless shit for snoring because it wakes me up at night, but I'll never tell him that I secretly love it, love his humanity.

Eyes still closed, Violet stretched, pursed her lips, and wrung her plump fists overhead. So tiny, so human. And without having the thought in my head beforehand, I bent down and touched my lips to her forehead. Her skin, her warmth—her being rushed through me. I felt how much I had been missing. How wrong all of this was—but how right my living daughter was. I loved her immediately and immensely, but it would be months before I fell hard and deep.

The day we brought Violet home, I curled her onto my chest and tucked the *NICU Grad* card into the crook of my elbow: one last photo in this place, with a blank monitor and empty plastic box in the background. There was no wheelchair to carry us out, no flowers, no balloons, but there was sunshine and a breeze. I rode in the backseat with her as Dale drove and she took her first breaths of fresh air, her first glimpses of the world outside the hospital. She was five weeks old—still not due for another three.

That first day, we placed her bassinet in the middle of the living room, under the wooden beams of our ceiling, light filtering in from our wall of windows facing west, as if she were on display. *Look, everyone: the baby… at home.*

Dale and I stood over her, already asleep on a sheet of pink llamas and green cacti. She wore a clean white onesie and was wrapped in muslin but appeared naked: no wires, no tubes, no stickers, no machines. A normal baby. At home. It felt, for the first time, that we could call her ours.

16

Maternity leave might be one of society's biggest jokes on mothers. It is a giant, foggy, leaking mess, unpaid and utterly unsupported. Dale took off six weeks; after working part-time through Violet's NICU stay and ending up in a fit of resentment toward my employer, I was taking off three months. But on Dale's second day back to work, I called the daycare we had registered with, asking how early they could take her. I was beyond exhausted, beyond overwhelmed. My brain felt fuzzy, my limbs crumbling, just standing and holding the phone to my ear.

"July 1st," the director said.

Our original start date—in two months. I didn't know whether to cry or scream. Either would have probably helped more than what I did: clench my jaw and fume.

When I hung up, I watched Violet rock quietly in her swing. I had discovered the magic of this contraption by accident a week before when I had nestled Violet into the plush white seat and buckled the four-strap harness around her; I was just testing to see if her five-pound body seemed secure in there yet. But the second I flipped on the switch and the swing began to sway, Violet's head fell to the side. She was asleep instantly and for two hours.

Resources, I thought and nodded at her. *I'm just going to have to get really good at this situation.*

•

One of my favorite columnists in the Albuquerque Journal—she does the human-interest stories—had a son who died of overdose in 2017. Now that I had been making time to read the paper again, I caught a notice in her column one morning: a child loss support group for Mother's Day. I smiled at the thought, tore the notice out of the paper, and tucked it into the black wire mailbox hanging on our kitchen wall.

The morning of, as I pulled on jeans, a crewneck sweatshirt, and my black Vans, I got a text from my cousin.

Happy first Mother's Day!!!

Thanks, I wrote back, my breaths long and slow. *I appreciate you thinking of me, but it's my third Mother's Day.*

Her reply: *Oh, I completely forgot.*

I knew she felt bad, but honestly, I didn't feel like managing anyone else's feelings that day. I would rather no one said anything, rather no one acted like this year was now worth celebrating and years past weren't. I would rather no one pretended like they were actually on this motherhood journey with me because they fucking weren't, never had been, never would be if they weren't willing to see the hard parts.

Seeing: It's the bare minimum. Forget asking, forget caring, forget helping. Just *see* me.

For any mother, this is the truth.

I pulled the paper clipping from the mailbox and stuffed it in my back pocket. The grief center was across town, right next to the mortuary where Sloane was cremated.

I drove in silence.

We still lived on that side of town the day that I had gone to pick up her ashes. I had thought of it like any other errand: The home would call and say they're ready; I would say, "Great, thanks" and head over there. I would walk in the front door, give them my name, and they would hand over a little box. I would get back in my car and drive home. Transactional—a process to go through.

But when I got to the funeral home that day two years ago, they had me sit down in a waiting area. It was set up like a formal living room: one long sofa facing two armchairs, high backs and curved legs, a low coffee table with a glass bowl of wooden balls on top, the entire space lit only by windows. On a card table off to the side was a half-full pot of coffee and a stack of Styrofoam cups. I couldn't imagine drinking coffee in a place like that—heightening everything I didn't want to feel. I sat on the edge of the sofa, elbows on my knees.

A man in a charcoal suit appeared. "The room is ready for you," he said, bowing his head and extending an arm down a hallway.

My chest stirred as I followed him; he moved me in a way I couldn't name. And then he opened a door—painted lavender with a small wooden wreath hanging on it—and closed it again as he left.

I can't say enough times that I wasn't expecting any of this—that living room, this private room, where against one wall, a wooden pillar stood between two white candles, laced in gold ribbon. They were lit, flames waving, and on the pillar stood a small canister, a drawing of a torn and bandaged teddy bear on its front. I didn't know rooms like these existed for people like me.

It took only a moment for the well that had begun to stir in the hallway to flood me completely. This was my little girl. Valued and honored, recognized and respected. This was a moment, a place, a gesture just for her. This was not a transaction, but a celebration of a life for a little girl who lived for only ten minutes, and me, her mother, who had come to take her home. Both just as worthy as anyone else.

I can't say enough times that I wasn't expecting any of that.

In the courtyard of the funeral home, on Mother's Day, I sat on a stone block and leaned against a trellis post. My watch ticked past ten. *Land of Mañana*, I thought with a smile. I closed my eyes, turned my face toward the sun. I was fine to wait; I was here. I wasn't happy, but I was ready. To hold the pain of a dozen other bereaved parents. To feel something beautiful move through my heart. To cry hard. I knew that I was lucky. I was there, waiting for a child loss support group, but I was lucky.

But then I was just waiting. Finally, I pulled the notice out of my pocket. I read it carefully, again and again, until I saw it.

Right place.

Right time.

And the date I had read a hundred times. The group was yesterday.

My heart suddenly felt ablaze. It all felt impossible—this mistake, this story, this attempt at living. Was it me? Was it all me? I had wanted one simple thing on this very complicated day, to be alone with Sloane first, before anyone else, because she didn't get anything in life, and I wanted her to know that she was *chosen first*, and I fucked it up.

It was a bright spring day, driving back home across the open expanse of Albuquerque, and my head was dark and tight.

"It was yesterday," I said to Dale as I huffed and puffed past him and slammed my stupid ass onto the couch. I didn't even ask where Violet was.

"I'm sorry, babe," he said. "Go somewhere else—a coffee shop, a park, the trails. I'm fine here."

I sat planted, elbows on my knees, wanting to just be angry. I didn't even know what I was mad at: myself for getting the date wrong; the support group for not being on the day I thought; greeting card companies for inventing this stupid holiday; all the moms without lost children; Sloane for being gone; Violet for being here. Myself for not doing this holiday right, not doing grief right, myself for not parenting or carrying or caring right.

Myself myself myself.

I left without knowing where I was going. Anywhere, anywhere other than this story. I just drove.

Before long—although how long, I couldn't say—I found myself sitting at a stone picnic table in the foothills, surrounded by yellow desert and flowering cholla, the pages of my open notebook fluttering before me.

For so long, I was a mother without a living child. Now I was a mother with both: a living child and a lost child. Both. These were both my children. A day for me as a mother meant a day that was *both*. Both hard and good. I couldn't be only one; that was not my experience as a mother, and it was not what I wanted to honor in myself as a mother.

For fuck's sake, I had my first miscarriage on my first Mother's Day. I was 5 weeks pregnant, four months after Sloane died, and Dale and I had gone to Boston for vacation. I had been bleeding moderately for a week, but I bled early on with Sloane, too, so I didn't know what to make of it. Then, thumbing through the Harvard bookstore, feasting on the colorful spines, a heat had suddenly swum through me. It shimmered in my head; I felt woozy.

"Let's go outside," I had said to Dale.

"What do you need?" he asked.

All at once I didn't want to be anywhere or do anything—not walk or sit, not inside or outside, and certainly not in Harvard Square surrounded by hundreds of people.

"I don't know," was all I could manage to say.

"Let's get coffee," Dale said, seeing a Peet's—his favorite. Inside, I waited by the prep counter while the smell of roasted coffee beans made me want to vomit, and when Dale poured a drizzle of cream into his black coffee, I followed the thin white trail around and around, blending...dissolving...disappearing... and then a warm gush rushed out of me.

"I'll be back," I said to the air.

In the single-use restroom, I pulled down my jeans, my underwear, the pad I was already wearing. Everything was filled with blood. So much blood. So much toilet paper, paper towels, recycled brown napkins to sop it all up. A mass, the size of half a thumb, wouldn't come out until later.

On the subway back to our hotel we sat across the aisle from each other, the only two open seats, and it was almost better that way—I could just dam the waves that threatened to swell inside. Because I still didn't know what was going on—would have Dale run to the drug store for a pregnancy test—and yet my heart beat wildly, out of sync with the car rattling in its tracks.

How could I not know, I would ask years later, the question haunting me until I understood: that my brain wouldn't let me know, didn't want me to know that devastation, again, so soon. The next day was Mother's Day, and I wouldn't find out until two days later that the baby was gone, and I felt like I didn't know anything about anything.

Two years later and I wanted to claim myself as the mother that I was while the world wanted to forget. The world wanted Violet to be the solution, the end—because she was the here, the now, the easy, the good. The world wanted clean, tidy, simple, when life was ugly, messy, complicated, and maybe part of me wanted that, too: the living child, the new chapter. What we all refused to see was that Violet didn't change anything. That *grief doesn't end; it just changes*. Violet was wonderful, and I was grateful, but she was my other daughter's sister— not my other daughter's replacement.

How to be this mother of both… was something I didn't yet know. Sometimes, it seemed, I didn't even know how to be a mother at all.

What even was a mother.

In the foothills, I closed my eyes. Inhaled long and deep.

On the exhale, I opened them. Lowered my sunglasses, looked out at the horizon. The slopes of three shallow volcanoes flowed between land and sky. A breeze caressed my face like a hand.

And I said aloud, "I will keep you alive."

My in-laws had bought a house in Albuquerque a few weeks after Violet was born. They had ideas about the kind of grandparents they wanted to be, and that meant living close, at least for part of the year; once they were both fully retired, they would split their time between Albuquerque and Maryland, where Dale's brother lived.

A week after Mother's Day, my father-in-law was in town. He had retired at the beginning of the year, while my mother-in-law was still working, and had been coming out here every other month or so to work on fixing up their new house. And helping us out: with Violet and Leo; with dinner and keeping up our own house. I stopped by their new place on the way back from counseling one day.

"How was your session?" asked Rich, a slight note of hesitation in his voice. I don't know if my husband and his dad differed on anything other than their hair color—Dale's dirty blonde, Rich's still dark brown—and their golf handicap. I always saw Rich as both who Dale was today and who he might grow into, as a father, a grandfather, and maybe a father-in-law.

That same good core, only smoothed out around the edges.

My eyes were bloodshot, my cheeks raw. I sat on their sofa—the only furniture in the living room so far—while Rich laid on the floor, propped up on one elbow, playing tug-of-war with Leo, who had slept over the night before, and a rope toy.

"Good," I said. "Got more emotional than I thought I would at some stuff we talked about. But that's good. All good stuff."

"Ok, that's good," he said, unsure.

And I can't explain it, but I felt an in. An effort, a bravery, like two weeks after Sloane died, when he asked to see pictures of her. An outstretched hand.

I took it.

"Mother's Day was hard," I said, swallowing. "I'm afraid that now that Violet is here, everyone will forget about Sloane. And she doesn't deserve that."

He swung his legs out in front of him and sat up, cross-legged. Leo rested with his chin on the floor.

"Theresa and I talk about it," he said, a quiver in his voice. "But we never know what to say."

"I know. No one does."

"We think about her a lot—about all you guys."

My belly filled with saltwater. "I always want to hear about that. To know that someone is thinking of her... means the world to me."

"Thanks for telling me," he said, pulling his ankles in closer. "We just didn't know. We don't really know about these things."

"I know—no one does. I read Sheryl Sandberg's book—you know, the COO of Facebook?—her book about losing her husband. It's called *Option B*. And in there, she said something that really struck me. She said people are always afraid to bring him up, as if they are going to remind me that he is gone. When really I am thinking about him and the fact that he is gone every minute of every day. All bringing him up does is make me feel less alone—that I'm not the only person thinking of him, missing him. I *want* people to bring him up."

I exhaled a breath I had been holding for months. My father-in-law asked questions—all the right questions. Inside me, rivers broke through dams, and I think, inside him, something happened, too. In that conversation, me on the sofa, him on the floor, I saw him peel back a new layer of life, of love. A new territory. Not something to fit into his current boundaries of life, but something he saw and understood and respected as new, unfamiliar. Something to learn about and learn from—an expansion of everything. And with a calm courage that I would come to know him for, he stepped into it.

He was in this with me, not to guide or advise or reassure, but purely to *be with*—which is often the hardest thing to be.

I learned a really stupid thing about myself during this time. I wish I could have also seen the bigger picture of what it meant, but I guess that would have been a lot to ask when the reason that it was so stupid was because I already knew it.

"It's just me and Violet during the day now," I said to my grief counselor. I sat cross-legged on the sofa across from her. I liked her office, if you could call it that. It was cozy—traditional New Mexican adobe on the outside, soft lighting and twentieth-century modern furniture inside. Out a sliding door was a small patio with potted plants—where I looked when I needed to process. "Dale went back to work two weeks ago. He stayed home today so that I could be here."

"How is that going?" she asked.

Her name was Blair, but she looked so much like Skyler from *Breaking Bad* that sometimes I forgot her real name. I had started seeing her after my second miscarriage, and since then, every three weeks had been more or less the same pattern: I would think I had nothing to talk about, consider cancelling, then, the morning of the appointment, think of thirty unresolved issues, and spend the majority of the hour crying. Since having Violet, she had been counseling me through postpartum.

"I was not havin' it in the beginning," I said, "but I said to myself: I gotta figure this out, or I'm not gonna get through it."

I was never fully honest in counseling. I mean, I was, and I wasn't. I didn't tell Blair about my suicidal thoughts in Georgia—or the entire year before—until after I found the website. *Look, look at this thing I did; now I will let you see all the shit that came before it.*

"What does that look like?"

"I feel like the biggest thing is sleep. I've been really solid at getting my five straight hours." When Violet was still in the NICU, Blair had told us—both me and Dale, sitting on the sofa across from her—that each of us getting at least one, uninterrupted five-hour stretch of sleep every night was a major preventative against postpartum depression, so once Violet was home, we had arranged our responsibilities to make that happen. "The problem is when I go back to sleep after getting up to pump and feed Violet—at say, two or three in the morning—then when I wake up again at five or six, I feel even worse. And I have to go straight to taking care of her, all day. I don't ever get time for *me* to wake up."

"What would you do if you had *your* wake-up time?"

"I've always been a morning person. I love taking time to make breakfast, drink my coffee, read the newspaper. Before I have to be anything for anyone else."

"It sounds like this time is really important to you."

"It is. I've been making the same oatmeal every morning since I was a senior in college. I make it on the stove—it takes like, an hour. Literally, every morning. I'm obsessed."

"Wow. So, you really like this oatmeal. You really like this time in the morning."

"I do—I really do. Not having that time just makes me feel off, like, the whole day." These days, I would say: ungrounded, uncentered.

"This sounds like part of your self-care. Self-care looks different for everyone, and this routine, this ritual, of yours might be part of what it looks like for you."

"Yeah," I said, turning my gaze towards the patio. The late morning sun only hit the top of the tan stucco wall, throwing the plants in shadow. "Yeah, that makes sense. I wonder if I would feel better if I just... stayed up."

I tried it the next morning. After I laid Violet back down in the bassinet next to our bed, I pulled on my robe and crept back out to the kitchen. 3:30 a.m., the clock on the range read. *Not bad*, I thought.

After nine years, my muscles could make coffee and oatmeal in my sleep. And after thirteen weeks, several times a day, they could set up my pumping supplies in my sleep, too. I'm pretty sure I had actually done that before. But that morning, I was strangely awake. A bit busted in the head, but alert. Calm. Happy.

I set myself up on a stool in front of the stove. With my oatmeal on the small back burner, coffee steaming in a mug on the counter, my robe open to an empty bottle hanging from each breast through a strapless pumping bra, I switched on my pump and opened a book.

I was reading *Super Sad True Love Story* by Gary Shteyngart—a book I had picked up, along with *The Hidden Life of Trees* by Peter Wohlleben, at City Lights Bookstore in San Francisco. Nine months ago, which now seemed like a lifetime ago. I had picked it up for no particular reason, and I had been liking it so far, but that morning, it hit me differently. The pump pulled and the milk dripped and, suddenly, in the middle of reading a sentence, I said aloud:

"I could write this."

Not *this* book, but *a* book. Something about its surrealism, its dystopia; something about its epistolary interludes and creative juxtapositions; something about its bright colors on a white cover— just made it all seem so *possible*. This thing, this thing I had been dreaming about since I was six years old suddenly felt extremely tangible, in my hands, under my fingertips.

There was a lot going on at the time—the milk, the coffee, the middle of the night; to say nothing of fatigue, stress, and hormones— but sometimes the clarity of something is undeniable. The quality of light unquestionable. And the difference this time, from the millions of other times I had dreamed this dream, was that I said *could*, not *want*. It wasn't a longing, but a certainty.

A certainty that almost made me feel as if it had already happened. My insides glowed; my heart surged. Suddenly, I was in love: I wanted to clean bottles and wash diapers and fold clothes; I wanted to rock and sing and snuggle. I wanted to read all the books and write all the books and live all the dreams.

I'm fucking happy to be alive, I thought, squeezing inside. *Right now. My morning. My milk. My daughter.*

My life.

I had been here before, knew what this was. One morning a year after Sloane died, I had sat in the middle of our couch, sleep still in my eyes. Everything outside was in shades of blue, the sun still thirty minutes away. I was writing in my notebook, about nothing at first, just small, mundane thoughts—how tired I was, how much I ached—but then my thoughts began to grow, and the blue outside mellowed into purple, and I wrote and wrote, and before long, the horizon was pink, and my insides were shooting rockets to the moon. I wanted to do everything in the entire world: start this project, visit that place, talk to this person, try that thing, and this hunger rose inside me like a bubble and suddenly, I was breathing hard, and at six-thirty in the morning, in our empty living room, I let out an audible "Oh…!"

My chest heaved in and out.

"Oh my God," I said. "It's me."

I wanted to cry and leap into the air, and I did some version of both as I set my notebook aside and took long skippy, strides over to the sliding glass door. I could see all of Albuquerque and sixty miles beyond. The desert, the mountains; the next day, and the next. Years from now. Decades. I hadn't even realized what had been missing until it came back.

"Feeling like yourself again is a major step in the grief process," Blair had said when I told her about that morning over a year ago.

It wasn't everything, I knew that—but it sure was something.

And now this, remembering what I had always known: that morning, when the rest of the world is still dark and asleep, is when I come alive.

By the time I got into a groove with maternity leave, it was nearly over. I had a freezer full of breastmilk, I was getting more sleep, and Dale and I had started to spend time together again, seeing new sides of each other—good and bad—and learning how to work together in new ways. We had also started Violet's developmental therapy, offered for free by the state for all preemies; her case worker, a mom of three named Jennifer who terrified me with her insistence on having a VBAC—vaginal birth after C-section—in her third pregnancy, came to our house for an hour once a month to chat about Violet and monitor how she was developing in all areas: gross motor skills, fine motor skills, eating, sleeping, social and emotional growth. Dale and I reveled in watching Violet grow and reach and want and try; having Jennifer as an objective third-party was comforting.

And behind the scenes, I kept a focused list of my most effective forms of self-care. I wrote and wrote and wrote.

When I wrote my first children's story in the final week of my leave, I had no idea what I was doing. I had been studying children's books of all kinds—classic, modern, good, bad—and reading up on the fundamentals, but when I started writing out this story, all I knew was that I knew this character, and I wanted him to live.

The story was about a rainbow who lost all of his colors. After a storm, he had turned gray, sad, unrecognizable, and by the end of the story, he got his color back. In a storyboard on dotted grid paper, I drew crude sketches of him walking through a city, climbing mountains, finding love. All trying to get back to himself.

Every day, as Violet napped on the floor, in her swing, on the couch next to me, I worked the story like I hadn't in years: a steady, urgent flow of capital letters across the pages of my notebook, the scritch-scratch of my pencil like a song. I worked it and reworked it and worked it some more, and loved every fucking minute of it, loved everything in the world: the paper, the pencil, the words; Rainbow, Sloane, Violet. My life. Maybe even myself. For the first time, I regretted having to go back to work the next week.

I sent Rainbow to Taj, asked him for his feedback. We had been working together for eight years by then; I knew he would give me the kind of input that would both terrify and excite me, burning holes in my chest either way. When I saw the return email come through on my phone, my heart leapt into my throat. I pulled my laptop onto my crossed legs and opened the file.

Why can't Rainbow just sit in the suck for awhile? read the first comment.

I exhaled. One of Taj's signature phrases—sit in the suck. *That's good*, I thought. *That's really good.*

I let my arms sink down my sides, realizing only then that they had been pinned there in the first place. Over the years, Taj had reviewed dozens of pieces of my work. We were both ones for storytelling, ones for words, and his feedback could either send me to the moon or smash me into a pile of crumbs. And it had, many times—like the time he said, "Your poise, your elegance—that was like a TED talk" after a presentation I gave to Nestle, or the time he missed the company holiday party to redo a report I had done for 3M. But those were mostly in the earlier days; I had since developed my own vision, my own voice, and could see how our work differed. Now I could learn from him without losing myself.

But this—this wasn't work. This was my life I had handed him. And it was the life stuff that he was always right about.

Why does he have to get rid of all the gray? Taj asked at the end. *Maybe he should keep some of it. It's part of him now.*

It was the life stuff I was most resistant to.

17

My first day back at work, I was already in tears. One of the research teams was halfway through a project for Glassdoor, the job search engine, and needed help with analysis, so I dove headfirst into pages and pages of stories that the research participants had submitted about their experiences looking for jobs—applying, interviewing, getting offers, getting rejections.

What a fucking privilege, I thought to myself, *that* this *is my job*.

Sometimes it's the most ordinary of human experiences that are the most interesting to learn about. Sometimes it's the most extraordinary.

Two months later I was out in the field for the first time since coming back to work. *In the field* means out where life is happening: the houses, the offices, the stores where our research participants actually lived their lives. This time, the field was the homes of people suffering from chronic illness—cancer, multiple sclerosis, heart disease. I'm not sure if I can fully express the privilege this was.

I drove through the sprawling suburbs of Houston, another moderator in the passenger seat, my client in the back. As much as I'd rather be leading the interviews, this time I was grateful for the easier responsibilities of analysis and client management. Sure, I had been back to work for a bit already, but Violet was only six months old, and everything was still exhausting.

"That's a nice playground," said my client, Rob.

I caught a glimpse of big tube slides and rope climbing nets as we drove past. Rob and I had been working together for two years; the first time we met, eating lunch in the cafeteria at his company's headquarters, he asked me if I had kids. I told him my daughter had passed away three months before, and he said he was sorry. He had three of his own. I liked him; he was a good guy.

"I've been taking my kids to every playground in Minneapolis," he continued. "We rate them all and post about them on Instagram. My kids help me. It's become kind of a resource for other parents."

"Oh, that's neat," I said. I didn't know jack shit about playgrounds from a parent's point of view yet.

"Yeah, it's been a fun thing to do on weekends. There are some pretty cool playgrounds out there."

The last time we were in the field together—interviewing small business owners in Dallas—he told me about his goal of eating barbecue with his kids in every state. His youngest was just a baby then.

"I'm so glad I could get out here for this project," Rob said. "Scheduling with my ex is a nightmare."

I nearly slid through a red light. *My ex?* I let Rob and the moderator carry on while I focused on how flat Texas was, how generic its green grass and gray roads; we could have been anywhere. My heart raced, wanted to speak.

"Rob," I finally said, "I didn't know. How are you doing with everything?"

"Thanks," he said. "The whole thing has been a mess, honestly. But I'm better off now. She just wanted to make everyone miserable."

I glanced at him in the rearview mirror. Adults in the backseat are always funny to me; they look like overgrown children. And he was tall, his head nearly touching the roof.

"I'm so sorry," I said. "That sounds tough."

"Yeah. The hardest part has been the kids. The days without them are so quiet. I'm like, what do I do with myself? Do I go out?"

"Oof, yeah—that sounds like a lot." I felt it in my gut.

"I've been on a couple of dates, but I don't know."

I slowed to the curb outside the house of our next interview. Hillary, a woman in her forties with diabetes and rheumatoid arthritis. Daughter, age eleven. I turned off the engine and faced Rob.

"Thanks for sharing with me."

He smiled.

Hillary was bubbly and gorgeous. She was tall and full-figured in black leggings and a bejeweled top, hair and make-up on-point. She felt more like a big sister than a mom. Maybe because I wanted to sit on her oversized brown leather couches and talk to her for hours.

The thing about this string of interviews was that we talked about everything: health, work, family, identity. Heartache and fear. Because their suffering never stopped at just their illness; it spilled into the rest of their lives, and the rest of their lives spilled back into it, and in that porous and vulnerable time of my life, I didn't know how to keep it all from spilling into me.

Hillary and the moderator talked. They sat angled toward each other on the same couch, while I discreetly curled up in a matching armchair behind the tripod, manning the video camera and scribbling notes, slipping effortlessly back into the flow of someone else's story. Rob sat in another armchair, listening.

Through smiles, Hillary described the pain in her joints. She showed us her manicured hands, stiff and swollen, and told us how she had to quit a job she loved—some regional manager something or other—because her arthritis kept her from traveling, even locally. Now she was awaiting test results for lupus. More pressing was the issue of how she and her father could make a family out of just each other; her brother had died by suicide some five years earlier, and eleven months later, her mother had taken the same route. Grief, with its many source waters, ran the current of her life.

"We still don't know why," she said, looking down, folding and unfolding a tissue in her hands. "He didn't leave a note. We didn't know anything was wrong."

I scribbled notes. Head bent down, a few tears slipped out of my eyes, landing audibly on the pages. The paper wrinkled under the splotches. I looked up and Hillary turned to me, her own eyes wet.

"She gets it," she said, waving her tissue in my direction. A smile, a twinkle. "I see you over there."

We both laughed—as if we were in on some secret together. She picked up a box of tissues off the coffee table, holding them out to me, and I unfolded my legs to lean around the tripod and grab one. The *whoosh* of the tissue brushing against the plastic opening seemed to echo. It took everything in me to sit back down, to not wrap my arms around her shoulders.

Maybe the secret was that she caught me pulled in deep to her story when I was supposed to be—quote unquote—impartial; maybe it was that we had both been dangerously close to suicide and the burn is quick to return. Maybe it was something else entirely—something knowable but indescribable. Like how it feels to be seen. Held.

Safe for one more moment.

Like her mom, Violet was wide-eyed in the dark before dawn. It was six-thirty a.m. on a Saturday in early October, the first year since Dale and I had gone to Balloon Fiesta in 2015 that I wasn't fatigued and nauseated by a first-trimester pregnancy, and our daughter was curled into a pack on Dale's front as we walked onto the fiesta grounds. I didn't expect her to stay awake after we snuggled her into her car seat and drove across town in the dark, but here she was, almost eight months old, in fleece footie jammies and a brown knit hat with bear ears, soaking it all up while I drank in the morning air.

We ate our breakfast burritos—mine still bacon and red, Dale's still sausage and green—and buzzed around the field. We showed Violet everything: the blooming envelopes, the flaring burners, the giant baskets, and as the sky lightened, the dark silhouette of the Sandias, the paler wave of the Jemez. She hardly blinked, and from the first handful of balloons that went up, her eyes never left the sky, the live kaleidoscope of shifting shapes and colors.

Being there with her, the magic seemed to multiply. Glitter folded into sparkle into shine. I twirled about, face lifted, in my own childlike joy, but then also watched her squeal and coo her way through the dream, reminded that this freedom, this belief in everything good, is her permanent state of being, like it was once mine.

Mid-morning, we made the long trek back to the car where we had hot water waiting in a thermos, Violet insistent on warm bottles. Dale cradled her in his arms, propping up the end of the fat bottle with his fingertips, as the three of us stood in the open hatch, watching the sky.

When her belly was full, I folded Violet into a hug and then sat her down in the open back of the car. Her eyes still glued to the balloons, she shifted in small ways—stroking a knee with her dimpled hand fanned out like a star, waving a foot and curling her toes—and for the first time, I saw her as wholly separate from me. In those eyes, those cheeks, that mouth, I saw wants and views forming inside her. Dreams and decisions marching out the days and decades ahead: her own life to do with what she will.

I put myself in her tiny round body, crafted out of my own flesh and blood, to see what she saw—blue sky, colorful balloons, Momma, Dada—and feel what she felt: a breeze on her cheek, fuzzy pajamas on her limbs, warm milk in her belly. Excitement. Security. Love. I felt her becoming her own person. And in that new space between me and her was where I fell head over heels in a deeper love than I had ever felt for her.

I don't know why it took so long. Maybe because she had been taken from me too soon, and I was stuck forever reaching back. Maybe because she was my daughter who lived, and I had spent so long with only a daughter who didn't. Maybe because this is just how long things take sometimes.

But now I knew that, no matter how painful life was, I would never leave her.

Which I also knew was not how any of this worked—that when the pain got so unfathomably big, it didn't matter who was in your life or how much you loved them.

But still—it was a hope to cling to.

18

I n the blue morning hours of early January 2020, I wrote in my notebook: *I think that the only way I might be able to cope with the human condition is to write about it. It's just too much.*

I felt that way often those days, wearing a lead jacket, head in a vise, an unknown pressure pushing on me from all angles. In the mornings—before work, before Violet—I tried to write, and sometimes every pencil scratch was agony, and other times my ribcage unlocked and I flew out, a flutter of wings. On the page, I tried to muscle my way into understanding why life had me in such a grip.

I'm too intense, I reasoned. *Everything I do has to drip with meaning; everything is laden with consequence.*

In November, for the eighth year in a row, when we had filled out our Secret Santa questionnaires at work, next to the question *What do you do to relax?*, I wrote *I don't. I don't know how.* Nothing to solve, produce, cross off—I didn't know how to do that. Something always demanded me: this project, that client, this initiative, that colleague; exercise, hunger, grief. Dale. Violet. Sloane.

At the time, I just called this life. I called it being promoted to Vice President and leading a company, being a mom and a wife and leading a family. I called it being an adult: responsible, capable, obligated. I didn't know life could look any different. Wasn't this the hill I had been climbing this whole time? Wasn't this... the dream?

And yet, my need for resources to live this hellish dream had taken on a new sheen of desperation since Balloon Fiesta—that *out* was no longer an out, but I still didn't know how to be *in* and be okay. Somehow the reality that I was going to stay here in this life seemed harder to swallow than the idea that I might not.

So, I focused on saving myself in the one way that I knew worked: living each day for the following morning. Forget afternoons, evenings, nights—I only wanted morning. Five a.m., sitting at a long counter-height table before a large window, with my notebook and a mug of coffee, and gazing out into the dark blue, this was when I could marvel at life. How we all wake up to this world that continued on while we slept, and yet its relative permanence makes it seem like it stood still overnight, waiting for me, for everyone, in their tiny beds in their tiny homes, laid out before me in a mosaic of neighborhoods—everyone at peace, asleep. Morning was the only time I felt grounded, the rest of the world suspended.

In those mornings, something started to stir inside me. An energy, a connectedness. Some days it just tingled in my belly and others it rose up like a wave—humanity, Earth, and all of time cresting in my chest. And when I stayed with that feeling—when I breathed in and out of it—I wrote and wrote and wrote.

"What do you have going on today?" Taj asked. He was sitting at my dining room table, forking eggs into his mouth. It was the second week of January, and he and his family were visiting; they had sold their house in LA last fall and were driving around the country in their van, trying to fall in love with a new city. Albuquerque wasn't on their list, but it was reason to visit us, meet Violet.

"Work," I said, half-rolling my eyes. I took work a lot more seriously than he did. "You?"

"I got some things," he said. Then he gestured a hand upstairs, where his kids were getting dressed. A fifteen-year-old and two thirteen-year-olds—not twins, adopted from different families. "And then whatever those guys want to do in the afternoon. You should come with. Maybe go hiking."

"I can't, dude," I said. I felt like an asshole—why, I wasn't sure.

"Why does it matter how many hours you work," chimed in his wife, Christa, "as long as you get the work done?"

Two, three at a time, she brought the dirty breakfast dishes into the kitchen. She had made a full spread: eggs, bacon, flour tortillas. Salsa and avocado, sliced and laid out on a plate. This wasn't a new argument from them, and yet, I still didn't know how to explain that there was always something more to be done. Taj knew the job; he knew the work. But he also knew me—often better than I did.

Six years before, he and I had sat outside a café in Reading, Pennsylvania. We had leaned back in wrought-iron chairs, a breeze blowing over our faces, decompressing after interviewing a woman who had been addicted to crack in her thirties and now ran a group home for mentally disabled adult women. We had spent two hours shopping with her at the dollar store, where she told us she had to buy the small ice cream containers because she'd been known to eat a whole gallon in one sitting.

At that time—like most times—I had been slammed at work, and Taj knew it. Knew that I was working my ass off but running on fumes. As we sat, an hour until our next interview, he pressed me on how I was doing.

"I'm fine," I had said. "This is my time to work as much as I can, get as much experience as I can. Plus, I love it. This?" I pointed my thumb in the direction of the interview we had just come from. "This is awesome. I love this shit. This is my life right now."

"Why?" he asked.

"Because Dale is still in Florida. Once he's done with grad school and moves out to LA—and then we're married—I'll be in a different phase. I won't be able to work twelve, thirteen hours a day anymore. Now is my time to do that."

Taj looked at me. He never wore sunglasses, just scrunched up his long face, his dark eyebrows. "The next time Eric assigns you a new project, can you just say no?"

I squirmed. Felt the muscles in my face harden. "I don't know."

"Can you let someone else take things off your plate?"

He was scratching at something tender.

"I don't know."

"Why can't you just ask for help?"

Heat sprang to my eyes. I squeezed my lips together to keep the tears behind my sunglasses, keep them from falling.

"I don't know," I said, louder than I intended, sharper than I felt.

I suddenly felt betrayed. I cried hard, and harder. Taj sat, silent.

I didn't understand—why I took everything on, why he was pushing me so hard, my torrent of a reaction. I cried in that chair, under the sun, until my eyes were swollen, like I did when I was four, in a *Dick Tracy* Breathless sleep shirt and scraggly hair, folded over myself on the floor. Hiccupping, gagging. Knowing no one was coming.

"That's just how much work I have," I said to Christa, back in my own dining room. "And anyway, I'm taking tomorrow off. It's Sloane's birthday, and Dale and I are going hiking in the morning. Then we'll have the afternoon free."

It's hard to remember now what the first signs were—what Dale and I noticed, what struck us as off. We know so much more now; it's hard to un-know.

The next day, Sloane's third birthday and a month before Violet's first, Violet woke up from her midday nap with her cheeks blooming red. That morning, Taj and Christa had offered to watch her while Dale and I went for our hike, but I had already lined up a babysitter. It was our first time with one, and I wanted to get it out of the way, have an option in place for when we needed it.

Sienna was her name. When we first chatted on the phone, and she told me how she responded to one of her charges hitting her repeatedly, I felt like I had never heard a more patient person in my life. Sold. Only twenty-three and with a four-year-old boy of her own, she had a gift with children. She nannied for two kids during the week and babysat on the weekend, always with her son in tow, who, she told me when she first came over and we swapped stories, was colicky for the first eight months of his life, only ceasing his cries if she bounced on an exercise ball. She and "his dad," as she referred to him, had gotten married, and she wanted another kid, but she was afraid of having to go through that again. Violet, unsure of all this, slept on Sienna's chest for the full two hours she was there.

Now, after napping again, her face was flush, and she seemed to have a hard time breathing. She sat on the living room floor, knocking down stacked blocks, biting into an orange rubber ball, her chest hitching every so often. But she gave me her new face: a thing she had started doing where she cheesed big and scrunched up her nose. She only did it when she was really happy.

As I watched her play, I found myself breathing hard.

"Let's just call the doctor," Dale said. "See what he says."

"Has she had any medication today?" a nurse asked over the phone.

"No," I said.

"Are her lips or the beds of her fingernails blue?"

I looked at Violet, swinging a rattle. "No."

"When she takes a breath, can you see her ribs?"

"Hold on, let me see," I said, holding the phone to my ear with my shoulder as I laid Violet on her back and unbuttoned her onesie. I pulled it up to her chest, watched her belly. I didn't really know what I was looking for. "I don't think so, but I'm not really sure."

"Can you count her breaths? I'll time you for thirty seconds."

Counting a wiggling baby's breaths was harder than it sounded.

"Ok, what did you get?" asked the nurse.

"Twenty-seven?"

"Ok, ma'm, why don't you go ahead and bring her in. We can see her in the Montgomery office as soon as you can get here."

A nurse wrapped a sensor around Violet's bare foot and scratched numbers onto a notepad.

"The doctor will be in in a moment," she said, leaving the room.

I slid my arms out of my backpack, leaving it on the bench behind me. Dale bounced Violet on his knee as she clutched a lovey—a white puppy with a gray patch over one eye—in one chubby hand. We had just weaned her off the pacifier, and the puppy was its substitute; so far, it wasn't really taking. I heard a knock at the door. The doctor walked in, a nurse trailing behind him.

"Man, she's got some cheeks," he said, sitting down on a stool and rolling toward us. "Kinda red today, huh?"

I smiled, squeezed Violet's leg.

"Well, guys," he continued, "she's not getting enough oxygen. O2 is in the high eighties. That's not really what we want to see."

"Ok," I said.

My voice echoed in the small room. Time seemed to stretch, and I felt a part of me pull away, float off into another exam room where I was just told I only had five millimeters of cervix left.

"This is not uncommon for babies of her prematurity…," the doctor went on, somewhere far away.

And then sound returned in full blast, the nurse shuffling through a drawer. She held up two clear plastic bags, one with a spool of clear tubing in it, the other with two round, brown stickers, and in what seemed like a glitch in the system, she was suddenly popping the stickers onto Violet's cheeks, wrapping the nasal cannula around her head, Violet writhing in Dale's arms, screaming, grabbing at the tubing, and I, without warning, was sobbing.

No hot eyes, no wet mouth—just the immediate, painful disbelief that we were back there again, in the dimly lit NICU, watching our daughter lie in a plastic box, surrounded by machines, her beautiful, sweet, innocent face hidden beneath stickers and tubes. It was the stickers that got me; it was once again not having the intimacy of her face, the soft skin of her full cheeks. They made her eyes seem like they were looking out at me from behind something.

Mama, Mama.

After the nurse had finally wrangled the tubing into the right place on the stickers, she looked over at me. "Oh, Mom—I'm so sorry."

"It's just like the NICU," I said, fresh tears wetting my eyes. I looked at Violet, Dale still trying to calm her. And then I laughed. "She was always pulling the cannula out there, too. So strong, even then."

I mopped up my face with my sleeves. Perhaps it was naive of me to think we had ever really left the NICU—that eight weeks premature could ever really be over. I reached an arm behind my back, found the side pocket of the backpack. It was automatic—this sixth sense of exactly where everything was. I pulled out a pacifier.

By the time they wheeled in the oxygen tank and connected it to Violet's tubing, her eyes were half-closed, exhausted. The elephant on her pacifier bobbed up and down.

Violet stayed tethered to an oxygen tank for five days. We learned a bizarre new world: terms for the different sizes of tanks, how to switch them out when they ran empty, the cadence of the weaning process. And to think now, that we thought that was all really something. It is incredible how one's sense of normalcy—one's lived reality—can become so warped that they can no longer even see what has become obscured. Like we would all learn soon.

I rolled the stroller over the bumpy grass. Parking it at the end of a row of folding chairs, I unbuckled Violet and pulled her soft, round body to my chest. Her chubby legs pressed through the cotton of her sweatpants and melted into my hands. My sweet.

It was a Saturday morning in early March—not yet into Albuquerque's windy season, not yet into COVID-19 lockdown. This wouldn't be Dale's last flag football game but close to it. He and his co-workers ran around the park, warming up their thirty-something bodies; girlfriends and wives set up camp on the sidelines. I spread a falsa blanket on the grass and plopped Violet down onto it.

She sat with her legs sticking out in a V, stacking and unstacking a set of brightly colored cups. She had just started crawling a few weeks before—three days before her first birthday. It was a relief, to say the least. Not only for her development but for parenting. Her world opening up meant ours did, too, even if only to be reined in again by clear tubing; the same afternoon she first crawled, she was put on oxygen again. And again two weeks later. But she was doing so well otherwise that we discontinued her developmental therapy with Jennifer, and today she was healthy and content, surrounded by all she needed: fresh air, sunshine, toys, Mom. All any of us really need.

Oh, to be her, I thought, *where life is simple and full.*

A light breeze blew. When it rippled across the brim of her blue sunhat and brushed the baby hairs by her ears, she looked up. Stared off into something. An arm floated up, fingers curled towards her ear. The movement appeared slow, absent, but felt like the most present in the world. Somewhere along the way, we forget how to do these things: breathe, sense, enjoy. In other words, just be. I felt myself settle.

The women got to talking. I had known most of them for a year or so, if "known" really meant anything at all. It was hard to make new friends in your thirties. The youngest two were engaged to players on the team—fiancées eager to become wives eager to become mothers. They watched Violet and dreamed aloud.

"I told Jack that as soon as we're married, I'm ready to have a baby," said one of them.

The other one laughed. "Same. I want a girl first."

"I only want girls," said the first, laughing. She smiled at Violet. "She's just so cute."

"Yeah, we are so happy to have her," I said, looking at Violet as she pawed a bowl of black beans. "Our first daughter passed away, so it was a hard road to get here."

From the first: "Was it just a miscarriage?"

I looked up at her. She wore big sunglasses, her head tilted to the side, face angled toward me. The sun had risen higher over the mountains from when we first got there, and in the high desert, the sun is strong, even in springtime. I sat cross-legged in black leggings, soft heat settling onto my thighs, but it was the center of my chest where a small circle burned, like the pinhole cameras we experimented with in my high school photography class. Six a.m. mornings in the darkroom. A simpler time in my life.

"No," I said. "No—she was born, and she died."

Maybe I went on to describe the circumstances a bit, but I'm not entirely sure because I didn't really go on. I was stuck on one word. *Just* a miscarriage? Are you serious? When is a miscarriage ever *just* a miscarriage? Even though what I was talking about wasn't *just a miscarriage*, that wasn't the point. This was so much bigger—than me, than my loss, than any individual, and any individual loss. This was a societal failure. People not knowing how to talk to each other; women not knowing how to be present for each other.

Was it just a miscarriage?

Who the fuck are you?

And yet, she was me, four years ago: young, in love, dreaming of babies. Not understanding anything about that part of life yet.

The summer before I got pregnant with Sloane, a good friend of mine was 6 weeks along with her third child. Dale and I had been in Tennessee at the time; we had done Memphis and Nashville and were heading to the Great Smokies for backpacking. As we drove the length of the state, the same never-ending line of trees, I followed the slow unravel of her pregnancy in a series of text messages. We were at a brewery in Knoxville when I got her final message:

I lost the baby, and I don't want to talk about it.

I was stunned, sad, but from a distance.

"Having a miscarriage," I had said to Dale. "I have no idea what that's like. I… don't really know how that would feel."

Emotionally, I meant. It sounded hard, but… how hard was it? It wasn't really even anything yet. Right? So much of this I couldn't have known yet—my body didn't have the felt sense of pregnancy or loss— but even intellectually, I was bothered by the fact that this wasn't more visceral for me. I couldn't feel the loss in my bones, in my gut, like I could with movie deaths. That distance—between me and my female body and my female friend and her loss of a child—got to me.

Maybe it was because she wasn't talking about it; maybe it was because so few of us do. So that we all stay protected, right? To protect ourselves from the shame and heartache of being inadequate, to protect others from the discomfort of bearing witness, we rid ourselves of our losses in private, bathroom door closed, on our hands and knees, mopping up the mess, alone. *Look at how strong she is*, they say, *dealing with this all by herself like a big girl.*

Each one of us, by ourselves. Millions of women, for centuries, such that a young woman in the twenty-first one can't even relate.

If it were up to me, I would have been able to feel the physical detachment of that embryo in my own uterus. I would have been nauseous at the thought of all the blood. I would have felt an abundant grief settle into my heart, for the baby, my friend, her partner, and their kids. If that's how it was, then maybe we, as a society, would actually learn how to hold loss and grief, how to fold these experiences into our lives, so that they aren't separate.

So that we aren't separate.

Miscarriage, ectopic, blighted ovum, abortion, premature rupture of membranes, placenta previa, placental abruption, stillbirth, preeclampsia, trisomy 18, twin transfusion syndrome, intrauterine growth restriction, IVF, IUF, premature birth, infant loss, loss, loss, loss—it's not that we need to know the ins and outs of each possibility; it's that we need to know how *real* loss is. That it *happens*. Not just in textbooks, but in real women's bodies, in real families' lives. And it is devastating, on a thousand different levels. If we truly knew that, we would never ask: *Was it just a miscarriage.*

I looked like I was watching the game. White uniforms running up and down the field in front of my eyes. Violet's arms batting around in my periphery. Blue sky overhead. But, for maybe the first time in... a long time... I was looking at myself.

What all had *I* been through?

Part Three

19

I clicked the red *more updates* arrow as soon as it appeared. New blurbs filed in, one after another: this state now with shelter-in-place orders, that many people now dead. Mid-March—the early days of the COVID-19 pandemic, and two weeks after Violet was last on oxygen support—was one of the rare times in my life when I did anything other than work during the workday. I sat in front of the two monitors on my desk, one with data tables, the other the news, and I watched compulsively as the world unraveled. My entire body had been tense for days.

When New Mexico shut down, we called Violet's pediatrician.

"Her lungs," we said.

And him: "Maybe keep her home for a while."

And so we began rearranging our lives. Dale set up an office in our guest bedroom upstairs, we assigned ourselves shifts for taking care of Violet, and we let go of the help we had been getting from Sienna. Dale stocked the cabinets with canned things we didn't eat—peaches, pears, soup—and I shifted a project that I was supposed to travel for from in-home interviews to online.

It was my dream project: interviewing people with behavioral health conditions—eating disorders, substance abuse, schizophrenia; bipolar, depression, anxiety. In an alternate life, I would have worked in mental health. Psychology was the only AP exam that I got a perfect score on. All those years watching *Intervention* on A&E, reading memoirs like *Girl, Interrupted* and *Smashed*—to know these experiences had always been an inexplicable desire of mine. I crafted the interview guide with care, packed it in warmth. I wanted everyone to feel safe with me.

It's different—moderating interviews online. No clients to ride around in cars with; no spaces to walk through together. But it might have been just what we all needed at the time, both craving and fearing other people, more comfortable in our own little boxes. Peering out.

It wasn't until later that I saw how those interviews broke me. Molded me, rewired me. Maybe even saved me.

"I'm a Babylon baby," said one young man I spoke with, two weeks into the interviews. His name was Kyle. He was transgender and suffered from bipolar disorder. He smiled at this term. "My parents met at Babylon—and then had me."

Babylon was the name of the institution where he was put in the psych ward at age thirteen, some eight or nine years before. Since then, he had transitioned, become a prostitute, and repeatedly blacked out during manic episodes. He was sweet and bubbly.

"What was your time there like?" I asked.

He smiled big, and his eyes widened. "Awful. They treat you like shit there. Like you're some sort of criminal. But I did come out of there with a set of coping mechanisms. These days, I'm trying to figure those out again—Do I like art? Do I like music, if it's not too loud?—but it was helpful back then."

"How did you learn those coping mechanisms?"

"They made me write them down, on an index card. Things that made me feel good. I carried that card with me everywhere. It's still in my wallet."

I suddenly got the sense that Kyle had lived an entire life already.

"What kinds of things were on there?"

"Breathing exercises they taught me—I still use those when I remember. Song lyrics. The Beatles. That's kinda what I'm getting back into now. See my sticker?" He pointed to a corkboard he had shown me earlier. It was covered in magazine clippings, torn pieces of lined paper, beaded necklaces hanging on pushpins. A sticker of the *Abbey Road* album cover.

I thought to myself: *Resources.*

"This board is kind of like your new index card," I said.

"Exactly!" He grinned. "The other morning, I couldn't get in the shower—looked at the shower and just said, 'Nope'—and I came and sat in front of my board instead. Finally, that afternoon, I was able to get in the shower."

I heard dozens of these stories, met dozens of these people—male, female, trans, gay, lesbian, white, Black, Asian, Latino, young, old, married, single—and I felt like I was meeting everything under the sun and it was all broken and glittering. The depth of suffering was unfathomable, the beauty of the people ineffable.

How—how was all of this possible.

"Aaaahhhh," was the sound that came out of my mouth. Out of my body. Half-sigh, half-yell. The full sun glorious on my face.

The four of us—me, Dale, Violet, and Leo—had just stepped onto Mars Court, a trail in the Manzanita Mountains just southeast of Albuquerque. It was early April, and the confines of the pandemic had been pushing us out into the wilderness every weekend. That wasn't hard to do in New Mexico; we could drive forty minutes and not see another person for four hours. Mars Court was a sweet little trail we had hiked many times over the years. It had a quality of home to it. The air was fresh, quiet.

I like to pass the first half mile of a hike in silence. Greet the land, establish a relationship with it. Not in any formal way, but in a very necessary way, like I do with the day: that grounding, that centering. And with how dense life had become lately—me, Dale, Violet, work, parenting, and a pandemic all on top of each other, all day long—I needed the space more than ever. Dale carried Violet in a front-pack while Leo trotted ahead. I took my time in the back.

Mars Court was everything we weren't expecting about New Mexico when we first moved here. Pine and broadleaf lined a rocky dirt trail, then fanned out into a lush forest as the trail widened and smoothed, and eventually thinned to a canyon floor of meadows and wildflowers. We had no idea there would be such green here, not that the trees and grasses were any better than the mesas and arroyos—just that they were secret, unexpected. The kind of yin and yang that you get in the high desert.

"My parents are still going to St. Louis," I said to Dale, when I had found my feet.

"Oh geez," he sighed.

"I know. I had texted them, suggesting that maybe that's not the best idea right now, and my mom basically said 'fuck off.' Apparently, she knows better than the rest of the planet about this virus."

"Sounds about right."

"Literally, I try to express concern for their well-being and that's what I get. Mark my words: When this pandemic is over, I am going to therapy for her."

I rolled my shoulders and squeezed the blades together. Exhale. "Anyway, I had that March of Dimes call. I learned a lot."

"Oh yeah?"

"Yeah. They don't have a ton of data so far, but what they do have is good." March of Dimes is the premier nonprofit on preventing premature birth; we had been avid supporters since Sloane died, even had our story featured in their 2019 holiday cards. The week before, they had hosted a call on prematurity and the coronavirus for their most dedicated donors. "I had submitted a question, and their chief medical guy answered it on the call. He actually laughed at it."

Dale laughed, too. "What did you ask?"

"I asked if the pandemic should impact family planning at all. Like, if we should wait." The trail turned down a long switchback, and the swaying grasses of the canyon floor came into view. We knew we wanted another kid, and we knew we wanted them to be close in age, but so far, I hadn't been ready.

"What did he say?"

"He said no—not at all." I don't know why he thought it was such a funny question. I guess I thought maybe more of life should have stopped during such a crisis—like maybe I finally wanted to stop charging ahead. But everything around me was still saying the same old thing: *carry on, carry on. This is life; carry on.*

"I think we should start trying," I said. "We just have no idea what could happen. It took us four months to get pregnant with Violet. I could have another miscarriage."

Even just saying all that felt shitty—this shitty, shitty process. But I know now that part of that was on me, still trying to force a timeline, force a perfect picture, still thinking I had control, that that was how life was lived, when the only reality was this: By trying to conceive, we were signing up for *anything could happen*, and we knew, intimately, the worst of those options.

"On meth, I could get everything done," a woman had told me early on in the behavioral health interviews. She had only been clean for three months, said she was white-knuckling it when she got her COVID stimulus check. "I cooked, I cleaned, I took care of my kids. My husband and I had sex every night. I could do anything."

"How did that feel?" I asked.

"I was fucking perfect. I was skinny, I was sexy. I didn't have to feel anything."

She, I would later discover in the analysis, was still in the self-abandonment phase of her illness.

"Want to stop here for a snack?" Dale asked when we reached the meadow, the air beset with the calmness we came here for.

I slid off my backpack and pulled out a falsa blanket. Tossed one end out into the air and let it settle onto the long grass. Dale unbuckled Violet from the pack and set her down on top. Handed her a pinecone.

"It's up to you, babe," said Dale. He had been ready for a while.

"Ok," I said, something coating the inside of my belly. The thrill of this adventure again, this life with this man. I smiled. "Let's do it."

It was amazing how much a day weighed in those times. Three weeks later—six weeks and thirty-something interviews into the pandemic— I was utterly spent. I didn't know how to not carry it all: all those stories piled onto my back, with full-time childcare for my living daughter on top, part-time grieving for my dead daughter on top of that, and the whole world dying on top of it all. My bones felt like dust, my nerves a beehive. I cried ten times a day.

I felt like I was on the verge of something. Some cliff.

But by then, a hole had been carved into the pandemic. Ways through: safety measures, protocols, data. We began to understand who was getting sick and who wasn't, which precautions mattered and which didn't. And so, one afternoon in early May, Dale and I sat on our couch, his phone between us, speaker on, and dialed Violet's pediatrician.

"We're thinking of sending Violet back to daycare," I said when he got on the line.

I listed all the reasons why, all the evidence we had that this was a sound decision. No cases at her daycare; all the cleaning and checking and distancing. Our work, my health. As I talked, another part of me asked, *who are you trying to convince here?* But this wasn't an argument; it was a necessity.

"I don't think this is a bad decision," the doctor said. "You can't parent her if you're exhausted. You know what to do if she gets sick."

Sometimes life does funny things, like switching out endings for beginnings. A clean transition: when life turned from this to that. And so it was that the day that Violet went back to daycare, I found out I was pregnant. Our first try. Not exactly what we had planned for—but maybe this would be the pregnancy where everything would go right.

20

So, Dr. Page reminded me of something today," I said to Dale when I got home from my pre-op appointment. It was late June, and he was still working from home, and I had trudged my tired ass up the stairs to his makeshift office. "I can't believe I forgot: I had an infection in my cerclage with Violet."

I flopped down on the purple couch. "What the fuck," I said, dropping my head into my hands. What the fuck were we supposed to do now.

My cerclage procedure for this pregnancy was in eight days. It was supposed to be our savior; this was the time that we were supposed to be in the 80-90% of cerclage pregnancies that go full-term. Huge belly. Fresh baby on my chest. Baby coming home with us. And now this: a reminder that the pathology from Violet's birth stated that I had had a placental infection and partial abruption *and* an infection at the site of the cerclage. The things that weren't supposed to happen, that were so unlikely, but were my reality.

We had found out early that we were having a boy. I was going to have a son. It was a thought that both terrified and thrilled me. But how were we supposed to protect him now? He had only been around for twelve weeks and already his life felt precarious. I felt a red heat spread across my chest.

This was fucking unbearable.

But looking back, maybe this was what I needed. Maybe I needed life to sharpen the edges of this thing just a little—to give me clarity, give me relief. Because my head had become a hard place to be lately. A dark jungle that I couldn't seem to find my way out of. I clawed endlessly at drapes of hanging vines, only to pull them back and find new realms of despair. It was the pull before the desperation—before the Jemez, before Georgia.

And yet, although I had been there before, something was different this time. Something hurt more than the thought that I didn't belong in this world, or that I didn't understand life since Sloane died. It was my head itself. A physical pain, yes—but more of a mental pain. Like it was made of lead, solid from ear to ear. Pushing outward in all directions. Hurting so badly I wanted to blow it off. A big bang. A soft, gray nothingness.

Release.

I needed a release from whatever was pulling me under, day in and day out, leaving me weary for the rest of life. I had work to do. I had a toddler to care for. I had a baby to grow. Part of me felt like I had come so far; another part felt like I had sunk deeper than ever. My own internal anchor tied around my ankle.

I lifted my head, rested my chin on my fingertips. Stared straight ahead. On the shelves before me, I caught sight of a familiar gray spine. The pregnancy journal. I had moved it up here after Violet was born. It suddenly occurred to me that I was still in my first trimester. That I wasn't sure that we would even make it this far. That, in fact, my son's life had seemed uncertain this whole time.

The truth was, I knew that a miscarriage was possible—even likely, given that I had been through two already—but I told myself that it would just be a delay. Something to get through. A complication, nothing more. I mean, that's how I saw everything back then. Everything except Sloane.

Two years earlier, in March of 2018, I had been in Chicago for work, interviewing women about beauty: how they shopped for it and how they did their look, but also how it shaped them, how it hurt. Their stories were raw and pulsing, like I was at the time. I curled into their wounds, let them teach me.

My client was a woman named Steph—a little older than me, but similar in her anxiety about life, about herself. I could often feel the tightness of her muscles. But I enjoyed her. We had spent time in the field together a couple of years before, so we had a rapport. In Chicago, we had gotten caught up on each other's lives; she listened to my stories with a bravery and a curiosity that buoyed my heavy soul. Which just makes me that much more of an asshole for what happened one night at dinner.

It was our last night in Chicago. Our interviews were over, my body drained, my head heavy. We walked to a restaurant a block from the hotel, and after we ordered—both salads, how gross; I almost changed to a burger so that we didn't look so oppressed, but truthfully, I was craving something green—Steph broke into an open-mouthed smile.

"So, tell me about Sloane," she said. She didn't know that that was the first—and to this day, only—time I had ever been asked that. That she was the first to assume—to know—that there were things to be said about my daughter, despite her short life. My stomach tumbled.

"She was incredible," I said. "It's hard to describe how wonderful it felt to meet her, to hold her, even after she died. It sounds wrong, but that's how it was."

"She sounds amazing. I'm so glad you got that time with her."

"Me too—she was such love and joy. Most of the time, thinking of her makes me so happy. Happier than most things, honestly."

"Wow." Steph's jaw still hung in that big smile, her eyes wide. It strikes me now how many people never got to share this joy with me simply because they were too afraid to see pain. How courage is a requirement for authentic connection.

"I would never say this to someone who has only had a miscarriage, but those were nothing compared to losing Sloane."

"I just had a miscarriage," Steph blurted out, "in January."

My stomach dropped beneath the table. Her eyes turned red, watery. I realized she hadn't planned on saying that.

"I am so sorry," I said. "Are you ok?"

"No," she croaked, sudden gravel in her throat. Her face twisted, so honest, so aching. "It was awful. Just so awful."

She told me the story: how it was her first pregnancy, and she was 6 weeks along and elated, and then she started bleeding. Dealt with it herself, kept her husband out of it. I imagined her in my own bathroom—rust-colored walls, blood on the tile floor. I thought of all the bleeding women do, alone in bathrooms all over the world—how we come face-to-face with our own blood every month; how we become numb to it. Take care of it. Discard it.

Discard ourselves.

Long after our bowls were cleared, Steph and I still sat talking. This slice of life is bottomless. But I wanted to give us both some place to land after all of it. I told her about the morning a couple of months prior, when I had the sudden experience of feeling like myself again. How Blair had said that was a big step in the grief process.

She stared at me.

From all my years of interviewing people, I can tell when someone is realizing something in the exact moment that they are uttering it aloud. The words come out slowly, perfectly, and the person always ends up looking you directly in the eye. Everything stands still. There is an untainted clarity in self-discovery.

Steph's eyes shined. Her lower lip trembled.

"I haven't felt that way since my dad died," she said.

I don't know if she would have gotten there had she not told me about her miscarriage, had I not fucked up. So, regret is a funny thing.

But so is truth, and even though I knew I shouldn't have said what I said, I didn't know yet that it wasn't even true. But my body knew. Knew it when it doubled over after we learned about the antiphospholipid antibodies with Violet. Knew it when I finally picked up the phone to start grief counseling after my second miscarriage hiking in Santa Fe. Knew it when I found myself at the top of a cliff in the Jemez after my first miscarriage in Boston.

My body knew that these were lives lost.

My children's lives.

Knew that that was something I couldn't bear to know again.

But this one—this one was still here.

In Dale's office, I let out an exhale. "Ok, what do we know?"

"Well," said Dale, "your cervix shortened with Sloane but stayed long the whole time with Violet."

"And the difference between those two pregnancies was that I had the septum removed. Which could have caused the cervical issues."

We laid these facts out before us like silverware at the dinner table.

"The likelihood of a cerclage infection is low."

"But I've already had one."

"And an infection automatically means delivery—no matter when it is. Lots of risk to the baby."

"Hey," I said suddenly. "Remember when Dr. Kwan said he didn't recommend a cerclage with Violet?"

We looked at each other. Said it in almost the same words, at almost the same time: "I wonder what he would say this time."

We called High Desert and left a message for Dr. Kwan to call us. And then we just sat there, waiting, and I tried to keep my head together, but all of this had started to make me feel sick. Get the cerclage, which might be unnecessary, and risk infection, preterm delivery, harm, even death; or don't get one and risk my cervix shortening, preterm delivery, harm, even death. Nothing about either of those options was unrealistic—and for us, the two options were exactly our history. What. The. Fuck.

When Dr. Kwan called back, Dale and I hunched over the speaker phone between us, once again laying out the silverware.

"I think you should get the cerclage," he said. No hesitation and no real explanation why—just that he thinks it's the right move.

We thanked him, hung up, looked at each other. We both knew the same thing: It was just another fork. He couldn't make the decision for us; we had to make it. The choice that we could live with.

"Let's sleep on it," said Dale. Ever more patient than me.

For the next twenty-four hours, the question rotted in my stomach. All the flatware began to disintegrate: rusting tines, brown spoon wells; it seemed like nothing could be taken at face value. It was all so incomplete, so imprecise—so laden with real fucking life-or-death consequences.

I dragged myself up to Dale's office the next afternoon. Sat on the purple couch. Sunk my face into my hands.

"Can we make a decision," I asked, my voice dead and muffled behind my fingers.

We talked it through again, as clearly and succinctly as we could, defining our pool of information and its limits. It was unbearably small. But it was what we had, and we had to know that: *This is all we have. This is all we can do. Nobody should ever have to do this, but here we are. Doing all we can do with all we have.* Accepting that is a human feat in and of itself.

And we agreed: The only decision we could live with, no matter the consequences, was getting the cerclage.

One more week.

We were water, me and Dale. Slipping in and out and around each other. Nothing but skin and muscle and heart.

Our last hurrah before the cerclage was both erotic and idyllic, a rousing promise to each other that we were in this life together. Afterward, I laid my chest on his. His skin, his being. *This man*, I thought, my body still alit, my heart swelling.

When I finally slid off of him and onto our bed, all I saw was red. Heart-thumping red. Fire engine red. Emergency red. We were both slaked in fresh blood.

"Whoa," said Dale.

I swallowed hard, eased off the bed, and made like a wounded gazelle to the bathroom—short, loopy skips, squeezed pelvic muscles, trying to hold everything in.

On the toilet, I relaxed my hold. Clots of blood and tissue fell out of me, their rush into the water pounding in my ears, thundering in my chest, sinking, swirling, threads of blood floating off the masses. The entire bowl was soon red. I stared at it between my legs, panting.

Something the size of my palm slid out of me and slipped quietly into the water. Sinking down, down. Settling, I imagine, on the bottom.

I slid my naked body to the tile floor.

Plunged my hand into the water.

Fished out what had fallen.

And held it in my hand, hovering over the bowl.

It was maroon—the color of liver. Both soft and firm.

"Dale," I called, barely recognizing my own voice. Too high, too raspy. "Come here."

His silhouette appeared in the cracked doorway.

"What is this?" I asked. The voice I heard broke in odd places. "Is this him?"

He edged open the door.

"Ohhh…," he moaned, leaning against the doorjamb. "Oh, babe."

I slid onto my left hip and dropped my head. Arm still resting on the toilet ring, red water dripping down my wrist. What had started to crack in my voice fully splintered inside me and I had nowhere else to go but the one question I had never asked, in three years.

"Why!" I shrieked. High, scratchy. "Why! Why does this keep happening to us!"

It was a question I had never understood but, in that moment, it kept coming. From where, I don't know—it wasn't my voice, wasn't my intention. I was nowhere to be found.

I don't remember cleaning up. Me, him. All the blood.

"I can't believe this," I said to Dale. I pulled a T-shirt over my head; my arms just hung. I looked him in the eye. "I can't do this again."

We both fell to our knees on our bedroom floor.

"I can't—I just can't," I cried, tears streaming. I balled my fists in front of my face as he pulled me into his arms. "This is it."

"It's ok, it's ok," he said through his own tears. Then he held me out at arm's length, our red eyes meeting. "I never realized it until now, but she is enough. Violet is enough. This can be it."

"Yeah," I said, looking down, nodding but not feeling it, and yet knowing that it had to be true. Because I was not going to do this again.

"It's late," I said, after we cried ourselves out, still sitting on our knees, on our shaggy white rug. "I should get to the hospital. You guys stay here."

"We can go—I can pack her up."

It was nine o'clock at night. Violet had been asleep for two hours.

"No, no—there's no sense in dragging everyone through this. It's the freakin' emergency room." I thought of my all-niter there after Violet was born. "I'll just go. I'll be fine."

It strikes me as odd that I chose to go to the hospital that night. Or maybe chose isn't the right word; it was more automatic, uncalculated, even though I had never gone for a miscarriage before. Boston, Santa Fe—those took care of themselves. I don't know why I felt compelled to drive down Montgomery, sit in the waiting room.

But the thing that really gets me now—and the thing that I promptly forgot as soon as I left the hospital—was that this should have been a wakeup call for me. A rock bottom that lays you out on your back, so that you can finally look up into the light. I had just spent three months listening to rock bottoms, analyzing them, designing solutions for them. But this wasn't mine—not yet.

Shortly after two in the morning, I crawled into bed. Swished my bare legs around in the cool sheets. Dale stirred. I leaned over to him, found his ear in the dark with my face.

"Everything's ok," I whispered. "I'll tell you in the morning."

21

What about Sal?" I said.

"Eh...," said Dale, looking across the park, eyes squinting behind his sunglasses. I knew I shouldn't have thrown out my frontrunner first.

"Saul?" I tried again.

"That's practically the same thing," he said, turning toward to me.

"I know—I like the sound of them. Saul Goodman. *Blueberries for Sal.* They're classics but rare. Fresh."

We were finding that balance hard to strike. It seemed like every boy's name was either too boring—Adam, Michael, Dylan—or too weird—Hunter, Maximus. Lately I had been feeling an urge to get a name picked out. Call me crazy.

It turned out I had placenta previa, where the placenta covers the opening to the cervix. It can cause heavy bleeding and loss of tissue and usually corrects itself naturally over the course of the pregnancy but if not, can lead to severe bleeding during delivery or the need for a C-section. Great. But thankfully, it did not impact my ability to get my cerclage; I had gotten it three weeks prior, as scheduled, and was feeling securely shut. Now I needed a fucking break. Everything else went into a box labeled *Future Problems.*

Except I wanted a name.

"Do you like Mickey?" I asked. I watched Violet shove her chunky blocks into each other. School bus yellow and sky blue. She was getting better at them.

"Not really."

"Ok, what do you like?"

Dale leaned back on one arm, uncrossed his legs on the falsa blanket. Watched the teens playing basketball across the arroyo. "Henry?"

"Definitely not."

A light breeze rustled the grass. The air was cool in the sprawling shade of the cottonwoods. Shade was gold in high desert summers; because the air was so dry, the temperature was significantly cooler out of the sun. None of that humidity nonsense, where even shade felt like wading through a hot, sticky pool. *The park*, I thought. *Maybe I could come here and eat lunch. Sit in the grass. Be outside, but in the shade.*

I had gone back to my lists. Like Kyle, the Babylon baby, trying to get back into his coping mechanisms. Even though a number of weights had lifted—the behavioral health project, the first trimester, the early days of the pandemic—I was trying to stay on top of things. Not let it get so bad. Again.

And I had gotten somewhere, or two places actually: a curated list and a new understanding. *Things That Help*, I had written in my notebook one evening, for what felt like the hundredth time. *Writing, walking, fresh air, yoga, meditation, a shower.* The meditation one was funny—I had only meditated maybe seven times in the last three years and had no idea what I was doing any of those times, but it always helped in the moment, so I wrote it down. But maybe its purpose was this: It helped me see that everything on this short list was a form of intentional quiet. I wrote that phrase next to the list, underlined it twice. *Intentional quiet.* Creating calm, slow spaces for myself—spaces that had never fit into my life before. My life based on productivity and achievement. My life that wasn't working.

Space. Maybe that was the real theme. Space for me.

In many ways, grief itself had been a drive towards minimalism. A clearing out—of things, relationships, time, and energy—to make space for these new emotions, new values, a new perspective on abundance. I was beginning to see all of this now—more of how my life could be, more of what I actually wanted—but I was still trying to have it all, old and new.

What the fuck was time anyway, and where was I in it. Grief had dra-a-a-a-gged for so long, and then the next minute, I had a toddler and another baby on the way. I wasn't ready for any of this, couldn't keep up with any of it, but here I was, painfully in the center of it.

Moving ever forward.

"How about I make a list?" I said to Dale. "And you can react to it. I'll make a little survey for you—give you a scale. Love it, like it, dislike it, hate it. You down?"

"I'm down."

I smiled. Not a romantic way of going about it, but a way I knew and could trust. Fuck if it isn't hard to change our ways.

It seemed like I was always sitting at the end of the same exam table, forever learning that my cervix was only five millimeters. Thick padding in dusty rose. Paper cover crackling under my thighs. Feet dangling. Except this time, I was at High Desert, and Dr. Kwan had just told me, casually, that my cervix was down to one-and-a-half centimeters. I had stared at him, expecting more. He gave me nothing. Now I was waiting to debrief with Ethan.

"Ok," he exhaled when he walked in, eyes wide. "Things are still ok right now. We don't know what's going to happen from here."

He sat down on the swivel stool, rolled toward me. I found it funny that now he was looking up at me, sitting on the exam table. Ethan was tall and lanky with a boyish face and tight brown curls. A physician's assistant—to Dr. Jeffrey, I think.

"Yeah," I said, dumb for words. I liked Ethan. I had seen him when I was pregnant with Violet. He seemed like one of those guys where every description of him always come back to: *He's just a good guy.* He met my eyes.

"But if you start having contractions," he said, "you need to get to the hospital. Before you rip through your cervix."

Sometimes doctors have a way of saying things so that they become seared into you forever. *The prognosis is terrible. Rip through your cervix.* Tattoos on my hippocampus.

But I just nodded. I had already started to drift away. Staring beyond the walls of the exam room, down the road we had walked with Sloane. Here we were again. And I was only 18 weeks along.

But the next one of us to go to the hospital wasn't me.

Flushed cheeks. Hanging eyelids. The bottom of her ribs poking out with each inhale. When Violet woke up from her nap the next Saturday, Dale and I looked at each other with the same thought: COVID. We had agreed to keep me away from people while I was pregnant, so he scooped her up and drove across town to urgent care.

I laid on the couch and waited. Turned on some dance competition show, sobbed at all of their talent, turned it off.

A text from Dale: *We're in an ambulance. Headed to the hospital.*

A minute later: *She is the most beautiful thing ever.*

I closed my eyes. Having one child in the ground, one gasping for breath, and one hanging by a thread was too much for me to bear. I willed myself to simpler times.

Every morning at Notre Dame, I walked from the south dining hall, across the south quad, to LaFortune. LaFun, as we often called it, was a small, quaint student center. It looked like a house but had a Subway, a Starbucks, and a mini-mart inside, above a big, cozy basement of tables and booths to study or hang out at. Surrounding the building, frog-green leaves, big as hands, hung high overhead, and the sun dappled the sidewalks, the breeze shifting branch shadows. Walking there every morning was a coming-home, a waking-up. I would get my black coffee, stir in a spot of creamer and a sprinkle of vanilla, and head out the side door toward my first class. And those first thirty steps out of LaFun, coffee in hand, was the best part of every day. Every time. My head brimmed with possibilities and a hunger for life; people swirled around me; life gathered. The world felt full and open and mine to have.

My phone rang.

"COVID negative," Dale said, "but she will be on oxygen."

"Oh, good," I said, exhaling. Life was fucked up.

"You should have seen her," he said. I could hear his wet eyes. Later he will tell me that it was instantaneous; as soon as she was strapped into the ambulance, he was choking back tears. Something between him and Violet started in that moment—something that would carry us all for a long time. "She was so brave."

When we hung up, I laid back down. Closed my eyes. Rubbed my hands down my small belly, ribs to waist. All I wanted was those thirty steps again.

Sometimes when I close my eyes, what I really need is to look up. Out. Beyond.

That evening we ate dinner out on the deck, Violet's oxygen tank laying on the table, the clear tubing snaking around her purple plastic plate. After dinner, Dale took her inside to put her to bed, and I stayed to watch the sunset. Most nights I tried to catch it at its peak; tonight, I wanted to watch it unfold. Or rather, it seemed, *it* wanted me to watch it unfold. It felt like an invitation.

At quarter to eight in mid-August, the sky was still solid blue. The sun a yellow ball in a band of gold touching the horizon. Brushstrokes of clouds swept in every direction. Some wispy, some feathery; others mere smudges like happy accidents. All of it, coming together.

This was the view of life that I needed: of things bigger than me and beyond my control. Of things at once lasting and fleeting and beautiful. This was a goddamn masterpiece, art on the ceiling of the world, and there was nothing as raw and poetic and breathtakingly bold as a painting being painted before your eyes, at times still and at times on fire, but always, always alive.

If only I could have held onto that view a little longer. That quiet, that space. For when the following weeks came rushing, tumbling down. A line of dominos.

22

ey babe," I said to Dale a week later. "I think we need to go to triage."

For two days, I had been barely able to focus on anything other than a dull ache in my pelvic area. I drank water, I ate; I laid down, I moved around. Nothing helped. I knew what this was. Ethan's voice was a pulsing strobe light in my head: *Rip. Rip. Rip.*

At the hospital, I lied to the admitting nurse. I had learned at my ER visit for the placenta previa that the cutoff for triage versus the ER is 20 weeks. I was a day shy. But triage was where I wanted to be, for all its familiarity—both the eeriness and the comfort of it. They say that the mind compulsively repeats even dangerous patterns, not only because the familiarity is comforting, but because it's also hoping for a different outcome, one that can act as a salve for all the previous bad outcomes. Turn the direction of the pattern. End it.

So, I answered all the historical questions and laid down in the bed that the nurse led me to, in the same room we had been in with Sloane. I closed my eyes. *We have been here before, and we have survived.*

But things tend to get weird when you go underground. After they took my vitals and checked out the baby in triage, they wheeled me down to the basement for an ultrasound. At least, it seemed like a basement—empty, quiet, stuffy, hallway dimly lit by a single light flickering near the end of it. I sat alone, parked next to the wall, waiting for the technician. Watching the end of the hall get thrown in and out of visibility. Light, dark. Light, dark. The lower half of my face was warm from my own breath, trapped behind a homemade mask. They were busy here. COVID.

A jolt to my wheelchair and then I was wheeled into a dark room.

"I don't know why they gave me you," the tech muttered as he fiddled with equipment, turned on monitors. "I don't know anything about these parts of the body."

I stared at him. And the whole time he was doing my exam, I couldn't stop staring. He was an older man with gray or white or otherwise light hair—it was hard to tell in the dark. Tall, broad, white. Angry. And then I realized: Lit only by the screen in front of him and mostly covered with a face mask, he looked like Trump. It was the hair. Suddenly, the world and everything in it seemed to expand outward and melt, like a Dali painting.

Everything was so far past the point of bizarre that it took all of me to not just burst out laughing. I was on the verge of losing another child, and an incompetent Trump look-alike was the one ushering me through it, while the rest of the world burned in Black Lives Matter marches and streets turned into morgues. What the fuck was happening.

Back upstairs, the world came back. The windows of my triage room faced east, the late afternoon sun on the other end of the sky, and the light that came in was mellow, warm. I watched Dale as we waited, and my body softened.

The nurse came in. We both looked up.

"Ok," she said, looking at me. "Your cervix is 3.2 centimeters."

Dale and I looked at each other. Everything seemed to lift; the room brightened, as if the sun had come out from behind a cloud. For that briefest of moments, I believed her.

"Are you sure?" I asked, turning back to her. "That seems weird."

"That's what the report says. You guys can start packing up your things while I get your paperwork."

She left.

It's amazing how many conversations Dale and I don't have to have—how often we know exactly where the other one is. It's most helpful when neither of us can find words anyway.

But before we moved, the nurse came back in. She held a phone out to me.

"The doctor wants to speak with you."

The phone was off-white from years of use. It was blocky and clunky and felt like a plastic brick next to my ear. An image of Zach Morris from *Saved By The Bell* flashed through my head, and again, I thought I might burst into laughter. That delirious, aching, crying kind.

"Hello?" I said.

"Hi Alexandria," a woman said, rushing. I realized I didn't even know who this doctor was. "I'm so sorry I'm not there right now. But I wanted to catch you before you left. Your cervix is not 3.2 centimeters."

"Yeah, we didn't think so," I said. And then I actually did laugh, as if we were all in on some joke. "The ultrasound guy even said he didn't know what he was doing."

"Yeah, he didn't. I'm going to measure this myself here. Hold on."

I kept my eyes on the floor, walked in small, lazy circles. I don't like talking on the phone. Anything could happen in this very pregnant moment, and I had only my ears to receive it and my voice to respond to it. No, I didn't like the phone at all.

"Seven millimeters. I'm getting about seven millimeters."

I hate the phone. Her radioed voice coming in through wires, loud and metallic in one ear, nothing but air in the other.

"Ok," I said. Like everything else, words seemed to be in short supply today.

"I'm going to call Dr. Jeffrey and see if he can get you in right away to talk about options."

I heard my voice somewhere, echoing.

Ok. Ok. Ok.

I was at High Desert first thing the next morning. After an ultrasound, I sat in a chair in a room that didn't make any sense. It had the same little corner set-up as all the other exam rooms—counter, sink, cabinets—but it was too small to fit an exam table. Ethan walked in.

"You have two options, and neither of them are good," he said before he had even closed the door. His eyes sagged with a heaviness I had never seen. But the whole time—even as he slid a wheeled stool between his legs, took a seat, set down his folder, drew out sonogram prints—they never left mine.

"The first option is to do a revised cerclage and place the stitch higher up," he continued. "The second option is progesterone suppositories. Neither of these has been proven to be effective in a situation like this, but they could help you get further along."

Still, his eyes hung but never wavered. I thought we both might cry if we were each alone.

"What are the pros and cons of each?" I asked.

Ethan nodded. "Always with a cerclage, the risk is infection. And with a revised cerclage, we are working in an area that's already been messed with and might be more swollen and irritated to begin with. We could be introducing new problems that aren't there already. The progesterone has helped prolong pregnancy in women without a cerclage but hasn't proven to help women who already have one. But it could help calm irritability in the uterus, like the contraction we saw."

I winced. I had been hoping that they wouldn't mention that again—that maybe they realized it was a fluke, or just immaterial. At one point during my ultrasound that morning, Dr. Jeffrey had pointed to the screen.

"See that?" he had said, and I had pretended to see. "That's a small contraction. That you're having right now."

Unsee.

"Yeah," I said to Ethan. "I was on progesterone with my first daughter, and it didn't make a difference. But I'm not really hearing any advantages of doing the revised cerclage."

"It's a very experimental procedure. There hasn't been much research done on it, so the benefits aren't clear yet." He tiptoed through his words, as if he felt tugged toward hope but knew it wasn't supported by the facts.

"Is doing both an option?"

"Good question," he said and paused, looking away. I could almost see the gears turning. I loved watching people think, found myself for a moment out of this room and in an interview. Finally, he looked back at me. "Let me go ask Dr. Jeffrey about that."

He left, and my gaze dropped down to the sonogram prints. Black and white shapes of body parts and profiles. I felt a wall come up between me and the images, me and my baby—a glass wall that I could observe him from behind but not connect with. Cody. That's what we had decided on. Cody Mateo, after the San Mateo Wilderness, where Dale and I got lost and had to find our way back. And here, on the counter next to me, was his face. Mouth open. *Singing*, I thought.

I was exactly 20 weeks pregnant, and 24 was the accepted cutoff for viability, when Cody could—maybe, possibly—live. And then came the chasm between 24 and 28 weeks, where most of the danger of lifelong complications lives. It was so long, so long to go.

Dr. Jeffrey and Ethan walked in, the same heaviness in their faces. But such kindness, such humanity, too. In my lap, I clenched my fists, holding on to that. Dr. Jeffrey slid the stool beneath him while Ethan hung back. They moved slowly, carefully, as if we were all under water but under it together.

Reverence—they moved with reverence. I thought of the funeral director and nearly burst into tears. These people—these people holding other people. Holding me.

God, it threatened to break me.

It could have; it should have.

I exhaled, looked down. Ground my teeth together. I needed to stay rational, focused. Behind the glass wall.

Dr. Jeffrey raised his eyebrows, opened his eyes wide. I loved his damn face—all the hair going every which way.

"Well, here we are," he said.

"Yeah," I said, something smoldering inside me. "It seems like Ethan was right when he said our options are not good ones."

"No, they're not. There are only a handful of studies on the revised cerclage, and none of them are statistically sound. Not double-blind, no control groups. Sample sizes as small as a dozen and as many as thirty. The results say the average gestational age for delivery is 30 weeks." He shrugged.

"I work in research, so I get that."

"Risk of infection is low—but it's there—and then there's the risk of ruptured membranes."

"How close is my water bag to the cerclage now?"

"Good question." He pulled out a sonogram image from the pile, blown up to half of a full sheet of paper. "These two white dots are your cerclage. Your cervix has a lot of funneling, but the membranes haven't pushed into the funnel yet. We would want to put the new cerclage a centimeter or a centimeter-and-a-half higher." With a pencil, he made two hash marks for the new cerclage. Then he drew a sweeping line across the widest end of my cervix. "This is where your membranes are. We would have about five millimeters of room to avoid them."

I gave an almost imperceptible nod, kept my eyes on the marked-up paper. Black and white when everything was gray. I finally looked up to see Dr. Jeffrey and Ethan staring at me expectantly.

In later years, I will think back on this time when life was so thin, and I'll get an inexplicable sensation of being flattened. I'll feel like a wood shaving, a knife blade, a long shore stretching out to sea, and when I come back to the present moment, everything seems so full— a drop of blue sky is as rich as paint, the breeze across my face a caress. When you've been to the brink, and then come back to the middle, you need so much less.

"I'm not really seeing any good reason to do the revised cerclage," I said finally. "It seems like the risks are high and the benefits are questionable."

I searched their faces, their bodies, for any feedback. Ethan hadn't moved in some time. Dr. Jeffrey did his typical: wide eyes, raised eyebrows, shrug. But he also slightly dipped the crown of his head, as if to compliment.

"I'd like to call Dale," I said.

Dr. Jeffrey nodded. "We'll be back."

I called Dale and explained the two options. As I talked, I realized that I desperately wanted him there with me. He had gone to work; we didn't know this was what the appointment was going to be like. But even over the phone—the stupid, stupid phone—we readily agreed: too many risks with the revised cerclage. Membranes get punctured and

Cody is gone. Infection and Cody is gone. I was only 20 weeks. We had so long to go before our son could live.

Dale came home from work early that afternoon. We sat together on the couch.

"Neither Dr. Jeffrey nor Dr. Page recommend bedrest," I said. "They both say that my cervix is gonna do what it's gonna do." I took a deep breath. "But I need to do what I can live with. I need to do as little as possible."

"Yeah," said Dale, nodding.

"I'll need help with walking Leo and making dinners. I can't pick up Violet. I can see if Sienna could watch her on Sunday afternoons, just to give us a break. We also need someone here for her if… something happens."

"Let's ask my dad if he can come out. Maybe he and your dad can switch off, a month at a time or something." His head fell to the side. "The first two weeks of which would be quarantine, every time. Shit."

"It's the best we've got."

Dale pulled out his phone, held it between us, and said, "Hey, remember when we had that crackpot idea to not do the cerclage?"

We both laughed. I smiled at him, kissed his cheek. Felt an opening into the next minute, the next hour.

We called my in-laws, explained the last couple of days, and asked if Rich would be able to come out.

A pause. A pause that I knew.

Breathless, he said, "Absolutely."

The next morning, I was doing the same gathering of myself that my father-in-law had been doing during that pause. I sat in a chair in an exam room, waiting for Dr. Page, lacing and unlacing my fingers in my lap. Remembering what words sounded like so that I could find them when the time came.

"Hellooo," sang Dr. Page after a soft knock, a note of reserve in her voice. "How are you?"

"Not so great," I said, meeting her eyes, our masks covering the rest of our faces.

"Yeah," she nodded, "and that's ok."

"I just can't believe we're back in this place again."

"I know, I know—everything had been going so well. Dr. Jeffrey called me yesterday and got me up-to-date."

"I just can't lose another baby," I gushed without warning. My head dropped to my chest and my shoulders collapsed. Tears flowed down into my mask. This was not what I had planned.

Dr. Page sat motionless, listening.

"You've been through so much," she said.

"I'm sorry," I said, grabbing a tissue from a box on the counter and blotting my eyes.

"No, don't be. This is a lot."

I pressed and wiped and dabbed my face from sopping to sticky. It felt like it weighed a thousand pounds.

"Yeah," I breathed softly. "It is."

She continued to hold space. I focused on evening out my breaths.

"I have some questions though," I said, zipping myself back together, remembering what I came here for. "I've been thinking about it, and if he comes early—especially too early to... save... I want to have a vaginal birth. I was all onboard with a repeat C-section earlier on, but with where things are now, I want to consider a VBAC." I paused, swallowed. "I just think it was really important for me to have that experience with Sloane, and I would want that with him, too. Because that's... all I would have."

I let out a big breath.

"I think that's totally reasonable to plan for. Everything will depend on how things look when you do go into labor, but we can absolutely consider a vaginal birth. Do you know what position he was in yesterday?"

"Mmmm.... no, I'm not sure," I said, deflating. I had forgotten about him possibly being breech, like Violet. My shoulders sank.

"Ok, I'll look at the report."

"Ok. And no matter what happens, I want to get my tubes tied. Can that be done at the same time as the birth?"

"If you have a C-section, for sure—we'll just do it while we're already in there. But if you have a vaginal birth, we'll have to schedule it separately. Sometimes you can get it done in recovery, but honestly, it's a lower priority procedure for the hospital, so more than likely, it will happen later. But we can certainly plan on it—there are some forms you need to sign first."

Later, in reviewing such forms, I would see just how much the government hates voluntary sterilization—one of the many choices in reproductive freedom that us women couldn't possibly be qualified to make. Still makes me seethe inside.

"So, the next question I had, I'm not really sure how to ask, but at what point—or under what conditions—would we try to… save him?"

I was breathing so damn hard.

"So, that's a tricky one. The factors are the baby's gestational age, the baby's weight, and if the NICU has the proper equipment for intubation—if they have a tube small enough. It will all come down to how everything looks at the time of delivery."

"Yeah, that makes sense," I said. I don't even know where those words came from—none of this made any sense. I wanted to gag at the thought that whether my baby lived or died could depend on the size of a plastic tube.

"Things are a little different from a few years ago when you had your first," she said. "Things have advanced a bit, so 24 weeks isn't necessarily a hard cut-off anymore."

I don't know if I actually closed my eyes, or if it just felt like I did, but for one long, slow breath, I was drawn inward, further and further inward, to a place so dark and deep I never went there. A stillness settled in: Nothing more could have been done for Sloane.

I don't know if I thanked Dr. Page with my eyes, but hers softened, seemingly in response.

"The best thing you and your husband can do right now is be prepared to make some hard decisions. If and when anything happens, you'll need to decide what is best for you and your family, and it's better to have those conversations now."

"Ok," I nodded. "We can do that."

"Are you seeing your counselor?" she asked.

192 | ALLE MUDRICK

"Yes, I see her again next week."

"Good—this is hard. I'll want to see you again in four weeks. But you can always come in sooner if you need to."

When I left Dr. Page's office, the August sun was harsh. My head swam in its heat. It felt as though we were dropping into a canyon—that first step toward descent, when the horizon jumps a step higher and, with every footfall, climbs higher and higher until it is overtaken by the canyon wall in front of it. There is no longer a beyond. Just the gaping mouth of the canyon before you.

23

Dale and I had done what you're not supposed to do in early grief. Don't make any big changes in your life, they say, like move, leave a job, or end a relationship, but we bought a house—our first house, our forever home—one week after Sloane died, and it was one of the best decisions we've ever made.

We almost didn't even go see the house we ended up buying. I had crossed it off my list; it had no backyard for Leo, for kids. But something made me tack it back on at the end of the day, after we had seen eight other houses.

"It has…. an x-factor," Dale had said. He felt it immediately; it took me a little longer. Built into the foothills of the Sandias, the house sat on half an acre of natural brush and rock, drawn up a steep hillside and off the street, so that it almost felt suspended in mid-air. Inside, that suspension was reinforced; the heart of the house was a great room with a thirty-foot wood-beam ceiling and a wall of windows looking out west. You could see for sixty miles—all of Albuquerque and beyond, to the desert, the mountains, the sky. A wraparound balcony perforated the walls, bringing the outside inside.

The wall-to-wall carpeting needed to be torn out, and the pink laminate countertops needed an upgrade, but the house had good bones. I know, one of those sayings that turns normal people into pretentious assholes, but it was also more than bones; for all the reasons we loved the house, it was really the synergy of them that captivated us—the bigger thing they amounted to, what was *more* but also impossible to define. It's funny how often perfect things feel indescribable.

Perfect things and horrific things.

In this time, I was hopelessly bound to both my house and my body. I spent most of each day perched on a high stool, brown leather, bucket seat and high back, in front of a high table pushed up against that wall of windows. I worked on my laptop, occasionally gazing out at the horizon. Lost, so lost. In every physical sensation, every emotional tug.

"Engage your prefrontal cortex," Blair had advised me when I updated her on my pregnancy. She tapped her forehead. "That's your thinking brain; it needs things that require focus and concentration. Helps to disarm the stress response."

I tried hard to recognize when I'd drifted away—an exceedingly difficult task. But when I got it right, I shifted from my stool down to my desk chair, now permanently parked at a plastic card table I had thrown up in the middle of the great room. There I had stacked boxes and boxes of jigsaw puzzles, no less than a thousand pieces each: mosaic jungles, watercolor cityscapes, abstract cacti. An Austrian riverfront and an empty café. I grounded my senses in each one—another technique from Blair—tracing the unique silhouettes of the pieces with my fingertips, inhaling the musty smell of cardboard dust sifting around in the box.

Every morning, I struggled to write. Most days all I could manage was: *I'm tired, I'm tired, I'm so tired.*

And every night, I dreamt. That Cody came too early, and I was scrambling to put him back inside me. That I had been dilated three-and-a-half centimeters for a week without knowing it, and my parents were my doctors, scrubs and all.

I dreamt that Cody and I built castles in the sky. Puffy, white clouds and silver linings on an expanse of blue. Castles for jumping and laughing and pretending; defending and raiding and rebuilding.

The day I turned 22 weeks, I found myself desperate. Spinning so fast I feared the ice might break. I needed something to grab onto, something new. The thought of a puzzle piece or a yoga pose or even one more moment of being trapped inside this body made me want to crawl out of my skin. More resources—I needed more.

On the high stool, before the windows, I placed my hands on my laptop keyboard and typed: *How to deal with a high-risk pregnancy.*

You know, for as vast and deep as the internet is, it's surprisingly fucking useless for a lot of things.

I scrolled and clicked and scanned, hitting the back button over and over. *Eat right, avoid alcohol, go to your prenatal visits.* Jesus. I began to wonder if there was any medical professional out there who understood that a woman in a high-risk pregnancy had to be awake for nine hundred minutes a day, every day.

This was all hauntingly familiar.

I started jumping through the search results, two, three pages at a time—skipping past all of the major medical sites and clinics—until I got to the tiny corners, the individuals trying to do good in this world, speaking hard truths without needing them to be vetted by a review board. And that's where I found her.

Parijat Deshpande's website was lilac and flowery. Simpler than it looks today—before her book, her community, her press—but clear on her background in clinical psychology, lived experience with high-risk pregnancy, and most importantly, her ability to speak like a human being to other human beings. Saying things that no one else was saying. Seeing me like no one else was seeing.

What struck me most in what she said was this distinction: Stress in a high-risk pregnancy is not baseless anxiety. It is fear grounded in the reality that your baby is at risk of danger.

This is the reality.

Not a little worry, not a passing concern. But a real fear founded on facts. Data. History. *The real world.* The constant presence of this fear keeps your nervous system in a state of fight, flight, or freeze. The weeks, months of pregnancy are too long to be in such a state.

I sat back. *Too long to be in such a state.* How long had it been, really?

How long had I carried this fear? Before Cody, before Violet; before loss after loss. Three-and-a-half—that's how old Sloane would have been.

For all the beautiful moments between then and now, fear had been there all along. Trudging up the mountain.

Wearing a mask.

Masquerading as so many things: grief, healing. Life.

Like when I thought spreading Sloane's ashes on her first birthday would be symbolic, meaningful—a letting go—and it was, but not in the way that I had imagined.

The day had started out all wrong. Dale and I had planned to hike to South Sandia Peak to spread her ashes in the mountains she was named after, and we had spent all morning shuffling around the house, getting ready, losing our socks, walking into rooms and forgetting why. I was finally starting to pack our bright red daypack, by just staring at it lying flat and lifeless on the kitchen counter, when Dale first said something.

"I don't know if I want to do it," he said.

"What?" I said, not softly. "Why not?"

"I don't know."

"But we already agreed to this." I could hear the desperation in my own voice.

"I know. But I'm just not sure anymore."

I clenched my jaw, sighed. I just wanted this day to mean something. Anything—I just needed something. But this was Dale's grief, too. "Can we still bring her ashes with us—just see what happens?"

He agreed. I remembered how to pack a backpack—water, snacks, first aid kit—and pulled the canister of Sloane's ashes off the shelf. It sat in my office, next to *What to Expect When You're Expecting*. I had just had the first surgery to remove the septum in my uterus; the next one was in two weeks. I wrapped the urn in a long-sleeved T-shirt and wedged it into the backpack so that it stood upright. Protected. As you would bundle up any child for a hike in mid-January. Coat, mittens, hat. In another time.

We left on foot. Half the reason we narrowed in on this neighborhood when looking for a house was direct access to the trails, the mountains. The other reason: the best schools.

We spent the first two and a half miles mostly in silence. We were heavy with a lot of things: grief, love, expectation. Even gravity seemed to pull harder over every foot of the one-thousand feet of elevation gain. Dale walked in front, finding our way up shelves of rocks; Leo moved in sprints, running ahead and then stopping to sniff. I'm not sure I was really even there.

As the trail reached a new height and then dropped into the forest, my shoulders began to loosen. Everything got quieter. I felt enveloped by something, held close by the pines hugging the trail. We passed through a shallow arroyo—like a ravine, but in the southwest—and something about it felt almost sacred, untouchable. It's funny how the shape of the land can make you feel like you're at the bottom of something, when really, you're eight thousand feet above sea level.

Out of the arroyo began another climb that would continue all the way to the peak, another three miles. The temperature dropped; old snow crunched beneath our feet. We were in the belly of the mountains now, hills forming cavernous bowls, trees stretching for days. And all of the space began to feel like a void. I stopped abruptly.

"I don't want to go to the peak," I said to Dale's back. "It won't mean anything."

Recalling those words now, I sounded like a three-year-old. But I can also feel how my head ached, how it felt screwed into my neck.

"Ok," said Dale, facing me. "We can turn around."

"How much more is it?" I asked, peering through the trees up ahead. Leo had stopped farther up the trail. I loved it when he turned around to wait for us.

Dale looked at his GPS tracker. "About two miles."

I thought I might vomit. How could we still have so far to go? How could we have been carrying this weight for so long—and still have so much farther to go?

Hot tears sprang to my eyes. "I don't want to go."

Dale stepped past me, back in the direction we came, and called Leo to come back. As we started off, I kept my eyes down. Stepping my feet back into the tracks we had just made.

I *was* three: young, small, and with emotions I didn't know how to handle. I wanted to kick and scream and flail my arms. Cry out, *This isn't what I wanted! This isn't what you deserve for your birthday! This isn't what I wanted for you, Sloane; this isn't what you deserve.*

I was furious and hurt and burning inside.

I wanted to be angry with Dale. I wanted to rage at him for making this day into nothing. But I couldn't. Lifting my eyes to watch him walk before me, I saw how his shoulders slumped, his back rounded softly, under the same weight of it all.

"I couldn't go to the peak and not leave her ashes there," I said, after some time. The words were soft and seemed to just slip into the cold air, as if they belonged there. "I just wanted today to mean something."

"Yeah," said Dale. I knew what he meant.

"Why did you change your mind about today?"

He paused. "I just felt like she is the only child we have right now...and I didn't want to let go of her."

His words hung in my ears, clung to the branches already heavy with snow.

"I understand," I said. "I'm so sorry it hurts."

"It's ok. It is what it is."

Our steps fell into rhythm. The earth around us brightened—snow draped over trees, pure white on dark wood, soft sunlight filtering through clouds that stretched and pulled—and this day that was here before us was suddenly right where I wanted to be.

"What if we just stayed open," I said, "to spreading her ashes. If we see the right place."

"I think that's a great idea," said Dale.

Easy—it had become easy between us again. We chatted and laughed. We wondered and dreamed. We admired the wilderness and relished our seclusion within it. And we gradually scaled back down to the forest floor, eight thousand feet above sea level.

And then I saw it.

As soon as we dropped into the arroyo: a tall, thick Ponderosa pine, standing alone, thirty feet off the trail. Basking in full sunlight, its face so perfectly in line with the sunbeams that it seemed to be thrusting its chest forward. Strong. True. Speaking volumes with its silence. I could physically feel where it shot through my chest.

"What about here?" I blurted out, trying to catch my breath.

Dale turned around and followed my gaze.

Nothing moved.

"This is perfect," he said.

Time slowed. We stepped off the trail, approached the pine. A five-foot wide flat clearing of dirt sat before it, shaped by roots. We lowered onto our knees. Moving as if underwater, Dale pulled open this moment: first, the canister out of the backpack, then the bag of ashes out of it, and then the bag itself. He poured half of our daughter's body into my cupped hands.

For a moment, I held her dust, her tiny shards of white bone. Then I let her slide through my spread fingers, cool and silky and puffing out into the air on her way back to the earth, clouds of my daughter taking up space in the world. I wept and wept as she slipped back into sunlight, into sound, into the very air that I was breathing.

Here she was, as big as the mountains.

At home. At peace.

And somehow, so was I. For at least this one moment, sitting in front of my computer screen, seeing my story reflected back to me: that my body knew fear. And what I seemed to understand but wouldn't truly know until years later: that this fear was here to protect me. From the places I had already been, the places I didn't want to go again. Even for all of their beauty—I had had enough.

I lifted my eyes to the window in front of me, gazed out at the horizon. It was a blue line of distant mountains. Every layer that came before it was a different dusty color: yellow desert, green *bosque*, orange rooftops, gray street. Our house at sixty-two-hundred feet.

The stitched hide of the stool pressed up against my thighs. I realized I was leaning forward, chest open. For fear wasn't the bottom. Beneath it was a whole mountain of love. And that was what I came here for.

I have a working theory that it's often the people most in need of love that seek to create it, no matter the cost. Because the promise of salvation—of finally being filled—is too sweet.

In early September, Dale and I went to High Desert for my 23-week appointment. I got an ultrasound done from the technician and then too many doctors filed into the room. Standing around its edges, leaning against cabinets and countertops were Ethan, Dr. Kwan, some others, and in the center, sitting on a rolling stool, Dr. Jeffrey. He slapped his thighs and raised his wild eyebrows.

"I can't believe you're still here," he said. His wide eyes looked directly into mine. They were so full, so kind. We had a silent conversation, a shared knowing that this journey was bigger than us and we were on it until the end. My entire body settled.

And then: "Three millimeters."

The room got heavy. Tones dropped as each doctor took his turn to talk about next steps. Their words were smooth, carrying—all of them—but also edged with imminence. The wide, flat blade of a butcher knife that eventually comes to a sharp drop-off.

From one: "We'll start steroid shots for the baby's lungs at 24 weeks. Two rounds, twenty-four hours apart. Then we'll do it again at 28 weeks."

Something in me winced and then relaxed. The shots I didn't have time to get for Violet. I silently thanked the doctor, thanked everything on this planet.

From another: "I think we should do something different next time. A transabdominal cerclage might be a better route for you."

I knew this term, had researched it a lifetime ago. A TAC was a sort of net placed in the abdomen, to keep the baby from moving down the birth canal; it was rarely done, and only if a cervical cerclage had been ineffective in past pregnancies. Like the cervical cerclage itself, or the septum removal, it only became an option after you had already lost. Oh, had I lost—but it was not lost on me that he was talking to us that day because he didn't think we would be back. When he continued, I held my palm up.

"Thank you," I said. "But we are not doing this again. No matter what happens, we are not going through this again."

He looked me in the eye, smiled. And then we all laughed. At I don't know what—the absurdity of it all, I suppose. They say people laugh when they're uncomfortable, to ease the tension. This wasn't that. This was a room full of people momentarily suspended over the top of life, looking down at how wild it all is. Knowing that all we can do is be along for the ride.

And yet sometimes, in later years, when I'm standing in my bathroom at five-thirty in the morning, brushing my teeth and gripping the counter, stomach boiling, I will have to remind myself that I survived these moments.

Blah. Blah blah. Blah blah blah.

That was more or less the focus group's reactions to the ads from our client, a major streaming service with a mediocre campaign. It was blah, and so were focus groups, unless you were leading them; that was the only way to really stay engaged. But I had had to ask Taj to moderate for me—just in case I was suddenly unavailable. So far, I was seemingly still here, at 24 weeks.

The conversation paused, and I tossed my pencil onto my notebook, loose lead plink-plunking inside the plastic tube. I needed a pause, too—from this mind-numbing group, this mind-frazzling world. I was perched on the same high brown stool I had been on for weeks, looking out the same window.

But today, instead of seeing the blue mountains and yellow desert and green trees, the earth had flattened out into giant green and blue masses, as seen from millions of miles away. I found myself wondering how lonely the astronaut got—how isolated, how disconnected. How cognizant of his rare perspective. I wondered what it felt like to come back to earth and know that he could never truly belong here in the same way again. I wondered if he just accepted that as part of the deal— that depth and fullness are rife with vulnerability and pain, and that they are worth each other. When he was out in the blackest of empty space, tethered only by a cord, I wondered if he felt the danger or the safety, or always both.

"Do any of the messages on these billboards resonate with you?" Taj asked the group. I knew the shifts in his face, in his posture, and I knew he cared just as little as I did. Muted and off-camera, I laughed, as if he were talking to me. *Does anything resonate.* I pictured a giant billboard high over Ventura Boulevard in LA, all black with a white-suited astronaut floating across it, tether snaking off the edge. *Does anything resonate.* I rubbed my eyes, shook my head in delirium.

There was one corner of the internet that sort of got me those days. I scrolled down my list of bookmarks and clicked. It was a discussion board called *Cerclage Mommies* on a popular parenting site. There were only a couple dozen of us in it, and even fewer who were actually active, but those of us who were there needed it. Because we had nothing else—that's the thing about a high-risk pregnancy. Who do you relate to? Who else knows what it's like to be holding onto your baby's life? Not healthy-pregnant women, with their complaints of swollen feet and round ligament pain; seriously, get the fuck out of here. Not even your partner, friends, doctors—they are all at least one step away from the experience inside your own body. But these women—they are, blessedly, only half a step.

In the group, we posted updates on our cervical length, funneling, dilation. How we were getting through our doctors' orders: no sex, no baths, no lifting over fifteen pounds; the gamut of bedrest restrictions. And then the women who made it to *DTS*, or "ditch the stitch"—when you get your cerclage taken out at 37 weeks and get to live out the rest of your pregnancy in plump bliss. Their gratitude, their joy.

Women were constantly looking for hope from the group. The most common post was almost formulaic: In a mad rush, the woman rambled off her gestational weeks and cervical length; then a bit of backstory—maybe her previous losses, or the circumstances of getting her cerclage; then her current state of mind—some flavor of doing horribly but trying not to; and finally, always, a request for success stories from similar situations. Even though there was an entire backlog of such posts with success stories that she could comb through, her aim was slightly different: She needed hope here, now. Tangible and close enough to touch—to have and hold and be hers for the seemingly endless stream of weeks to come.

But I didn't go there for the success stories, for what could—maybe, hopefully—be. I went there for what is, right now, in each of these women's lives. Every one of them was heartbroken in some way; in their words, I could hear grief, fear, stress, sadness, depression, anxiety, anger... alongside empathy, kindness, hope, support, faith, and most of all, love. A deep, fervent life-source surging toward all of their children and all of the other women and all of their children, too. A love that was not overt or gushy or light, but solid and quiet and deep.

Today there was an update from Lisa. We had all been following her pregnancy, rooting for her. She had lost her first daughter at 22 weeks two years before, had had trouble getting pregnant since; now she was 24 weeks along with her second daughter.

Except... she wasn't. Her update: Her daughter had died yesterday. Infection. Placental abruption. Her doctor recommended a TAC next time. She wanted to know if anyone had experience.

In our stories, it was painfully obvious how alone we all were back in our real lives—our homes, our families, our social circles. The grocery store. School drop-off. Bed. There were canyons opening in our bodies and no one else really knew how much of ourselves was falling into them. This was what I found comforting; these were the stories that made me feel like I could still live on this planet.

These stories—shown only through a collection of black letters typed into a white box, standing in a great void, shouting to know if anything existed beyond it.

I stared at Lisa's post, her picture next to her name. She reminded me of Hillary, sitting on an oversized brown leather couch. Dark, moussed hair, full makeup. I looked up from my laptop and out the wall of windows.

Life feels like the twilight zone for a long time when you're on a journey like this. You think about things you never knew existed, make decisions you never knew could be made, have conversations that you can't believe can be shared between two people, even as you're saying the words aloud. Every day in the twilight zone—or several times a day, on the worst ones—you come to a moment where you question if this is all really happening. *Is this really my life?* you ask. And it takes everything in you—and maybe something that is beyond you—to say, *Yes. Yes, this is really it.*

This is life as you know it, as you have lived it. Normal life feels alien. You can't relate; it is not what you have experienced. Your experience was from the twilight zone. You are on the fringe, looking in. Separate.

I looked back down at my screen. *Cerclage Mommies* was sandwiched by dozens of other groups: *Baby Names, First-Trimester Woes, Fit & Healthy Belly*. All of these women—I wondered what planet they felt they were on. What life they were living. I thought about Cherie and her fat arms, Kyle and his corkboard. I thought about Shannon's father, Rob's divorce. Hillary. Steph. I wondered if everyone felt alien in some way. And then, for the first time, I wondered if I needed all of their pain to keep me from feeling my own.

Years later I will hear an interview with a real astronaut about his experiences. About how seeing Earth from space made it viscerally clear how we are all made of the same stardust. And I'll think, *yeah—that's it. That was it all along.*

When my father-in-law came over to make dinner that evening, he hugged me tight.

"24 weeks!" he said, beaming.

"I know, I know," I said. I smiled too, because he was.

He walked over to Violet, already sitting in her highchair. "How's my girl?" he said, wiggling a finger under her armpit.

She giggled and squirmed, dropping a handful of brown rice and crumbled sausage. Dale walked in from the kitchen. We looked at each other, and I rubbed my lower lip along my upper teeth.

"So, you've been here for a month now," I said, turning to Rich. He looked up from Violet to us. "And we couldn't have done this without you. But we know that's how long we asked you to come for."

"So, we can ask Alle's dad to swap out," Dale jumped in.

Rich looked at us, eyebrows raised. His eyes moved back and forth between me and his son until he stopped and said:

"I'm not leaving until this guy is home."

24

The day I turned 28 weeks was the first time I came up for air. Dale and I seemed to look at each other that morning and do a double-take: *Oh, there you are*. I began to wonder if I was going to be one of those miraculous success stories. I ordered jigsaw puzzles that felt like the remaining months of my pregnancy: a harvest scene in oil paint for November, a busy alpine ski hill for December. Hope surged in me like a geyser.

A few days later, a Sunday afternoon when Sienna and her son were playing with Violet, I sat cross-legged on the purple couch in our guest room. My overfilled belly brushed my ankles. I had developed polyhydramnios—excessive amniotic fluid—so I had been at High Desert twice a week for the past couple of weeks. I didn't mind; I liked the extra monitoring. But the extra fluid put more weight on my cervix, so I had been trying to sit down as much as possible. That, unlike bedrest for incompetent cervix, was a real thing. Some stuff just came down to physics. Gravity.

But it was mid-October and if I couldn't walk around the neighborhood, I at least wanted to feel fall on my face. October was my month—turning leaves, warm smells, cooler air. Fresh but cozy, like the world came in closer, gathered 'round. I had the sliding doors open on either side of me so that the breeze could blow through, unencumbered. I wanted to just sit. Listen.

I inhaled, long and slow. Not knowing how on earth we had made it this far. Exhale. Not worrying about how much further we would go.

I closed my eyes.

In, out. In, out.

Violet's gooey voice bubbling up from downstairs.

Laughter.

Air moving, inside of me, outside of me.

The wind began to rise. It soon became a symphony, at once booming and ethereal. It rushed through the full branches of tall pines, rustled the tinny leaves of low bushes. I could hear it from miles away, singing through the city before rushing up the foothills to meet me. It blew through the room, rattling the French doors and lifting up corners of loose paper. A reckoning, a movement, from the outside in.

The whole world felt alive with something older than time.

And I—I was a part of it.

A week later, my dreams started coming true. In the fucked-up way that they do in the twilight zone, but at that point, if fucked-up was the best I was going to get, I was going to take it. There is something to be said about accepting the journey you are on; there's even more to be said about actually letting yourself *enjoy* it. It's so fucked up—*beyond* fucked up. Everything in you screaming that *this isn't right*. But if you follow that scream all the way through to its end, you find that on the other side of it... is peace. An immense, exalting peace, like holding your daughter for the first time, already dead in your arms.

How is it that we can forget the lessons that tear us open?

Even better: How can we remember?

Oddly, I had woken up late the morning that I turned 29 weeks, still stirring my oatmeal when the rest of the house started waking up. I gripped the long silver handle of the pot in my right hand, a wide flat wooden spoon in my left, folding the oatmeal over and into itself. I cook it so long because I like it drier, with chewy edges, the texture halfway between cookie dough and baked cookies.

I had an early appointment with Dr. Page, so I was already dressed for the day. Navy blue joggers, a long-sleeved gray maternity shirt—

both gifts from my mother-in-law, the first during Sloane's pregnancy, the second during Violet's. I was bad at buying maternity clothes; the only new piece I had bought during Cody's pregnancy was a short-sleeved yellow shirt that made my belly feel like the sun. I first wore it two weeks ago, with the same blue joggers and my black Vans. I had stood in front of the full-length mirror in our bedroom, hands moving up and down my belly. A tattoo of grayscale leaves fell out of my left sleeve, roses blooming on my tricep; *Sloane Sandia* in script, tucked close to my expanding ribcage. My face was pale, weary. But so proud—so fucking proud of me and this guy for still being here. I had taken a photo of myself that morning, in the mirror. It was the last photo I would get of my pregnant belly. The very last one.

I swept the wooden spoon around the side of the pot, piling the cooked edges into the hot, soupy middle. Frequent stirring was the secret to getting the texture uniform. I tapped the spoon handle on the edge of the pot, and as the excess oatmeal slid off, a small gush slid out of me. Something softly clicked into place.

Ok, I thought. *Here we go.*

I laid the spoon across the top of a small cream-colored bowl—where earlier I had blended the dry ingredients before pouring them into the simmering almond milk. Oats, vanilla protein powder, cinnamon. And then I zipped my legs together and shuffled to the bathroom.

It's hard to describe how okay this all was. How okay that my water broke eleven weeks early; how okay that it broke at home, like I had always wanted. How okay that I got to hold a few precious drops of the dream in my palm: the excitement, the frenzy, the *normalcy* of rushing around the house to get off to the hospital. And like with Violet, maybe that *okay* was part of the problem. It was as if I had stolen a few moments from another life, forgotten the life that was mine. Forgotten to come back to it. Because sometimes still, I can go back to that moment—standing at the stove, stirring my oatmeal, fluid leaking—and feel only the joy of being one step closer to meeting my son. Only the surging love of being a mother. I can feel none of the heartache and fear and grief that motherhood had been. Only love.

Perspective is a beautiful, dangerous thing.

•

I didn't realize that I had been discounting my own motherhood up until this point. Even after all those years—two that felt like ten—when I held steadfast to the notion that I was still a mother, just one without any living children; even after having a living child and mothering her through breastfeeding, bottles, purees; rolling, crawling, walking; smiling, laughing, talking. All the things—all the things that children learn to do, that I was there for, and yet, I still didn't see myself as a mother.

Something shifts in every mother with the second (living) child. She begins to see her own skill where she once saw only guesswork and luck, her own capacity where there was once only a thin margin. Her experiences start to mean something beyond sheer history. She glimpses her own depth.

I started to see mine in triage, where the nurse didn't believe me that my water broke. Thought maybe I had just peed a little, despite the rundown of my history: fifth pregnancy; incompetent cervix; history of premature birth at 22 weeks (loss) and 32 weeks (emergency C-section); cerclage at 14 weeks; cervix measuring three millimeters at 23 weeks. Oh, what I would have given to have just peed myself.

Still, she had me put on a gown, get hooked up to the monitors. Again, in the same room where we had learned we would lose Sloane, and nine weeks earlier, I had laughed in delirium. I lay patiently, soaked it up. I knew I would never get to be in this room again.

For all of its depth, all of its horror, I loved it down to the paint on its walls.

In that room—again and again—the world became clear to me. As if the coordinates of those four walls were at the axis on which we spun, one rotation sharper each time we were in there. It was like what they say about airplanes: how life seems to tunnel when you're inside one, up in the sky. You're not here, or there, or anywhere really, so new perspectives can rise up unbidden and jarringly honest. Not just views of gridded farmland, or the tops of clouds, but of your real life, back when you're somewhere. It can all come at you at odd angles, or just fall away completely, leaving you with a sense of what matters, and the urgency to land changed.

"Hand me my phone?" I asked Dale, reaching my arm toward the counter-like shelf behind him.

I opened my work email, scanned my inbox. Nothing important. We had sent the report on the advertising campaign. On all of my other projects, my team and I had intentionally cast me in supporting roles. I clicked *Compose*.

I could be in here for weeks. Months. But here—here was where I wanted to be. For once, for now, for this last chance I had at everything: I wanted to be here.

I thought of the last time I had felt that—the intense need to be *here*. It was in the Redwoods, a hundred lifetimes ago, amidst the sweet chlorophyll, before so much, after so much. And still, so often: I was nowhere and didn't even know it.

I sent the email off with the subject *Mat leave*, and when the nurse saw that the quilted paper beneath me had been soaked through with amniotic fluid, I was admitted to the hospital with one goal: keep me pregnant for as long as possible.

My hospital room was made for a fucking queen. It looked like a master bedroom—at least twice the size of any hospital room I had been in before, tall honey-colored cabinets on either side of the bed, a sitting area off to one side. High ceiling and huge windows with golden sunlight filtering through. Bits of dust floated in and out of the rays.

Ginny was my new nurse. Her face was pale against her black scrubs, her light brown hair thin and uninteresting. She was pregnant and looked like she had been through things, quietly. I liked her instantly. I let her COVID-test me—back then, still a sharp drill up the nose to swab my brain—so that I didn't have to wear a mask, and she didn't have to wear a yellow plastic gown.

"The mag is going to make you feel horrible," she said. She reached up to hang a bag of clear liquid on the metal pole next to my bed. "You might get hot and feel really drowsy."

"Oh… yeah…" I said, my voice suddenly far away.

Ginny's hands shuffled around the IV in my right forearm, clipping, unclipping, clipping.

Then my voice again: "They tried to stop my labor with magnesium with my second daughter, but it didn't work."

Ginny pulled a stool up next to my bedside and sat down. She looked me in the eyes. I could really only see her eyes, with the rest of her face behind a KN95 mask, but her eyes were enough. Baby blue. "We're going to do a 24-hour course. I'm going to sit here with you until you start to feel it."

It didn't take long. We had barely swapped stories—mine about Sloane, hers about breast cancer—when I felt the lava. Ginny had just gotten to the part about going through chemo post-partum—the cancer had developed during her first pregnancy—but her eyes had been watching me the whole time, and I must have suddenly looked red and warm.

"Tell me what you feel," she said.

"Hot," I said. "Thick."

"Good," she nodded, then smiled. "Well, you know what I mean."

"I know what you mean. At least it's all... slower... this time." I don't think she knew what I meant but I just left it at that.

"They say it could come back with this one," she said, patting her small, round belly.

I wanted to ask her all the questions. *What did it feel like? Were you scared? How much harder was everything? How scared are you now? Do you see your own depth?* But I had suddenly turned to lead, and all I could do was close my eyes.

The afternoon dripped down the walls, thick and slow. In the honeyed sunlight, we were like flies in amber, my head lolling on my pillow, Dale's nodding off in an armchair. Magnesium was limbo; nothing was really happening, but we couldn't do anything either. But if we were stuck, with nothing happening, then so was Cody, with nothing happening, encased in the warm gold of my womb. Calm. Happy. Rolling about. The line printed on the running strip of paper jagged without hills. Movement, but no contractions.

It is in this slower unfolding of things that Dale and I got what we had never had: our version of a hospital bag and a birth plan. The mag for Cody's brain; more steroid shots in my hips for his lungs. A visit from the white-haired head of the NICU. And with a slew of other doctors, the opportunity to ask questions: what about my cerclage, can I have a vaginal birth, does he have enough fluid, what is the plan.

"This first twenty-four hours is critical," said one of the doctors that afternoon. I couldn't remember any names, but every now and then was a familiar face: Dr. Baca, who had reopened my C-section incision, and the guy from High Desert who had tried to talk to me about a TAC. My head rested like a bowling ball, turned toward the doctor of the moment. "Getting through it will cover the full course of magnesium and two rounds of steroids. Then, we wait."

"Will I be hooked up the whole time?" I asked.

"We will monitor you every two hours, as long as everything is looking good. If we can get you to seventy-two hours without labor progressing, there's a good chance it won't happen." He pointed upward. "There are some women up there who have been there for weeks."

"Ok, so first get to seventy-two hours, and then that's the goal, right—to be here for as long as possible?"

"Yep. After that, every day you are pregnant is a win. We're gonna do everything we can to get you there. If anything happens—anything at all—tell someone right away."

That first twenty-four hours, nothing happened: not sleep, not food, hardly even rest. By morning, I felt I was made of pixels—tiny vibrating cells, neon energy in a field of black—but when the mag wore off and I finally slept, I emerged as if brand new. Back into that sun-filled room, back into my mothering body. As if life, for all of us, was a series of births—cocooning, growing, evolving; surviving, arriving, thriving. Man, that drug was a bitch.

That evening, I moved to a more permanent room on the fourth floor. Not quite as homey, but still oversized with windows facing west and a padded bench running beneath them where I could sit and write and watch the sunset, every day a win.

"The other women up here do all kind of things to pass the time," my new nurse said. She opened a tall cabinet opposite my bed. "You have all of these shelves here to bring in and store anything you want."

I immediately envied these women and wanted to be in their club. Another fucked-up club to belong to: first the loss mom club, then multiple losses, then preemie moms, NICU moms, now hospital bedrest moms. I should really get one of those little black books to store all of these membership cards in. But truthfully, I did want to be one of these moms: in the safety of the hospital, slowing time down to day by day by day. I imagined whiling away sunny afternoons, reading, writing, painting-by-numbers. This was my time to be a blissful idiot. Or maybe just: This was my time. The only thing that tugged back on that was Violet.

We had my father-in-law to help take care of her, but because of COVID, she wouldn't be allowed to visit. *Where would she think I was? Would she wonder if I was coming back?*

And then, as I put myself into her soft, little body, looking for mama, pulled all the way back to the dim, lulling NICU, I wondered: *How long had she already gone without me really there?*

"We're not really supposed to do this," my nurse said, as if reading my mind. "But some of the women here have other kids, too, and we let them have a little picnic out there on the weekends."

I knew the little stretches of grass she was referring to, had driven past them a hundred times to and from the NICU. I imagined being wheeled down there on weekends, the sun and breeze welcoming me back into the world, like the first time we brought Violet home. Dale would pack fun things—sliced apples and peanut butter, honey mustard pretzels, salami spread with cream cheese—in our little blue cooler; we'd lay out a blanket. Violet would be overjoyed, waddling and giggling and pulling up fistfuls of grass. Rich would lean back, smiling, watching. Telling me how proud he is of me.

After the nurse left, and after my dinner came, and after I called Dale to give him an update, and after they cleared my dinner away, it was just me and Cody. I laid in my raised bed. Left the blinds up across the room, let the black night give the room a warm glow. I looked down at my belly, now smaller, with less fluid, placing my palms at the sides, where he usually kicked, and spreading my fingers wide. Holding everything. My son, my son.

That one slow moment was a gift that I had been unable to grasp this entire pregnancy. Because now, I felt safe.

25

At sixty-seven hours post-rupture—two o'clock on a Friday morning—the distinct sensation of tunneling between my legs woke me. I opened my eyes and squinted under the harsh light of the monitors, slid my hand around on the sheets until I found my glasses. In the bathroom, gobs of pink mucus streaked the toilet paper.

Crawling back into my hospital bed, I collapsed on my side for a moment. And then I grabbed one of the containers Dale had brought me the day before: superhero muffins—oversized, made of oats, zucchini, carrots, walnuts, and a handful of chocolate chips—that I had made before my water broke. Not my oatmeal, but I savored every bite of the chewy edges and soft middle, knowing that if they needed to start an epidural soon, I would tell them I had eaten nothing since the day before.

When I was done, I lay back in the dark. Eyes closed but awake, letting the waves of contractions roll through me, hollowing me out. Everything—everything—receding with the tide.

This was it. The last time I would have a baby inside me. The last time I would feel my child's bones on the underside of my flesh. Every pregnancy I had tried to describe it to Dale—what it felt like to grow another human, to feel its safety, its love, its happiness rolling around inside you. It is an unrivaled intimacy, comparable to nothing. A connection I longed deeply—*deeply*—to hold onto longer but felt unduly privileged to have experienced at all.

I held onto those final moments, knowing they might stretch into a forever longing. Knowing my belly might never be full again.

You never feel heroic in the moments that you are. Never know what you are asking of yourself, what you are sacrificing. Sometimes the best you can hope for is knowing the moments to hold onto: in your body, in the quiet, in the dark. Knowing what is yours.

I waited until six to text Dale: *I'm in labor. No rush. Just get here after you get Violet to school.*

When my nurse finally came in for shift change, she chided me for waiting so long to tell her about the contractions. I couldn't explain that I knew what I was doing. That through all this I had developed a relationship with my body like I'd never known before.

Maybe that was the beginning of the relationship that would come.

Oh, her depth—*there's so much more to come, dear one.*

The nurse flipped on a small light to reconnect all the wires and straps. The light warmed the brightness of the monitors, melted into the surrounding darkness of the room, a golden glow. It felt intimate, cozy, the world large but kind. I spread my hands over my belly.

Then more nurses, a technician—all floating in and out of the dimness, checking my vitals, drawing blood, while the world continued to open inside me, faster and deeper. And then into the fold swam Dr. Page, her blue scrubs fitted to her womanly body, her thick brown hair pulled back into a half-loop. I could see a smile behind her mask, in the corners of her eyes.

"I was on the night shift," she said. "I heard what was going on."

"I think it's happening," I said, sucking in air between my teeth. Although I couldn't believe *this* was happening—her, here, just like I needed. At the end of 2017, I had gotten a letter in the mail from my health insurance company saying that, come the new year, they would no longer be covering the practice Dr. Page was a part of. I had written them an impassioned letter in response, detailing our story—how Dr. Page had shepherded us through losing our daughter, miscarriage after miscarriage, and imminently, into uterine reconstruction and trying again to conceive. How she was more than my doctor; she was my safety net that kept me from a dark freefall. Now, I smiled at her. "I'm just glad we made it this far."

She nodded. "For a while there, we didn't know. But I hear he's doing great."

Please don't leave me alone in the dark, I had written in the letter. *I still have the rest of my journey to see through.* I don't know what eventually made them change their mind; maybe enough women told their stories, and maybe they listened.

Dr. Page watched me grimace, wrinkled her face in response. "You're really feelin' it, aren't you?"

"I'm ready for the drugs."

"Let's check your cerclage—see if it can wait to be taken out until after we get an epidural started."

I wasn't in a labor bed—the kind where the lower half drops out—so I watched as Dr. Page poked around for something to prop me up on. She and a nurse laughed as they worked together to get the height right, the angle right, and I wondered what it would be like to really know these women. In the warm glow of that dark room, I felt like I was witnessing magic.

Dr. Page held up a shallow bucket of some sort, flipped it over in her hands. More laughter. And then she helped me bridge my hips, slid it beneath me, and now I was a part of the magic, too; I was in on the absurdity, the humanity.

"Everything looks good down here," she said.

When she stood back up, she pulled off her latex gloves, tilted her head to the side. I knew she had to leave; her shift was past over.

"Sorry about the ramshackle exam there," she said, meeting my eyes. I couldn't explain that I wished she had fumbled more, laughed harder. Stayed longer.

"No worries." And before I even thought the words: "I'm just so glad you were here to be a part of this."

Suddenly I felt washed upon the shores of my beginning, bent over on hands and knees, forehead to the wet sand. Humbled, loved. More completely than I understood.

Dr. Page was a container. Holding all of this for nearly four years.

Dr. Jeffrey was a container.

My father-in-law was a container. Dale was a container.

They just held. In ways I had never been held.

The journey pierced my eyes.

Dr. Page wiped away a tear before it fell behind her mask. "Me too," she said.

And then she was gone, and the container stayed.

Finally: an epidural. Third labor and I finally got the calm I always wanted. I was back on the mag for one final effort at brain protection but somehow, this time, it was better. I was in a spacious, sunny room, and I slept for hours, warm and heavy. Dale nodded off in a loveseat.

Dr. Cabrera, who had delivered Violet, was on duty.

"It's rare that a doctor gets to deliver two babies from the same family," she said, a slight smile. The comfort of her familiarity was worth her lack of warmth. Maybe if we had had more time together.

At three in the afternoon, movement burrowed through my sleepy haze. It was deep and rough, like my cervix was being scraped out with lobster claws. I called in my nurse.

"Yep, you're ready," she said from between my legs.

Sometimes you wait all day—or weeks, or months—for one singular event to happen, and then all of a sudden, it's happening and you're still trying to catch up, wondering how you got there. This wasn't that. I was more present, more ready than I ever thought I would be.

That depth.

What a trip it all was. The mag—meant to stop labor—kept my contractions five minutes apart even during active pushing, making that final phase of labor as slow and languid as the day had been. After every contraction, when Dale and my nurse relaxed their holds on my bent legs, Dr. Cabrera stood and stretched, and five or six people from the NICU milled about in the background, we chatted, we laughed. We made magic.

And every now and then, I glanced over at what would become Cody's spaceship. I had never seen one of the incubators outside the context of the NICU, and out here, it looked different. Bigger, sleeker, shinier. Its top was raised up high, so the box seemed completely open, bright, inviting. For the first time, I had a moment to just be in awe of what it really was. Its magnificence, its stature, its ability to do what my own body no longer could. I wanted to take a picture—to capture this creature in its most majestic state. Chest out, jaw wide, ready to carry my son in its mouth.

This was our life. The only one we knew.

What a trip it all was.

I snapped back to another contraction coming down the lane, and then Cody slipped into the world.

"Sixteen-thirteen!" someone shouted.

And then more numbers: *Ten. Twenty.*

And then my son, wrapped in a white cotton blanket, a medical cap pulled down low on his forehead, was placed in my arms and Dale was at my left shoulder and we were cradling him together, and I heard myself saying "Oh, oh, oh," over and over again.

Someone, somehow took a candid photo, and the numbers pierced back through: *Forty. Forty-five.*

And then I realized they were counting the seconds that Cody had been alive without oxygen support. So that we could have this moment before they took him away. This final dream.

I grabbed it, fiercely—my fucked-up version of getting to hold my child right away—and with equal ferocity, thought, *Take him, take him, it's ok, it's ok.*

And when they got to sixty, they did, and I was full.

I thought that was where this story ended. Our reproductive journey over, a pepperoni and green chile pizza from Mario's delivered to the hospital, a big hug and an *I'm so proud of you* from my father-in-law when we went home the next morning. This chapter—that could fill a whole book—of our lives closed, done, over.

Just shows how much I still didn't know.

Eight inches of perfect white snow fell two days after Cody was born. It was late October; snow this early was rare in central New Mexico. But it had snowed for Sloane's birth, for Violet's birth, and I couldn't help but think of Edward Scissorhands being somewhere *still up there.*

My heart sang those first several mornings as I drove to the NICU, sliding back into the familiar tracks we had worn down Montgomery. Thick pelts of snow edged everything like icing on a gingerbread house: buildings and shops, benches and trees, the curved roofs of the bus stops. Everything hugged by magic. Life felt still and wonderful and contained. A snow globe.

Cody, too, was still and wonderful and contained in his own world—his plastic box, covered with a thick fleece blanket; on it, campers and pine trees and lake waves. We weren't allowed to hold him for the first three days to protect against brain bleeds, and for a while after that, only an hour every other day to prevent overstimulation. So, day after day, I drove to the NICU, sat by his covered box, drained my breasts into little bottles, ate superhero muffins, and wrote. Starting with the end, every detail I could remember: the hours in the hospital, the conversations with Dr. Jeffrey and Dr. Page, the timeline of my shortening cervix. And back and back, as far as this story went, and every few pages, when I needed to come up for breath in that dark, warm womb of a place, I wrote a memory of a simpler time.

Like, in college, waking up in Dale's apartment, where we both slept in his twin bed, a mattress on the floor. It was a serial memory, one that happened over and over again, on as many days as we could find: In that slippery morning haze, we would slide around between the sheets, holding each other in new ways, as if we had each yearned for the other while we slept, and when we finally crawled out, we'd pull on thick, soft sweats, both of us in his clothes.

Dale would make a pot of coffee—Folger's Black Silk he used to drink back then, when he thought he was becoming an adult—and pour us each a mug. As it steamed, he'd pull on a knit gray cap with a narrow bill and unfold a bag of American Spirit tobacco, a pack of Rizla rolling papers sliding out from the fold. On the couch he'd sit hunched over the coffee table, clearing a space with his round, nail-bitten fingertips, the cardboard coasters and fast-food receipts shushing across the wood. And this was the part of the memory that I savored most, the reason I came back to it time and again: every meticulous movement of his fingers, his soft eyes as he pushed and rolled the stringy tobacco into place, his deep inhales to absorb the aroma, the slide of his pink tongue along the seam. Now, neither of us had had a cigarette in over a decade, but how deliciously full an act this still was to me in memory. By Dale, only by Dale. And when he was done, he'd stand up, tuck both papery cigarettes behind one ear, and cup his mug of coffee in both hands. On the balcony off his living room, the air out of reach from the sun, gray but not unbeautiful, we would nestle into outdoor chairs with creaky woven seats and cold metal armrests. Dale would light both cigarettes together and hand me mine, exhaling a long, full stream of smoke. And then he'd give me his soft, twinkling eyes, for a few beats longer than any girl could ever hope for, and bring his mug to his lips.

This womb.

The remembering wasn't quite nostalgia, but more a reminder of truth. A slight but vibrant ache, reawakened, for where I come from. For falling in love and the thirty steps out of LaFortune. For reading *The Secret Garden* and *Island of the Blue Dolphins* as a little girl. For wind and trees and sky forever.

In the beginning, I found myself being there, in the NICU, more than I had been with Violet. This time, I wasn't healing a C-section wound, or working part-time. It's one of the first times I can remember just being a mom.

How are you today, Mom? the nurses asked. *Do you want to give him a bath today, Mom?*

And every day, I lifted one side of Cody's blanket and lowered my face down across from his—just in case he opened his eyes, looking for Mom. When they stayed closed, I covered every inch of his three-pound four-ounce body with love from my own coveting, searching eyes: his skinny limbs, his barrel of ribs, the scruff of strawberry blond hair sprouting from his oversized head. He was devastatingly handsome, my son. And mine was the first heart he would break, the first time I changed his tiny, folded-over diaper and saw the loose skin hanging over the backside of his pelvic bones where his plump bottom should have been. His little bird bones. Too small, too bare to be here yet. My heart flattened and slid into my belly.

The delirium of Cody's survival was the sparkling surface on a vast and brutal sea: the reality that he was, truly, still fighting every day to live. We were lucky—he was healthy so far—and that made it possible to forget that he still needed a feeding tube, high-flow oxygen, a warm incubator, various drugs, and a team of nurses to survive. And there was something about the familiarity of it all—that we had done this before, that we knew generally what to expect, that he even had many of the same nurses as Violet—that made it all seem… normal. And for us, that was the truth: This was the only postpartum experience we ever knew. Our life was still—still—the twilight zone. But we had gotten through it once; we could do it again. I didn't consider how I had come out of the last experience, or how I might come out of this one, or if I had ever come out of anything, really.

As the weeks wore on, and I canceled my counseling appointments with Blair—*Cody is here; I'm just so tired*—and I carried the mesh purple bag of milestone cards in the front pocket of my backpack every day, even though I had only taken a photo of Cody with two of them—*I'm in an open crib!* after twenty-seven days, and *6 pounds!* after forty-three— there was only *through*. Only the mountain to climb.

Isn't this the shit we tell ourselves over and over again?

Gotta get through it, just get through it.

One of my co-workers had a saying for when our project load got too heavy, our workdays too long: "I can see the light at the end of the tunnel… but I know it's just the light of another train coming."

Nobody ever talked about just getting the fuck out of the tunnel.

Why does it have to be a tunnel, a mountain, something to endure?

Hadn't I already made it *through*?

When does *through* end?

What ever happened to cigarettes, to dolphins?

26

It was a week after Cody came home, after seven weeks in the NICU, that Dale found Violet breathing far too fast in the middle of the night.

"Her coughing keeps waking her up," he said in the light of my bedside lamp, after he had roused me from sleep. I rubbed my eyes, slid on my glasses. My head bristled with exhaustion. Cody was a noisy sleeper, so we had moved the bassinet from my bedside to the little sitting area beyond the foot of our bed; I peered over at him, caught his tiny face through the mesh lining, and softened to a dull ache, my breasts now heavy.

"Ok," I said. "Let's go look together."

I pulled on my robe and followed Dale upstairs. Violet had just started sleeping in a toddler bed: dark wood, small pillow, a light comforter with graphics of stars and penguins and blue elephants. It was hard to believe how much older she looked laying in it—how much older an almost-two-year-old could get in the right, or wrong, circumstances. We crouched down next to her on either side of the bed. Her egg-shaped nightlight gave the room a soft glow.

We had gotten better at seeing the signs by then, although we still questioned ourselves because who ever wants to admit that this is really happening. For me, the saving grace was knowing that we came by it honestly: that I was raised in a household where medicine expired and boo-boos were ignored, and Dale was raised in one where a bad cold warranted a doctor visit; any decision we made together was a compromise of those extremes. That, and we had a certain knowing: that there was so much we didn't know, couldn't know. That mucus could mean labor, that vomiting could mean placental abruption. The lungs were a whole new world—and imagine all there was to know. But that night, the reality without imagination was enough: her heaving chest, the wheeze in her throat, and when I unzipped her footie pajamas, her soft skin being pulled through her ribs.

"You were right," I said, looking up at Dale. "She needs help."

"Where?"

This is where the things you never dream of come in. The things that are maybe even your worst nightmares, like they were mine. But that would come later. There was still so much we didn't know.

"There's a 24-hour urgent care on Paseo," I said. I was imagining it like the pediatrician's office: she gets checked out, hooked up to oxygen, sent home with a tank.

"Ok. Who should take her?"

I looked back at my daughter. Her full cheeks, her round, button nose. I had started calling her *angel*, as in *Good morning, angel* and *What do you want to play, angel?* It came out of nowhere—just one of those terms that feels like the closest thing to squeezing all of a being's preciousness into one word. I liked it; it seemed to fit, to capture something that I didn't yet understand, or maybe never would, but knew to be true, and there was an unmistakable opening in my heart every time I said it, as if the word itself were breath.

And now, I thought: *I'm sorry, angel.*

My shoulders sunk. A knot in my heart where breath should have been. I looked back up at Dale. "I have to pump."

From there, everything unraveled slowly and then quickly. Dale recounted the long, foggy hours spent in the lobby of the urgent care, where Violet was oddly awake and playful, followed by the rush to a hospital downtown, the ambulance blaring the siren when it needed to, and then the flurry of admission, and finally, mid-morning, sleep. Violet awash in an ocean of oxygen, Dale laid out on a fold-out chair.

And five days later, there we were, still in the pediatric intensive care unit, Violet and I staring at each other through the slats in her hospital crib. Because of COVID, only one parent was allowed to be in the room at a given time; Cody wasn't allowed at all, but the nurses had been gracious enough to let us bring him in when Dale and I tagged in and out for each other. Rich was still in town—wasn't leaving until after the new year—but he happened to be sick, and we couldn't risk Cody, who still wasn't due for another three weeks, contracting anything. By day five, we had gotten past this all feeling like a puzzle, and then past this all feeling like a trap, and now it was just a total mindfuck.

As if I had blinked in one hospital, down Montgomery, and opened my eyes in another one, downtown.

As if we had walked out the security doors of the NICU, down the hall, and then in through the security doors of the PICU.

As if I had untethered my newborn from all of his tubes and wires, and then hooked them up to my almost-two-year-old.

The revolving door was spinning too fast, too fast.

The PICU felt elaborate compared to the NICU. The rooms were large and individual, with lounge chairs and padded benches that folded out into beds. And windows—this room had one that faced west, looking immediately, from six floors up, over the motel from *Breaking Bad* and *Better Call Saul*, then over the easy-moving lanes of I-25, and beyond to the yellow desert and distant mountains. All of that was dark now, at eight-something in the evening four days before Christmas, but I knew it was there. Depended on it being there.

Before I sat down, I had turned off all of the lights. Except for one: in the back, behind a curtain, to give off the same warm glow as the egg-shaped nightlight at home on my daughter's bookshelf. Here, her books were stacked on the floor, against the wall: *Where's Spot?*, *I Love You Through and Through,* a bundled set of Llama Llama. Beside them sat a tub of blocks, a 64-count box of Crayola crayons—the one with *robin's egg blue* and the sharpener in the back—and two coloring books. Then a gray plastic highchair and, hanging above it, a small square painting of a pink feather. Overhead, stars, moons, and rockets on every third or fourth ceiling tile.

I didn't know yet that this room would come to feel like home, all of its peculiarities familiar and endearing, like the padded seat in the back that folded up to reveal a toilet, or the awkwardly-placed central column that everything plugged into. For now, I only wondered if this room was some fresh hell or if we had ever really left the old one. It had all the same wires and tubes as the NICU; all the familiar monitors with their blinking numbers and running lines; all the alarms that booped and shrieked. Only the plinking drip of the high-flow oxygen system—not muffled within an incubator, but exposed and visible and confusingly calming—was new. That, and the hand-drawn sign on the door: a chocolate ice cream cone, cherry on top, next to rainbow-colored block letters that read *Violet*.

She laid on her belly, up against one short end of the crib. The end nearest me in my armchair. I had zipped her into her purple and white flowered footie pajamas; this was back when I thought that piece of home would be comforting, before we learned that it was better to keep them unclothed—easier to watch their chest and back, see how hard they were having to pull for breath. Her wispy blond hair was pulled into a tiny sprout on top of her head. A cannula stretched taut across her full cheeks, oxygen pouring into her lungs at several liters a minute. Eyes not blinking, eyes clawing at me. Her tiny being arrestingly beautiful and unreachable.

How did we get here?

Weren't we supposed to be *through*?

I had just ordered four picture frames for Rich, as a thank-you for the past four months with us. Each was in the shape of a puzzle piece, with its own engraving, and they all fit together:

On Sloane's piece: *Thank you for honoring my memory*.

On Violet's: *Thank you for teaching me what the watch says*.

Cody's: *Thank you for bringing me safely into this world*.

Leo's: *Thank you for letting me hog the bed*.

We were done; we were grateful.

But suddenly I didn't know if I had gone anywhere at all in the last four years, been anywhere at all. Or if I was still nowhere. Still standing on top of a cliff, utterly alone.

Georgia wasn't the first time I had felt suicidal after Sloane died. The first time was brief, just a moment: two weeks after she was born, when we went up to Taos in northern New Mexico with my in-laws, and I walked across the bridge over the Rio Grande Gorge, looking eight hundred feet down the rough walls of rock to the crack of river at the bottom, my stomach somewhere down there with it. My heart pounded, and a flicker of a thought ran by: *It's not safe for me to be here right now.*

The second time was three months later, May 2017. My in-laws were in town, and we had taken them and Leo to the Jemez Mountains fifty miles northwest of Albuquerque. I wanted to hike, needed to hike—needed to just be out there. I had had my first miscarriage in Boston the week before.

The trail had started out rather unremarkably. An expanse of pines covered either side of a wide path scattered with dried needles, forever and ever anon. Dale was always so much better at these stretches than I was, breathing in the different scents of the trees, getting high off the juniper. Occasionally throwing an arm up toward the canopy, pointing and saying, "Look! A bird." I could never see the birds back then, even when he would stretch his arm farther, point harder. *So, it's a bird*, I had always thought. *We see birds all the time at home.* It wasn't until later, when I finally started to see their broad chests and feathery wings perched on branches, that I realized I hadn't seen them because I hadn't cared to see them.

The next stretch was the kind I thrived on: a steep rocky climb with a view. The five of us made our way silently, carefully, one foot in front of the other over big white rocks, the view first popping through small breaks in the brush and then widening over long stretches of low bushes bordering the trail. In the distance, everything came into focus: the uneven shape of a mountain range now outlined against the solid blue sky; every tree on the face of that mountainside now clarified in detail. As if they were drawn by a charcoal artist—a line for every trunk, every branch, every needle, thousands and thousands of times over. I stopped to take a picture at every new angle, needing to capture this intensity. This world so much bigger than me, looming so large and untouchable but breathtaking all the same.

Rich reached the top first, then me. I looked back, Dale and his mom still climbing. On that same trip to Taos, I had sat outside Taos Mesa Brewing in the middle of the afternoon with Dale's parents while he and his brother skied, the three of us crying behind our sunglasses.

"How is Dale doing?" his mom had asked.

"He's heartbroken but ok," I said.

Her voice cracked: "He doesn't tell us these things."

"I know, I know," I said, not knowing how to express the mass of everything that was in my heart, but knowing that I would carry it all with me in an image: her long, bony fingers with oval-shaped nails, sliding beneath the lower edge of her sunglasses and across her cheek, sun glistening off the wet.

From that vantage point at the top of the trail, I could fit everything into the frame: Dale and his mom climbing up the rocky edge in the foreground, the miles of trees stacked up the mountainside in the distance—as if the gulf between wasn't so vast. And yet, everyone's posture said we were climbing, climbing, climbing; we have been climbing and we don't know if we will ever really stop climbing.

We keep on, we keep on—the view at the top no different than on the way up.

We found perfect seats for lunch. The air was still and warm as we sat on two large flat rocks, pulled four burritos out of our red backpack, and peeled back their foil. Dale had made them that morning: brown rice, black beans, corn, canned chicken, shredded cheddar, green chile. Mixed together in a big silver bowl and then piled into whole grain tortillas. They were lukewarm by midday, but everything tastes better in the wilderness.

I don't know if I said five words the whole time we ate; I felt somewhere else entirely. Mindlessly bringing my burrito to my mouth, I was overcome by the view to the south: a smallish, rounded mountaintop, so close that I could see every individual pine tree and where it came out of the ground, the circular shadow its branches made on the dirt. Seeing the trees head-on this way, they looked like sticks— their branches so much farther apart than when viewed from below, where they seemed dense and full. But the thing that really got me about that hilltop was that I could see its entire shape—from edge to edge and rounded in the middle—and against the wall of blue sky, the round top looked like a slowly inflating balloon, expanding ever upward and outward. I stared and stared at that hill, letting it rise and rise. Both marveling and faltering at the illusion. Wanting desperately to swallow it whole, so that it was both inside me and out of sight.

When we got back on the trail, it meandered along the crest for a bit. Little shifts this way and then that, seemingly going nowhere in particular, until suddenly it opened up to a wide, flat overlook—yards and yards of dirt covered in dried needles, edged on one side by juniper bushes and tall pines, the other by large boulders and a drop into whatever lay beyond. We spread out like roots searching in soil.

I didn't know what to make of anything back then. Why, surrounded by people I loved, I felt completely alone. Why, even in the peace of nature, I felt overwhelmed. Why, even amidst all of this beauty, I felt dark and vast and empty inside. Everything—everything—felt miles away.

I hung back a few yards while everyone else neared the edge to take in the view. They stood on the big rocks, at shades brown and yellow and gray. Leo trotted along the rocks, too, sniffing, exploring. The drop-off was steep, their hiking boots three feet from it. Beyond, a blanket of trees up to the rippled mountain line. I think many of us know how breathtaking the bitten crust of anything can be: the shore before it dives into the sea, the final moments of a goodbye. These places arrest us, shake us into attention; *something is happening here*, life says. *It will be brief; don't miss it.* If only we could know, sometimes, just how brief.

I realized my feet were moving. A few steps one way, then back; another way, back again—the two-step of the lost. A mild wind batted my face and ears, blew my insides around. I rubbed my tongue along the back of my teeth and swallowed, my mouth suddenly dripping with saliva. My eyes were glued to Leo, my heart shuddering every time he stepped a paw onto the outermost rim of boulders. I called him back, over and over, trying to balance my sense of urgency with an irrational fear of frightening him over the edge. Or maybe the fact that I didn't know whether it was irrational or not was what was making my stomach boil.

Suddenly I saw myself running toward the cliff. Trampling over the boulders, flying at the trees beyond, legs kicking and arms flailing, suspended briefly in the center of that arresting expanse, those open jaws, before plummeting down into them, below the cliff, and down, down, down.

My chest heaved. Screams echoed off the walls of my skull. I shuffled forwards and backwards over the dead pine needles. I looked away, looked back, saw me jumping; looked away, looked back, saw Dale standing. Three feet from the edge, one foot propped up on a boulder, hands on his hips. Steady gaze across the chasm. I felt the wind blow, saw it ruffle the hem of his gray flannel. I snapped off six photos in a row of him standing there—his calves, his shoulders, the mesh back of his Bosque Brewing hat, Leo moving in and out of the frame—in case this was the last time I saw him.

I wanted him to know who he was.

And then, in my mind, I took his place. Standing there calmly, taking in the smell of pine. Then feeling the air shift as my wife charged swiftly past me, the soles of her hiking boots grating against rock as they left solid ground. And with all of my organs fighting their way up my throat, I turned and walked toward the trees because I couldn't do that to him, I couldn't do that to him. I blinked hot tears behind my sunglasses. I couldn't do that to him.

Tall juniper bushes took me in. I took deep breath after deep breath, my head, my shoulders, dropping.

Sitting in my daughter's hospital room, her eyes now closed, I was back on that cliff, that precipice of death. Not my own but still that of my children. Not panicking and ready to jump but completely still and unmoving. Tight. Frozen.

I stripped off my wool shirt. Gooseflesh covered my arms and chest and belly as I pulled my full breasts out of my maternity bra, fingertips brushing the small curves of blue veins. I hooked myself up, holding the bottoms of the twelve-ounce bottles in my palms so that they didn't pull as I drained and they filled. Before I closed my eyes, I saw my blue Vans sitting on the floor next to the plastic gray highchair. The pair I had bought as soon as we got back from Georgia, to replace the ones I tossed.

Do we just go 'round and 'round this thing until it stops?

When my breasts lay limp and doughy, like half-empty flour sacks, I poured the milk into little plastic bags. Smooth, rich—this could still come from me. I lined up the bags in the mini-fridge, scrubbed my pump parts, laid them out on a paper towel. Set my alarm for midnight.

27

I don't remember much about the months that followed. January, February, March... I remember the milk—the entire chest freezer in our garage full of thousands of ounces of my breastmilk; sopping it up from the floor several times a week when Cody would get so upset he would vomit. The way my breasts deflated to less than they had ever been once I finally stopped pumping.

I remember the nebulizer—the seemingly constant whir of its motor and clouds of vapor. Violet had come home from the hospital with no diagnosis of what went wrong—prematurity her only condition—but when she got another respiratory virus in January, her pediatrician put her on a daily steroid for her lungs. Every morning and night, we had to hold a mask over her screaming, writhing, still-not-two-year-old face, the drugs carried in through her nose and mouth on breath and breath alone.

And I remember Cody's sweet face—how when he fell asleep in a semi-upright position, like in his car seat or the swing, he tilted his head slightly to the side and held his tongue between his lips and looked exactly like Sloane. Dale and I both saw it, both paused every time.

April, I remember in the pit of my stomach. By the light of Violet's nightlight: her chest, her ribs, the pinhole of space it sounded like she was trying to breathe through. I hadn't believed Dale when he had woken me again in the middle of the night. Thought I would tromp up the stairs, declare her fine, and let us all go back to sleep. She had only had a mild cough earlier that day. But even when I saw it—when I knew she had to go—I also knew that I couldn't be the one to take her.

The story I told myself was that Dale did better on no sleep; he had the stamina to withstand the middle-of-the-night urgent care, the wired toddler. We never thought things would go as far as the hospital again. But what I didn't tell myself, because I couldn't bear it, was that Dale had what really mattered: the compassion to grease the skids of it all. He had what I couldn't give. Because if I gave a crack—a jagged sliver to let love out—I just might fully break.

And at all costs, I had to remain intact. I had a newborn to care for, a workload to cover, a house of cards to hold together. I sensed it even then: that as much as that sounded like digging in my heels and standing up straighter, I was in nothing but quicksand. Sinking inch by inch into a new, deeper twilight zone.

Our kids had lived.

This was supposed to be over.

When was this going to be over.

Urgent care. Ambulance. PICU admission. Oxygen.

I can ship your dad out! my mom said on Day One, and desperate, we said yes, even though what I really wanted to say, but never would, was, *Could you come instead?* Because I just assumed it would be a *No, I have to work,* and I didn't need that, not now. So, my dad was there on Day Two, but it seemed that what I would overhear him say a few months later, after all of this had gotten much worse, was already true for him then: *I just don't feel the need to help anymore.*

We spent five days in that same room with the funny toilet and the awkward central column; five days of tagging in and out, solo parenting, even with my dad there, on either side.

And always, the most tenderness—the true *care*—coming from Dale. Me, the bull; him, the heart. I asked him one time, years later, about his special bond with Violet.

"It has a lot to do with all the time we spent in the hospital," he said. "We did a lot of bonding then. The first 24 hours were always the hardest... only a few hours of sleep, nodding off through waiting and getting evaluated, then admitted. All she would allow me to do for the first day was hold her. And always standing."

But he did it. Mostly tenderly, occasionally numbly, but always with valor. I was there—we split the time—but I can imagine the metaphors: a block of ice, a hollow suit of armor.

She deserved more than that.

Even in the rearview mirror, this whole time seems impossible. It is a slick smear of water on a windshield, the world behind it unreal, too painful to touch.

And then came June.

I suddenly felt out of breath. Like I was trying to catch up with something, even though I was sitting on my living room floor. Cody laid on a blanket in front me, on his back, one arm sticking up to the ceiling and swinging a toy moose around erratically. We had started his developmental therapy, his case worker the same one Violet had: Jennifer. That was a funny phone call—on her end, *I was so excited to see your name!*, and on mine, *I had a VBAC!* It was, once again, a relief and a comfort to have her involvement, even if she could only watch Cody's movements through a computer screen once a month; COVID protocols kept her from in-person visits. Still, she tried as hard as we did to get him to spend time on his tummy; failed just as hard as we did. But we all just let it go: *his vomiting*, we said; *his big head*, we said. *And look how happy he is otherwise.* And silently: *He's already had to endure.*

The moose crinkled and rattled; a small bell around his neck jingled. Cody, unfazed, seemed to be looking at the ceiling.

He was home sick for the day, presumably with the same virus that had landed his sister in the hospital two days earlier. She was still there, needing oxygen, but this time out of the ICU, at a hospital in northwest Albuquerque. So far, Cody just had a mild fever, low energy—only a slight cough. But when I realized I was breathing too fast, and my gaze drifted from his soft face down to his chest, I also noticed the slight panic that had started thumping in my own. Even through his onesie, I could see his ribs pushing through his skin. Begging to be seen.

There was no question—no matter of believing or not believing. I had felt it myself.

My seven-month-old.

Urgent care. Ambulance. Hospital admission.

An ocean of oxygen that knocked him out cold.

My son and daughter overlapped with adjacent hospital rooms for less than one surreal day. It had been a stupid sort of nice, the four of us there together, large windows in each room looking at the same view of the Sandias, Dale and I swapping between rooms even though we weren't supposed to without gowning and de-gowning each time. But that evening, Violet went home, and around midnight, Cody got transferred to the PICU downtown. He needed more oxygen.

"How is he?" I asked Dale the next morning when I pushed open the door to that old familiar room, a hand-drawn sign with *Cody* and a rubber duck fluttering in my wake. We kept our voices somewhere between a whisper and normal.

He nodded. "They have him at fifteen liters."

I slid my backpack to the floor, moved to the crib. The room was dark; I would keep it that way for most of the day. Cody lay asleep on his back, arms stretched out in a T, his tiger lovey clutched in one hand. An IV stuck out of his head at the hairline, like Violet early on in the NICU. His bare skin, so fresh, so pure. Later I would learn that that rate—fifteen liters of high-flow oxygen per minute—was the highest level possible for someone of Cody's size; the next step was intubation.

"I'm sorry about the midnight ride," I said, looking up at Dale across the crib. "Maybe we should have just come here first. I just thought with Violet up there…"

"It's ok." He held the back of his head with one hand, arched his back to stretch. "We got settled in here around two, slept until seven-thirty. And then he was only awake for an hour. Still can't eat or drink."

The doctor had warned us the day before that that could get hard, but they didn't want to risk him taking milk or food into his lungs on that high of an oxygen flow.

"But he gave me this look," Dale said, "when they were loading him into the ambulance. Like he needed me. Like he was looking to me to take care of him."

I smiled. I knew Dale had been waiting for something like that from Cody. I also knew those child eyes—how they could tear at your soul. And I knew Dale as a father—how he would stand up and hold them. Be a container for them to pour into.

I walked quietly over to him, slid my arms over his shoulders. Pulled my mask down under my chin and pressed my face up against the warmth of his neck. He covered my back with his arms, pulling me into his body. *Hearts touching*, he always said.

"I'm so happy for you," I whispered. "You deserve that."

"Good luck today," he said as we pulled apart.

I handed him the car key. "Halfway between D2 and D3."

When Dale left, I picked up my backpack and swung it onto the built-in bench at the back of the room. A shaft of sunlight came in from beneath the half-closed shade—the only light in the room. I bent down, peeked under it. Saw the broken concrete of the empty motel parking lot. The highway of cars rushing about their day. The distant yellow desert.

All still there.

I unzipped my backpack and pulled out my laptop, slid it onto the bench. I had a report due.

In the years to come, the quality of light in that room in June 2021 will be one of the last things to leave me. Day after day, I kept the lights off, the shade raised only a foot, perhaps so as to not see, even as I stood over Cody's crib and watched his chest. His round boyish face always asleep, his sweet giggle a mere echo.

The gray was quiet; the gray was heavy.

We're just going to have to get really good at this situation, I had texted a co-worker that morning when he asked how I was doing, if my dad was going to fly out. *This is our life.*

That's really admirable, he said. *To have that kind of mindset.*

I didn't think it admirable so much as necessary. The only path up the mountain. And I could see it: We would nail down our care plan, get help early, know where to go when. We would set a schedule for swapping in and out, have standard lists of what to bring. We would figure out how to work, take minimal time off. We would keep going.

This was our life, and we had to do it.

The real world.

Didn't we all have to?

The report I was working on was for a mental health app, and the project was on how stress and anxiety looked in real people's lives. Wasn't this that? Just real people's lives? What right did I have to not do it just like everyone else—with a tension in my jaw and ice in my limbs? What right did I have to say this was all too much—had been too much for far too long? What fucking right did I have to drown?

I saw a glimmer of something in that report—some glancing blow of light on my laptop screen, coming in below the shade, obscuring the graphics but illuminating the fine particles of dust. Something between the data on how people dealt with stress and the data on how people avoided it. Something in the list of resources that people use to handle it—*resources*, I noted, the word almost a distant memory now—and how all the most common ones were just distractions at best, and at worst, they compounded the problem. Added stress. Multiplied it.

And then buried it so deep you forgot it was even there.

It was like truth: how sometimes we see it, and sometimes we avoid it. How it can both help and hurt; how it is multitudes. How it can grow so big that it escapes, impossible to wrap our arms around, fold back into us.

With this report on deck, I could spend the long hospital days somewhere else. Somewhere where my son wasn't lying motionless, unable to eat, drink, breathe; somewhere where the quality of light didn't hurt. And I didn't have to sit still and enclosed; I could soar on insights and implications, weaving together data points and interview quotes into something new, something beautiful. Something helpful, worthwhile. A story.

That was all the truth that I knew, which wasn't even half of it.

I called Taj on the third day, excited by what I was seeing in the data. We had been working on the project together, him moderating the interviews while I was still on maternity leave, me running the survey and data collection.

"I wanted to run something by you," I said.

"First, how are you doing?" he asked, his voice as heavy and smooth as wet sand. I could practically hear his hair, tied up in a bun; his shoulders inside his T-shirts. I hadn't seen him in person since that January at our house the year before, when Violet was first sent home on oxygen. Hadn't seen anyone, really, except through a screen, or from behind a mask. And in that moment, through the intimacy of just a voice in my ear, I ached for a warm body.

"I'm fine," I said. "I'm fine."

"Why won't you let me help you with the report?"

I was standing in the back of the room, behind that central column that everything plugged into. Beyond it lay half-darkness and the constant rush of oxygen like white noise. I saw it again, like in Atlanta: the outside reflecting my insides. My body felt pulled toward the floor, while the tinny zip of adrenaline buzzed in my head. But when it came to work, this separation of mind and body was familiar, unalarming. Part of the process of doing great work.

"I'm fine," I said again. "Cody is mostly sleeping, so I'm getting a lot done here. I can do it."

And for better or worse: I believed it.

But for better or worse: So did everyone else. Even when I finally said I couldn't.

The cycle had started to become clear, even to me: We seemed to never fully recover from every hospitalization. As if it took so long to climb back out of the pit of exhaustion—recovering only in the snatches of space between parenting and work and household—that by the time we were back in the hospital again, we were already a foot deep. I knew this because, every time, at the sound of the first cough, something inside me would tumble like a stack of blocks, and Dale would get a sharp edge in his voice. *Not yet*, we were saying; *we're not ready to do this again yet.*

And as time rolled into July, we almost decided not to.

"She keeps getting sick from daycare," said Dale one night.

We sat on our living room couch, our bodies slumped over the cushions. This was not an original conversation, and I didn't think I had the stomach for it *again*.

"Yeah," I said. "But what's the alternative? A nanny is too expensive, and I don't want that situation here anyway. That would be a disaster for work."

"Yeah..." He trailed off, and in my head, I filled in all the things he wasn't saying.

You're being selfish.

You're not sacrificing enough.

Wouldn't you do anything for our daughter?

My stomach felt like a gutter, dark and murky, saturated with rainwater. I could hear the walls, the air.

"Maybe we could just keep her home for a little while," Dale ventured. "Let her get back to healthy."

Why was he so much fucking better at this than I was?

"I can't do what we did at the beginning of COVID. I nearly had a nervous breakdown."

"I know, I know."

"And what about Cody? He'd be bringing home all the same stuff."

Dale sighed. "Yeah, you're right."

The defeat in my husband's voice felt like crushed glass in my chest. I thought about Violet—how, despite all of her illnesses, she could now hike two miles at a time through the mountains, loved racing up and down the balcony on her truck in just her pink undies, and was perfectly content pouring dirt back and forth between cups, smudging her round face when pushing blond wisps out of her eyes. Those were moments and memories, yes, but it was hard to view them without my own context: the exhaustion, the frustration, the overstimulation.

But for as many truths as there were, there was really only one: The soft, animal body of my two-and-a-half-year-old was being worn down, and I cared for that body deeply.

Dale and I had been daycare-parents long before we ever had kids. If there was one thing I had inherited from my mother, it was that I would be a working mom, as she was. *You can have it all*, she always said, empowering me out of the same mouth that disempowered all working women, saying, *I can't, I have to work.* There was a clear hierarchy in having it all, and my high school volleyball games and college graduations and even the births of my children fell somewhere near the bottom of it.

I took a deep breath. "If she gets sick again this month, I'll request a medical leave of absence. Six weeks. And I'll just stay home with her."

"Really?"

"The way I see it, your job is what is keeping us in New Mexico, and this is where we want to be. We have to protect that at all costs. I'll figure it out."

I didn't know how, and I really didn't want to find out, but I was starting to learn the kind of mother I wanted to be, even if it wasn't the kind I was taught. Because I knew it even as a kid, looking over at empty seats in the crowd: Everything is a choice, even when you tell yourself you have none.

July passed without incident. But perhaps buoyed by the undercurrent of agency that that conversation with Dale had evoked, in early August, I did something I had never done before. Although it didn't feel monumental—more like taking that first nauseating sip of water when you wake up with a hangover in your belly.

Oh, to just be hungover—to just be an idiot who had too much fun. To just need water and sleep and twenty-four hours.

Instead, us adults in the *real world* often need *desperation* to get us back on track. Feeling so in-need that we finally break in ways we should have broken long ago.

I was in an impromptu meeting with the rest of the senior team. The report for the mental health app had gone fine; and if I'm being honest, that's all it was: fine. But in the time since, it seemed my workload had multiplied faster than usual, and the timelines for my projects kept shifting until they slowed to a stop, all stacked right on top of each other. Now we had a brand-new account—a national retailer—and our first project with them needed to go somewhere. Project North, they were calling it, because it was investigating potential in the Canadian market.

"What's the timing on it?" I asked.

"The last they said was that we could be ready to start recruiting in September," my co-worker Benny said. "So, field in early October, everything done by Thanksgiving."

I looked down at my notebook where I had jotted down notes on my workload. Too many lines, all jumbled together. I took a deep breath. "Ok, what are you thinking?"

"I can lead the account," Benny said. "But I'd love for you to moderate and do the report."

I swallowed, my tongue sticking to the roof of my mouth. I loved Benny. Thirty years older than me, with a storied career in research and advertising, he was one of my favorite people. And I one of his: he gushed over my work, over me.

"The last I heard," I said. "The report wasn't going to allow for much storytelling. Their segments are super basic, not very human."

"Yeah, but if anyone can pull more richness out of them, it's you."

Exhale. "I'm worried about the timing with what I will already have going on at that time." I looked down at my notes as I read them off, sticking out a finger for every project. "I have the X retainer with Taj—his part will be ramping up more in the fall, so I'll be in charge of the ongoing stuff, which is pretty unpredictable. Y will be coming out of field in October, and that will be heavy on my plate through the end of November. Z will be going into quant reporting—TBD on who is doing that, but I'll be leading the analysis regardless. Then A follow-ups. And whatever is going on with B—if they want to finally get started with the Hispanic research. With all of that, I just don't have the capacity to add this on."

I was holding up a whole hand, cold to the touch even though I was sweating. No one said anything.

"The biggest thing is Y," I said, jabbing towards Benny. It was his client, his project, and he knew that I was the only one with the skillset to do what they wanted. *Let me go, let me go*, I silently begged. "It's four decks and a whitepaper, and they've got lots of eyes on it. It could lead to a whole new avenue of work with them."

No one said anything. Five faces all staring at each other in a grid on a screen. Five faces that used to be fully fleshed-out bodies, working together in the same office, sitting together at the same table.

"For now, let's just see where the timing nets out," said Eric, my boss. "We're talking to the client on Friday."

"Ok," I said, my voice shriveling to a tiny thread, already distant.

If I only knew—if I only knew that none of this shit mattered. None of it: not the project assignments, not the workload, not the flattened-out faces. But I guess I'm saying that for the sake of all the years prior because it was only a few days before this all started to crack—and I started to know.

28

Ten years before, on the morning of August 9th, 2011, I had woken up in my studio apartment in LA and started a pot of oatmeal. While it cooked, I pulled on a stretchy high-waisted denim skirt, a loose goldenrod top with a front pocket, and cream-colored heels I could barely walk in, and sprayed my hair—bleach blonde, still coming back from four years as black—into unnatural curls, sweeping my side bangs back in a brown barrette. After I ate, I drove three miles down Ventura, parked in a basement garage, rode the elevator up to the eighth floor, and walked, heels knocking, into an office. A wall of windows overlooked the valley. Everything inside me flipped and buzzed. My first day at my first *real world* job.

On this August 9th, in 2021, I woke up to a *Happy 10th Anniversary!* email from our office manager and the sound of Violet coughing. I still started a pot of oatmeal, but instead of pulling out my notebook and catching the last bit of blue morning before the sun came up, I trudged up to the den, unplugged the nebulizer, and brought it into Violet's room. Her daily steroid was also a stimulant—just brilliant for her bedtime dose—so we never did it while she slept, but with her already coughing at five a.m., it seemed worth it to give her lungs a boost. And maybe to ease the sick feeling that had already sunk into my stomach.

Violet stirred as I knelt by her bedside, pouring the solution and screwing together the parts. I pulled her small body into my arms, laid her head on my chest, and leaned back against the bed. Switch on, mask to her face. Plumes of vapor swirling in the dark.

For all the shit that had gone on lately at work—we were a small business; there was always shit going on—and all the years of a demoralizing workload, I was damn proud of today. Ten years is an accomplishment. Ten years of loyalty, of dedication; ten years of another family, dysfunctional as it was at times. In those ten years, I had never thought about leaving. And I still didn't—not on that day.

Instead, I thought about the time when Taj and I went to Philly and accidentally took a car from the wrong rental company, and then later lost it in a parking garage, and then later got tattoos. I thought about the time Benny and I were doing a fit test for a new cut of Levi's and the woman I was interviewing let her pants drop to her ankles to show me just how much they didn't fit. I thought about working with Eric on re-branding the company the fall that I was pregnant with Sloane; how, at the launch party, he had given a toast in the form of a rap, and I had given one that implored everyone, as we embarked on this new chapter of the company, to take off their masks and be their full, present, wonderful selves.

I thought about how none of that would have ever happened had I not switched my major in college from English to Business because I was too scared to pursue my heart, after which my parents sent a card in the mail, delivered to my dorm room, my mom's perfect, loopy handwriting telling me in blue pen how proud they were of me.

But most of all, I thought about how this company had been the backdrop to everything I had gone through over the past five years. How it held it all, better than I could; how it could have held more, would have held more, had I let it. For the moment I allowed myself to forget how the pandemic had fucked up a lot of that: how we couldn't be together in-person, how we were all in survival mode, all had to wear masks. For the moment I allowed myself to forget how deeply exhausted I was. Instead, I thought about how ten could become twenty—how this place, these people, this work could become fused to my bones.

I loved it fiercely, although the intensity itself was something I didn't fully understand. But I never questioned it either.

•

Sometimes I think of all we didn't know back then—how Violet still didn't have a diagnosis, how we didn't have the right tools to care for her. It seems obvious now what should have happened—what eventually did happen—but I guess if anyone had learned how amorphous the medical practice was, it was me. And truthfully, I thought this was a case of inaction *being* the decision—that because she hadn't been given a diagnosis, that meant there wasn't one. That this was just her life, as it would be.

What the fuck do any of us ever know about anything.

It's such a game—this ladder we are always climbing, trying to get to the top of it all. And then to *stay* on top, we huff and puff, trying to keep the lid closed on an overflowing chest of trinkets. Things breaking inside from all the pressure. Springs popping out.

It's exhausting.

Naturally, without discussing it, it seemed that by this time in August, after four pediatric hospitalizations, Dale and I had reverted back to the mentality that we had surrendered to after Sloane died: hope and adapt. Sometimes, get lucky. Always, together. Somewhere along the way—probably when Violet was born, even though her birth fit all the tenets, especially luck, but the shock of it all blew us to pieces—we had drifted away from that plan. But I guess everything changes when it's no longer about you but your kids.

But does it have to? Or is that someone—something—else talking? And what if we listened, but then remembered our own wisdom? What was given to us when we were in rapt attention, wondrously overcome by birth and death.

To not know what we already know—now there's something.

So, Dale and I monitored Violet together the rest of the morning: counting her breaths, lifting up her shirt to watch her ribs. And during her midday nap, because we had learned that our oxygen levels dip when we sleep, we crowded around her bed, slipped a tiny finger into a pulse oximeter, and watched the numbers together.

We had practiced with this thing. This small blue plastic block with a blinking red sensor inside its jaws and a face that told us her heart rate and blood-oxygen level. It seemed like a savior when we first got it—*we can know her oxygen level without going to the doctor!*—but the tininess of her two-year-old fingers in its mouth rendered it more finicky than reliable, which sometimes felt worse than having nothing at all. Until, that is, we practiced: placing her finger just right, making sure she held still, not throwing the damn thing against the wall. It worked best when she slept.

Which is all to say that when the numbers finally settled, and they were not good—I don't even remember now what they were; everything started to move so quickly after—Dale immediately called the pediatrician and paced the hallway outside her room.

I sat on the edge of Violet's bed, watched her sleep. She was on her back, round face turned up toward the window. She pressed her white and gray puppy lovey into one cheek.

"They said to hang up and call 911," said Dale, flying back into the room, already dialing.

And of all the things we had been through, this was when my own worst nightmare came true. I suppose it's because I didn't know about all the other things, but this—calling 911—had been ingrained in me as the thing you never wanted to have to do. I remember long, languid summers laying on the couch with my sisters, making macaroni and cheese in the microwave and watching daytime TV. We had a daily lineup: *Facts of Life*, *Maury Povich*, *Days of Our Lives*, and reruns of *Rescue 911*. Watching the reenactments of 911 calls made my whole body feel sick inside, but I felt I needed to know all of the life situations when I might need to call. Because what if I didn't know to call? What would happen? Who would I fail?

I was eight, nine, ten—already starting to want my own baby to care for, to love, to steal my heart. A baby like the one whose red skin fell off in sheets after it was put in too hot of a tub.

Would I know when to call for them?

Somewhere in the back of my mind, I heard Dale on the phone with the 911 operator, but I couldn't hear what he was saying. I realized I was still looking at Violet. And her lips were blue.

The whole room became water—semi-dark and cool, like sinking farther and farther below the surface. I never knew how blue they meant whenever they went through the list of questions: is she coughing, wheezing, retracting; are her lips or fingernail beds blue. I didn't know if they really meant purple, like warm, smashed blueberries, or maybe more of a blue-gray, like the sky brewing a thunderstorm. But no—they meant blue. *Blue.* As blue as the world before dawn. All those mornings I'd gazed out the window, right here in my daughter's lips.

I saw my hands paw at Violet's shoulders, pulling her up and out of sleep. I heard myself shout to Dale.

Her lips are blue echoed through the room, from me to Dale, from Dale through the phone. Off the walls and into the floorboards.

As she began to wake, blue deepened to purple. She was wobbly, sweating profusely, locks of blonde hair matted to her face.

"Stay with her," I said to Dale, as I flit about the room, pulling her things into her llama backpack.

I was flying down the stairs to the living room when I heard the siren. I flew to the sliding glass doors that opened onto the balcony, as if there was something I might be able to see beyond the houses, the trees. I had never heard a siren heading toward my own house; never knew how different it would sound. How, rather than jagged and jarring, it felt smooth and undulating, pregnant with sorrow. Demanding attention, deference. Like the mother orca who carried her dead calf on her nose for over a thousand miles, showing the world what had happened to her and her baby.

Listening to the siren as I stood at the sliding door, before the same view of the west that I spent weeks looking at while pregnant with Cody, the same view that I still watched turn from black to blue to bright every morning, my chest cavity filled with something otherworldly—something thick, heavy, capable of moving mountains.

This is our life, I had been saying, resigned to all of its twists and downturns, from preemie funeral gowns to our own dead infant; the NICU to the PICU; *Rescue 911* to calling 911. This precipice of death. But for the first time, hearing that rolling, surging song, I felt that life had a place here among the living, not just the dying and the dead. Maybe I could belong here—and maybe it could be beautiful.

●

Hours later, after the nurse left and Violet fell into a deep slumber, wadded up in alphabet-covered hospital sheets, I sat cross-legged on the built-in bench, watching her.

It's RSV, the nurse had said. We knew RSV—knew that it had the highest child mortality rate of any respiratory virus. Knew this because we had talked at length with Violet and Cody's pediatrician about the RSV vaccine. Back then it was only covered by insurance if the child was of a certain prematurity—which ours were—and had a chronic lung condition—which ours hadn't been diagnosed with. Yet. Otherwise, it was ten-thousand dollars a shot, five shots in the full course. We had considered it and declined.

And now, here was Violet. With RSV.

At home, there was Cody. Still an infant.

And for the first time during any of their hospitalizations, I cried. Sobbed into my hands, waves rolling through me. Something—the blue, the siren, the nightmare—had cracked me open. Fear had spoken, and I had listened. And then, I had remembered.

This is what's here, what's alive.

The terror and the love.

My beating, aching heart.

29

s he raking food with his whole hand, or picking it up with two fingers?" the physical therapist asked.

"Mostly raking," I said, rubbing a palm over Cody's belly.

Her long pink fingernails made an audible click on her tablet screen. She was the big guns: round, loud, and sitting with legs in a V on my living room floor. She was here for an in-depth evaluation of Cody's development—the first time he was able to be seen in-person since they relaxed their pandemic restrictions, a week after Violet was discharged from the hospital. Bea was her name; her mask was deep purple, sparkly.

"But he's eating everything," I said, knowing full-well that wasn't relevant to her question. "We're adding coconut oil to his oat cereal, and butter to his purees, like Jennifer suggested." I paused, looking over at Jennifer—the one who knew my kids—then back at Bea. "We've been going slow with solids because of all the throwing up."

I hated this—this assessment by questions. Or maybe it wasn't so much the questions themselves, but the empty space that surrounded them. Bea spoke like a textbook. Crisp black letters in serif font; glossy white pages. Me—I read any book with a pen and a highlighter, marked my own being into the text. Could we talk about how he just miraculously evaded the hospital—less than two months after he was in there for five days?

Yes, yes, of course, we had talked about that. *But could we go back to it?* I wanted to ask. *Because I'm still there, in the hospital and the miracle.*

"He seems to be hearing okay?" Bea asked. "Sometimes a head tilt like that can indicate a hearing problem."

"I think so," I said, looking down at Cody sitting on my bare leg, bouncing him. Lately his head had been hanging to one side—not always, but often. But his proportions hadn't changed at his nine-month check-up: head size in the 98th percentile; height and weight in the first, even for his corrected age. His neck just wasn't strong enough yet, we thought.

"Can I see him?"

"Sure," I said. I held Cody's round face up to mine. Animated my eyes since he couldn't see my mouth behind my mask. "You're going to see Miss Bea, okay? Just for a minute. Mama will be right here."

I set him down in front of Bea, and she placed a hand on his back before I let go, knowing that he still couldn't sit up on his own. She had already asked that question.

"I can feel some tightness here," she said, feeling his neck, shoulders, upper back, her pink nails flashing in quick movements. I knew she was a physical therapist but there was something I didn't like about her hands on my son—as if he could feel how cold they were, and I wasn't ready for him to know that part of the world yet.

"You can take him back now," she said. "Let's get his hearing checked. It can take a while to get an appointment, so go ahead and call. In the meantime, start noting when his head tilts—certain times of day, after certain activities. And give him little shoulder massages every time he wakes up—in the morning and after naps."

I nodded. What? His hearing?

Anyone—anyone in the whole world: could anyone just give me a little more heart. *Mine is raw and aching*, I wanted to say. *It can't take any more picking and raking.*

Bea looked at Jennifer. "I think we need to start weekly visits." Then she turned to me. "Can you do that?"

"Yes, I can do that," I said, my stomach sinking into the rug.

"Good. We need to get him sitting up on his own and spending time on his tummy. Holding his head up." She folded her tablet case cover over the screen, snapped it closed. "No preemie is every really 'behind' at this age, but he needs a lot of extra work."

I nodded, picking up Cody as we all stood. I hugged him to my chest, willed his tiny, soft body to melt back into mine. *This kid?* I thought. *But this kid is perfect.*

No—none of this was his fault.

I was the one who reported on him to Jennifer every month.

I was the one who was just happy he was alive.

I was the one who had a meeting to get to.

After I closed the front door behind them, I pulled my mask under my chin and grabbed my laptop off my desk. I propped Cody up in a curved pillow, shimmied his activity cube in front of him; he had been really into dragging the wooden beads along the curved rails, letting them slide into each other with a clatter. They would keep him busy during my meeting.

I don't remember anymore what the meeting was for, who was in it—honestly, the level of memorability of most meetings. All I remember is sitting in front of my open laptop, faces in a small grid of squares—three-by-two at the most—Cody's pudgy hand reaching for the beads, and my phone buzzing beside me on the carpet. It was a text from my co-worker. The same one who called me admirable.

You're on Project North, it read. *Eric just announced it.*

As if someone had turned on the broiler inside me, it took me less than a week to inappropriately rage at Eric in another one of those fucked-up face-grids and then start a new company Slack channel titled *women*.

Eric said: "Your team said they thought you could handle it."

I said: "I am the only one who speaks for me."

I wrote: *Does anyone have any recommendations for feminist literature?*

Women wrote: *The Yellow Wallpaper* by Charlotte Perkins Gilman. *Feminism is for Everybody* by Bell Hooks. *Untamed* by Glennon Doyle.

Glennon wrote: "A woman becomes a responsible parent when she stops being an obedient daughter."

●

It was October again. That month when everything stretches out—deepening, heightening, coming alive in the middle. Cool dusk, tall grass. Space for me to be in this world. How was it only a year ago that Cody was just barely still in my belly; it seemed we had lived a lifetime since. And yet, being back here—knowing that the earth had returned to this place and would again and again—filled me with something new.

On the first morning of Balloon Fiesta, Violet and I had pulled blankets off the couch and sat on patio chairs on our balcony. A different view than being on the field, but with its own glory: that spread of balloons all contained, in one pocket of sky above the horizon. And most importantly, the sheer joy of Violet's squeals.

It was still magic—and with maybe further of a reach than I knew.

One afternoon, between meetings, I found myself sitting cross-legged on my bedroom floor, my back flat up against a loveseat, too tired to hold myself up.

I don't know where the drive to meditate came from—other than wanting my head to just shut the fuck up for a minute. It seemed to have been less of a conscious decision and more of a sudden remembering. From when, I think longer ago than I even knew; I had done it a handful of times in early grief, and it had always helped, but in that fall of 2021, I found myself turning toward it more often. I had no idea what I was doing… but I don't think that mattered very much back then.

What mattered was that outside the leaves were turning and falling, returning to the earth, and inside, I, too, felt a call to return. To get heavy, quiet; to let everything wash through me in what the meditation teacher, through an app on my phone, called *deep healing*. Sinking, sinking into the floorboards, eyelids falling, every muscle in my body collapsing against something harder beneath it. Twenty-something minutes of relaxation—because I didn't yet know how to stay alert—and then, when the meditation was over, stillness.

The kind of stillness where you can hear silence. Where you can see how blue they meant, how the siren is a song.

I lifted my head from where it had fallen onto the loveseat, felt it settle back onto my neck. Opened my eyes. And in that instant, as I took in the yellow walls and the bedspread like a darkened sunset, the fine grains in the wooden dresser, and the curious folds of clothes dropped and left, I thought: *I don't need any of this.*

And after that thought came and went: space, endless space.

I didn't know exactly what that thought was referring to, but what it meant to me was that what was missing in my life wasn't external. It was something inside me—a void, a need, a hole leaving me unfulfilled. All this time, filling my life with so much—a wonderful husband, two amazing children, a beautiful home, a successful career—to cover up the feeling of incompleteness that I thought started with Sloane dying but was really so much older than that. And once I saw that hole, I saw everything I had tried to stuff into it over the course of my life: research for the past ten years; before that, three different areas of study in college; before that, multiple part-time jobs in high school; and all the way back to the beginning: advanced placement, academic clubs, leadership roles, learning, studying, acing. Work work work, so that I could look out and away from everything inside, the only place that mattered. And at that time in my life, that meant only one thing.

I thought about it the rest of the afternoon. Slowly, methodically, honestly, as if I were underwater—not drowning, but diving deep into something mysterious and beautiful.

I planned out a strategy: two years, and we'll see what happens.

I listed the benefits: I'll have the flexibility we need for our kids' medical needs; I'll have more energy; I'll be happier.

I'll be living the dream.

My dream.

After dinner that night, I fluttered about the kitchen as Dale did the dishes. I hadn't planned what I was going to say, but when I finally started with, "Hey babe," and Dale looked up at me with those eyes, his hands still scrubbing, I realized it didn't matter.

I tried not to smile. This moment didn't feel serious at all, felt nothing short of ordinary—the kind of ordinary that warms you from the inside, like the smell of pumpkin in the dark. I guess what I mean by ordinary is *true*. Pure. Uncomplicated.

That's how it has to be when you pull out the card that's holding the whole house together. Because then there's no force pulling everything down—no gravity, no pressure. It all just releases upward and outward, into open space.

"I need to make a big change with my career," I said.

Dale stopped washing. A full-blown grin. "Are you retiring?"

I loved him more than I could handle.

"I just have one condition," he said. "That your pen name be Cynthia Brownshoe."

Part Four

30

New Mexico is covered in arroyos, or dry streambeds. Long, snaking gullies of soft soil, walled on either side by eroding earth, empty of water. They are somewhat otherworldly, both ominous and magical—something you're not supposed to be able to experience, walking on the bottom of a waterway. But then when the monsoons come, the arroyos fill, rushing and pounding and flooding in less than a minute.

And so it was with the newfound empty space I had carved into my life: Everything seemed to pour into it. I didn't realize just how burnt out I was at work until, in January 2022, I was no longer there, and the exhaustion that had been the silent undercurrent of the past ten years, and then deepened in the past five, flooded my body and laid me out. My head pounded; my limbs deadened. And every time I turned on a guided meditation called *Deep Rest*, I wept and wept at the words slipping sweetly out of an old woman's mouth.

Rest.

Rest.

Deeply rest.

Every time, when the meditation ended and I re-collected my bones, I wrote it in my notebook: *Rest. Rest.*

Things That Help: Resting. Meditating. Writing.

That became my new normal—resting, meditating, writing—on weekdays, during the hours of eight a.m. to four p.m. That is, when my kids weren't home sick and Cody didn't have therapy and I wasn't managing all the invisible work of the household, or taking on freelance research projects, because I couldn't fully let go, not yet.

It's dangerous to try to walk in that empty arroyo, reaching for what is forbidden.

But it's true that when you start to gather yourself up, more of life gets gathered up, too. It had taken over two months to get an appointment with a pediatric pulmonologist, but when we finally did, it proved to be an inflection point in our lives. Really all because of a tree of sorts.

In late fall 2021, Violet and I had sat in an exam room at the local children's hospital. While we waited for the doctor, she chewed on a homemade pumpkin muffin and pushed her blue denim shoes off and back onto her heels, over and over. I looked around—another hospital to befriend. A wavy blue line cut across the middle of all four walls, their lower halves covered with decals of fish and seaweed and bubbles, their upper halves stark white. A strip of wallpaper showing the alphabet bordered the ceiling. The scale was shaped like a rocket.

When Dr. Kohl came in, she got to know us through a detailed walkthrough of Violet's medical history. My pregnancy: why she was born early, did I have steroids; her NICU stay: was she intubated, how many days was she on CPAP, how many on high-flow, how did she do on room air; her illnesses: common symptoms, typical progression, length of each hospital stay, level of oxygen support needed, how she responded to various treatments.

We had gone over this history during every hospital stay—with every doctor, every nurse, every respiratory therapist—but this was the first time that I saw that the beginning of *her* medical history was *my* medical history, too. That we started as one, and then became two. When it hit me, I winced, that splitting like a brief, distant shriek lost somewhere inside me.

I snapped back to a long list of new questions: how does she do with exercise, pets, dust; outdoors; when the weather changes.

"All fine," I said. "She plays hard at the park, can hike two miles on her own. Loves her dog. Would be outside all day if she could."

"Anyone in the house smoke?"

"No." We were grown-ass adults now.

She scribbled some notes, then bent down to pull a manila folder out of a drawer. It had a stack of papers inside. "It sounds like viral-induced asthma." She looked at Violet. "She's only being sent into respiratory distress once she already has a virus. Not triggered by any other allergens. That could change over time, so keep an eye on those things, but for now, she just needs extra monitoring as soon as she starts coming down with something."

I exhaled. Finally, a diagnosis.

"I'm gonna put her on a new steroid. You can get rid of any budesonide you still have." She pulled out an inhaler—a long plastic tube, covered in teddy bears, with an orange face mask on one end. "Two puffs, thirty seconds between, twice a day, six deep breaths with each puff."

And then she pulled the top sheet of paper from the folder and slid it over to me. Boxes and lines, questions and instructions. It was a map; a decision tree.

"You will be able to manage 90% of illnesses at home now," Dr. Kohl said. She walked me through every box of the flow chart. *If these symptoms are present, give six puffs or one nebulizer vial of albuterol; if symptoms ease, repeat in three hours; if they persist or worsen, repeat in twenty minutes*; etc., etc., all the way down to *Call 911*. "I'll put in an order for the albuterol and the prednisone so that you have them on hand. She might still have a case that lands her in the hospital, but it should be far less frequent than it has been."

I scanned the page in silence, re-reading everything she just told me. Rubbing Violet's small back. Feeling everything we hadn't known fall away, over the side of some cliff.

"This is amazing," I said, looking up at Dr. Kohl. I couldn't even pretend to have it all together. That net that Dr. Page had always held for me—it felt like this woman had just placed it beneath me again.

She smiled. "It should help. And most likely, as her lungs mature, she will grow out of this by age four or five. Until then, you can expect her to get sick every four to six weeks. But it will be nothing like what you've been through."

I hung the tree up on the wall in the kitchen, next to Cody's finger paintings and Violet's holiday crafts.

On a Saturday afternoon in December, after Violet helped me roll warm snowballs in powdered sugar, Cody woke up from a nap breathing rapidly, sucking his belly all the way under his ribs. We took him to the pediatrician, thinking, *Oxygen—we just need oxygen. At home.*

"I can't send him home like this," the doctor said, and we nodded.

Ambulance—so tiny, in his car seat strapped to the gurney. Hospital admission—in that same room with the central column and the hidden toilet. Oxygen.

He spent four days in the PICU and was diagnosed on the spot: viral-induced asthma. Sent home with the same steroid, inhaler, and treatment plan as Violet.

Now all three of us had our lists—mine of resources, theirs of action steps—for when we were drowning. Just in time for when COVID finally hit our household in January 2022, and we could stare into its face and howl, running albuterol through the nebulizer every three hours around the clock and coming out unscathed. The beginning of a string of knockouts, crushing virus after virus, always staggered by a handful of days between the two of them, so that there was almost always someone sick, and it was stressful and exhausting, and I was not resting nearly as much as I needed to, but it was working, *it was working.*

"Is he raking food, or picking it up with two fingers?" Bea asked. She and the sinking feeling in my stomach were back in early February, again making themselves at home on my living room floor.

"Mostly raking," I said. "Sometimes using his fingers, but usually three, not two."

"Does he point with one finger?"

"No—he'll gesture with his whole hand. Or his arm, really."

Jennifer had asked Bea to come see Cody because he was almost sixteen months old and still wasn't crawling, still hated being on his tummy. He could sit up on his own now and his hearing screen had come back normal, but his head was still heavy, and he got tired of holding it up. *I feel you, buddy*, I thought when it would start leaning to the side, telling me his neck and traps and back were done. *I feel you.*

"But he's been really into standing," I said, sitting up a little taller. "He holds onto the coffee table and sometimes takes a couple of steps to the side. I hear some kids skip crawling and go straight to walking."

That had been my secret hope ever since Cody started showing interest in being on his feet. He found it thrilling, stretching towards the rubber farm animals I placed just out of reach, figuring out how his legs worked.

"Ok, we don't want him to do that," said Bea, the glossy textbook page back in her voice. "Crawling is actually the only time in our lives where we are actively learning to coordinate the left and right sides of our brain. Babies who don't crawl often turn into kids who struggle with dyslexia and other learning abilities. In school, they can't read what's on the board and write down notes at the same time."

Well, that's that, I thought. *This kid will crawl.*

Jennifer hopped in. "We've been trying really hard. She sets up these obstacle courses for him, where he has to knock down the blocks, and she figured out that he's more cooperative if she sings while he does it." She turned to me. "I still think that is so amazing that you discovered that."

I smiled, silently thanked her.

"We tend to think of crawling as using gross motor strength," Bea went on, turning the page. "The big joints and muscles like hips, back, legs—but it actually starts with fine motor strength. Without strong fingers and hands and wrists, he can't hold himself in the proper crawling position. That's what we need to work on most with him— things like smushing hair gel around in an airtight Ziploc bag, or putting Cheerios into a water bottle."

Fuck, I thought. Not to anything in particular, just generally: *Fuck*.

"Ok," I said. "So should we also be trying to practice crawling?"

"Yes," she said, so matter-of-factly that I became confused as to how all of this was actually going to happen. "I'll show you some things you can do. Can I see him?"

I sat Cody down in front of her, and he looked up at me, his eyes drawn down at the outer corners. "Miss Bea is going to help you learn to crawl," I said. "I'll be right here."

Bea pulled him onto her lap, forming a zipper of pink nails down his middle. Then she flattened his back, shimmied his hips, tucked in his knees, and held all of him into place as she rolled him slowly off her lap and toward the ground, where he shot out his arms and caught himself on his palms.

"You want to practice this motion," she said, moving him in and out of her lap, like a VHS tape playing and rewinding, playing and rewinding. "And then when he gets comfortable on all fours, just rock him back and forth, like this."

You know that thing kids do where they behave for everyone else, but with their parents, they feel free to be their most difficult selves? That's what I was thinking about as Bea moved Cody around like a plush doll, completely unaware of how he collapsed into a rigid, wailing mess half the time during these types of exercises. Yes, Bea, I know about the rocking—that's the damn thing I've been watching for to tell me that he's getting closer to crawling. But just when I was about to save face—for no reason other than I still hated her lack of heart—she came out with the one thing that would eventually save our hides.

"He's having a hard time getting on top of his knees," she said, setting Cody aside to rest. "To keep them from splaying out, you might want to try what they call 'mermaid pants.'" She did the air quotes, her fingernails flashing up and down. Then she mimed in the air: "You can just make them yourself—take some stretchy pants, like an old pair of leggings, and cut them at the knee, then sew them down the middle and across the bottom. They'll hold his legs closer together. They're used for kids with low muscle tone—like kids with Down Syndrome—but I think they might work for this, too."

"Ok," I said, my stomach now nowhere to be found, some blurry image of a bull scaling a mountain resurfacing in my mind. Not because it had gone away but because it now seemed untenable as a way of life. Undesirable even. Bulls didn't see blue or hear songs; didn't feel the sky crack open when their nightmares came true. And yet, I said: "I can do that."

•

"Nothing is going to change unless something changes," I said to Dale that evening, when I told him I was going to start picking Cody up two hours early from school every day for dedicated crawling practice.

Two weeks into our new routine, I looked forward to three in the afternoon every day, when I scooped Cody up off the daycare floor and into my arms, pressing my nose into his pillowy cheek—and then dread three-fifteen, when we walked into our house and had to start what Dale called "the gauntlet."

The gauntlet was a circuit I had designed with exercises for his tummy, back, knees, and hips. Ten minutes at each station, with a five-minute break in between, and all that fine motor crap—poking buttons, squeezing sponges, pulling pipe cleaners through a colander—sprinkled throughout. Cody in the mermaid pants the whole time. It was grueling—for both of us. But Jennifer had seen it, and she agreed: this was what he needed.

And I had seen some change so far: longer stretches willingly spent on his tummy, more strength in his fingers and hands. Some days he even seemed to forget he was in the middle of an exercise—the easier ones, at least—blowing past the timer and actually enjoying himself. I didn't look at the changes in myself: how I felt even more tired, how I was growing resentful toward Dale for not having to go through this, how a deep well of something black was beginning to form in my chest.

It was hard to keep telling myself that this was for Cody's well-being when there was so much screaming, writhing, wailing. Like when Violet had her nebulizer stercid, or when either of them had to be pierced for an IV. These weren't the normal sounds of childhood. And they echoed in my skull.

"Be a mom first," Taj had said to me when I told him I was leaving the company. Inside, I had bristled at the advice, the same as I had six or seven years prior when he and I had sat at a restaurant in Chicago, in the field for Nike, spooning cookie pie out of a bowl sitting halfway between us, and he told me his belief that a mother's role is to be with her kids, especially when they are young.

That's partly what I was trying to do when I left—be available for all of my kids' extra medical needs that stemmed from their prematurity, which stemmed from... I didn't know, but it was hard to fully separate whatever it was from my own body, my own being. This was the house that couldn't hold them long enough. But what was underneath that house—its foundation? Where was I? That was the bigger thing I was trying to do with quitting my job, and it felt like I was just sinking further and further into the ground.

As if the house had no foundation to begin with.

31

So, how's the writing going?" asked my dad. Each word came out slowly, as if he wasn't sure how to form the sentence. He sat at one end of my living room couch—a wide, plush semi-circle—my mom at the other. They were in town for Violet's third birthday.

"It's amazing," I said from where I knelt on the carpet, pulling thin sheets of tissue paper off a stack. I pinched each one in the middle and plunged it into a gift bag so that most of the sheet stood up and fanned out, like a paper bouquet. On the front of the bag was a llama wearing sunglasses; inside were markers, chalk, paints, and brushes for her big present: an easel. "Everything I've ever wanted. It's hard to get to some days—what with everything going on—but when I do, it's the best."

"I'm still just so happy for you," said my mom, clasping her hands together, her voice like a song. I knew this voice—her genuine voice, when her words came out smoothly and softly, a ribbon from her heart through her smile. It was the same voice she used when I first told them I was leaving my job, back in October, when they were in town for Cody's first birthday. I had waited until the last day of their visit, when I could no longer stand the panic rising in my chest, but it had gone nothing like I had feared, and my mom cried, and no one chastised me, and to this day, I still don't understand it.

"What about the research?" asked my dad.

"Good. Doing a project right now for Benny and getting paid more than I was full-time. Also, my old co-worker Cosmo is at a new firm, and he connected me to their guy in charge of contractors. I chatted with him, and it seems like they might have some work for me."

He nodded, staring straight ahead. The outer corners of his eyes slightly pinched; the gears turning. "We should talk about estimated tax payments while we're here."

Money was my dad's love language. He had been a CPA, then ran finance for a transportation company before retiring at the age of forty-nine to become a day trader for his own finances. When I had started working as a teen, he had taught me how to balance a checkbook and save for a car; the way he spoke to me like an adult in those conversations was the first time I ever heard pride in his voice. It would still be some time before I stopped telling him about every penny I earned, hoping it would mean something. That I finally knew something, finally was someone in his fading blue eyes.

"Sounds good," I said and turned to my mom. "I got all the cupcake stuff yesterday. Liners, mix, icing. We have a bunch of sprinkles in the pantry, but I also got some special unicorn ones."

"Ohhh, that's ok," she said, in another one of her voices—the fake sugar cover-up. "I was going to take Violet to the store and get everything with her."

"Oh, cool!" I said, smiling. "She will like that." My own fake sugar cover-up—for all of the other sugar that I rushed to pick up from the store on my way to the airport, so that I would have everything prepared, no cause for conflict or disappointment, but that would now sit in my pantry, unused. Money was her love language, too, in the form of gifts: both the unexpected, personal ones that leave you in tears— like the half-body mannequin the Christmas I was seventeen, for working on my own sewing projects at home—and the forced, substitutional ones that leave you wishing for the real thing instead— like the jacket she made me get when they both came to visit me in Austria my sophomore year in college, just before she told me to go to dinner with just my dad, even though I hadn't talked to her in months.

"Pick something out and I'll buy it for you," she had said, skipping all courtship on a narrow cobblestone street in Salzburg, everything in her voice saying she didn't want to be there. It was only a day after she had raged at my dad for telling me the wrong arrival time of their train, so I was hours late meeting them; a month after she had unexpectedly quit her senior-level job, ending a career she loved; eight months after her brother, one of her ten siblings, had killed himself with carbon monoxide, sitting alone in a car. There she was, herding me into a clothing shop, suffering silently, trying but unable to love me.

She, the original bull.

"I'm telling you," said my mom, looking up at my in-laws and jabbing her pointer finger towards Violet. "She is exactly like Alexandria when she was that age."

We all laughed, watching my now three-year-old gleefully bite her little rabbit mouth into a chocolate-frosted chocolate cupcake. All afternoon, she and my mom had traded squeals in the kitchen, standing next to each other, my mom frosting and Violet pouring on a dozen different kinds of sprinkles. I think even Violet knew that was the real gift—that sweet, full drop of time together. Grandma had always been my mom's best role.

"Do you remember what you wanted for your third birthday?" asked my mom, turning toward me, at the opposite end of the table.

"A cake with pink frosting and race cars on top," I said, not actually remembering but having heard the story enough times.

"Yep, and it couldn't be any other way."

I clenched my jaw, inhaled long and slow, knowing what was coming. That voice—I didn't have a name for it. Had always tried to keep my distance from it. But was now hearing it in a new way—clearer, louder, than ever before.

"She was like that from the day she was born," my mother said, now booming, everyone listening. She thinks she sounds other than she does, comical or endearing; even I used to mistake it for pride, until now, when I could really hear the harshness of the enunciation, the gravelly drop-off of some sentences—how everything was supposed to land and land hard. *This is how it was*, she was saying. *This is who she is.* One hand held rigid, chopping down on the other laid flat with every emphasized word. "She *knew* what she wanted, and *that's* how it had to be. Even when I breastfed—it was going to be on *her* terms."

She was looking directly at me, seeing whatever she wanted to see. I couldn't bear to look anywhere else, had no stomach for what I might see. The kind faces of my in-laws, the frosting around my daughter's mouth—they would only make the shame sink deeper.

"Do you remember when you walked into the principal's office in seventh grade and *demanded* that you be put in a different math class?"

I caught my mother-in-law's face out of the corner of my eye; she had raised her eyebrows, the whites of her eyes glossy. "Really," she said, a slight question.

"Oh yeah," said my mother, shimmying in her seat to lean forward. She had her audience now. "'Um, Mr. So-and-so is going too slow with the lessons,'" she said, her voice now imitating thirteen-year-old me, who sounded like an entitled brat. "'Yeah, uh, you need to put me in a better class.' Do you remember that?"

I shrugged, pulled my cheeks back into a simulated smile. Played my role. "I wasn't learning enough."

"And then when you emailed your freshman English teacher a few years ago, apologizing for how you acted in his class," she said, grinning, shimmying.

My mother-in-law, I could tell, feeling pressured to continue her role: "Oh, wow."

"I did," I said, straightening up, out of breath, but a strange combination of shame and pride rising up in me. "Mr. Van Dam. He had made us do an assignment that I, at the time, thought was stupid, and I had told him so—in different words. Ten years later, I found his email address on the district website and sent him an apology."

No speculation from the peanut gallery on why I had so little respect for authority, or why mistakes like that ate me up inside for years, or how I ever learned how to fucking repair when it was never modeled to me.

I retired to my room that night at eight o'clock, exhausted to the bone. My parents and my in-laws had each other to entertain themselves. Me, I needed to be alone.

I collapsed on my bed and rolled onto my back. Held my phone above my face as I opened my meditation app. I scrolled through my bookmarks, not sure what I was looking for, until I got to the end—or rather, the beginning. The very first guided meditation that I saved, on a whim, in February 2018, four years before. It was called *Loving and Listening to Yourself* by Sarah Blondin. I vaguely remembered it—remembered more so her tender voice, like white sugar poured from a cupped palm. I pressed play and closed my eyes.

Vibrating violin strings. Single piano notes.

And then:

I love you. I am listening.

When is the last time you closed your eyes and said these words to yourself? When is the last time you took the time to give to yourself what you endeavor to give to others?

As tears leaked down my temples, I remembered why I had saved this meditation, and why I had never listened to it again since.

"Where are your parents?" Dale mouthed to me the next day. He had just woken up from a midday catnap and come into the living room where I was working on crawling with Cody.

I pointed a finger up, for upstairs, and mouthed, "Packing." They were leaving the next morning.

Dale raised his eyebrows, a shit-eating grin spreading across his face. "Soooo, I had an interesting conversation with my parents."

He spoke barely above a whisper, like we did in the hospital. He had taken both kids hiking that morning with his parents while I slept.

"Apparently, your mom was going on and on about you last night."

"Oh yeah?" I said, not surprised, my heart quickening anyway. I stood up from where I was kneeling next to Cody, let him off the hook for the time being. Groaned internally as he rolled onto his side and then up to sitting.

"Yeah, and I had actually heard some of it after you went to bed, and I was still cleaning up the table. Your mom was saying, 'I don't understand why she's so exhausted all the time. The kids are in daycare and they're so good.' So, I went over there and said, 'Alle does a lot for everyone. And teaching Cody to crawl has taken a lot out of her.' And she goes, 'That's only been for two weeks.'"

My head felt drained of blood. As if it had all sunk down to my belly where it now boiled.

"So, I just walked away—she wasn't going to get it. But then I guess after I left, she just went off, saying that you were making our lives harder by making all of the kids' food and not allowing screen time and... there was one other thing... Oh, cloth diapers."

I stared at him, locking eyes. "Cloth diapers?"

"Yeah," he said, punching the word with the same force that my mom used to chop hers. "*That's* what she thinks makes our life hard."

My shoulders fell.

"I know," he said. "I know. It's terrible."

The burn in my stomach was almost unbearable. Thinking of everything I had told her over the years—about Sloane, about the miscarriages; the surgeries, the complications, the births; the NICU, the PICU, the oxygen keeping us all afloat—and now knowing with certainty that she never heard a word of it, never saw me for anything other than what she wanted to see for her own damn story about how I was a baby who dared to cry when it was hungry.

"Oh," he said. "And I guess she also told them some story about how you snapped at her about something, and then apologized...? And when she asked why you've never said sorry before, you said, 'I've never been wrong before.'"

Now it was in my chest, white-hot. "'I was wrong'—that's what I said. She was bitching about how Aunt Cheryl didn't go to the benefit that Uncle Mike's friends put on for him. I got fired up, saying that it was nobody's business how Aunt Cheryl handled her grief."

The previous summer, my uncle's decline from ALS had been fast, and then unexpectedly rapid at the end; his funeral ended up being the morning of a fundraising event his friends had planned months before. Another of my mom's brothers—her fifth sibling to die. But her lack of compassion for the bereaved—after all the grief she had endured, after all of it I had endured—rubbed a wound.

"Anyway," I continued, "I fucking apologized for snapping—literally said, *I was wrong*—and this is what I get? Is she fucking nuts—is that what she actually heard? How the hell am I supposed to—"

I threw my hands up, unable to even articulate all the things I couldn't do right for her. Instead, I followed an echo: *lack of compassion for the bereaved.* Toward my aunt... toward me... toward herself...

Hearing about my life, seeing my life, but not grasping its gravity.

Not feeling it.

Trying but unable to love.

I took a deep breath. Steeled something inside me. Then said: "Remember what I said when the pandemic started—about going to therapy for my mom when it was all over? I think it's time."

The first available appointment with Blair wasn't for another several weeks. But I was full of a nervous energy that I needed to pin down before it blew my insides to bits, the question running through my veins: *What role does my mom have in all this?* I meant this story, our reproductive journey, but what I didn't realize at the time was how every story within the bigger story is the bigger story, too. Like how our fingers aren't separate from our hands; it's all the hand.

All the body.

It's all the story of our lives.

So, I spent hours scrolling back through our text messages—the only way my mom and I communicated, unless we were together in person, where we talked for hours—all the way to the beginning, when I first found out about my cervical insufficiency. And as I crawled forward in time, the messages frequent and deep that first year of grief, I realized that 2017 was the tenderest time in our very tenuous relationship. I turned to her with sadness and heartache, joy and hope, and she sent back words of comfort and support, celebration and encouragement. But that's all they were: words. Even though I had been waiting my whole life for more words from her—more *I love yous*, more *I'm heres*—I now saw the shadow that came with them, the tall thing lurking just behind: I didn't believe any of them.

I said I did—and even thought I did at the time. I told her she was the best, thanked her profusely for her love and support. But there was something about the urgency in her typed voice—the paragraphs of text, the exclamation points—that made me feel wrong. She had never been a container—was often quite the opposite, pouring me out onto the floor when my seas got too rough.

Even into my adult years, she would heave her shoulders and mock blubber five-year-old me: "B-b-barney says it's o-kay to cry-y-y." Again, she thought she was being funny; again, her words stabbed at me, and in this case, also reminded me that, as a kid, I had learned more about life from a purple dinosaur than anyone else.

You know the song—*I love you, you love me, we're a happy family?*

As the years went on in the text chain, and my kids were born and lived, it became clear that death was the only circumstance that warranted her full support, lacking as it was. Through the pregnant months, the NICU weeks, the PICU days, her empathetic words lessened, sometimes stopped, and occasionally reversed, like when I was 27 weeks pregnant with Cody, at the beginning of October 2020, and we had already been hanging by a thread for eight weeks—Cody, the cerclage; me, crippling fear—and I told her that if I made it to November, I was considering starting my maternity leave.

To relax and focus on my mind and body, I had written to her. *Is that selfish? The idea makes me feel kinda guilty.*

And she had responded: *I can see why you would say that. Violet is in daycare, Rich is in town, you have a wonderful husband, and you have people clean your house. Why shouldn't you be able to work?*

From me: *Yeah, maybe it's not a good idea.*

And now, it had become clear after Violet's birthday party, the words she had for me and my problems were fake sugar cover-up in front, cutting shit-talker in back. She, the shadow; she, the one who didn't believe in *me.*

A year later, when Dale and I were driving up to the Jemez for only our third weekend ever away from our kids, he said, as we rounded a curve through the red cliffs, "You know what I hate when people say? 'There just are no words.' It's like—sure, there are. Just find some."

I laughed. Him, always the one to say *I don't know* before even trying to think of an answer to a question. "I hear you," I said. "But I also get it. Sometimes words can feel inadequate."

And that's true, but I think what I meant was: sometimes words aren't the thing you're looking for. No, you're looking for your mother, instead of your father, sitting in your hospital room as you become a mother to your dead daughter. Your mother, instead of your father-in-law, playing with one of your kids so that you can rest while your cervix shortens with the other. Your mother, instead of your father, holding your newborn son while your daughter is in the hospital. As a substitute, words come out lacking.

And some people use words to just avoid the thing altogether.

Words, or gifts, or things other than the thing itself.

The thing provided by presence.

And where had I been all this time that my mother wasn't there? Hadn't I, too, given only death its due? Hadn't I, too, lessened, stopped, occasionally reversed?

Sat in a chair, looked into Violet's eyes through hospital crib slats instead of holding her.

Holed up on a bench, looked at data instead of my son.

How do we learn what we are never taught?

32

strapped my mask over my ears and pulled open the front door with a big exhale, as if I, not Jennifer, was the one who had just trekked up our steep driveway. It had become automatic now for Thursday mornings: a sickness built in my stomach while I played with Cody until she arrived, then I steeled myself while we worked with him and he fought and cried and still didn't crawl, and then, after she left and I brought him to school, I systematically deflated myself, muscle by muscle. Or sometimes I just rotted until a new dawn made me hopeful again. But this Thursday was different: after six weeks of the gauntlet, and nearly seventeen months old, Cody had finally crawled.

"How's he doing?" Jennifer said, slipping off her shoes.

"Great," I said, squeezing Cody into my side and finally feeling a breath of excitement. I had sent her a video right after it happened, but I wanted, needed, her to see it live. "We went to the zoo on Saturday, and then he crawled that afternoon. I was so happy I almost cried."

"That's great," she said, drawing out the vowels. "I'd love to see."

"Cody, do you want to show Miss Jennifer how you can crawl? Let's show her." I set him down on all fours near his yellow school bus and gave it a push so that it rolled a few feet away. "Can you crawl to the bus? Go get the bus."

Cody wobbled forward a couple of paces, his sweatpant-covered knees slipping around on the wood floor. I hated this part: the show. *Perform, perform.* I'm pretty sure kids hate it, too, evident in their frequent non-compliance. And yet, we parents set ourselves up for this binary of extremes: soaring pride when they do the thing, personal failure when they don't. Meanwhile, the kids don't give a shit. You want them to crawl, and they're taking in the way the sunlight falls onto the floor in patches, how their first pair of shoes makes their feet feel suffocated. And they're right.

There is nothing more humbling than a child—nothing that shows you just how much you don't understand about life.

Oh, all the shit we laden ourselves with as adults. When does it end—when, when does it all end.

Cody grabbed a foam soccer ball and shifted onto his bottom, leaving the bus parked.

It took a while, but Jennifer eventually got to see Cody crawl and stand and cruise a few steps along the curved rim of the coffee table. And without Bea there, we chatted: about her kids, about Violet, about where we were hoping to go camping in the summer. But it all felt wrong. Muted. Still rife with tension. Not between us, not hanging over the room—just all within me.

"Ok, so let's keep working on getting his knees under him when he's in that crawling position," Jennifer said at the end of the hour, slipping her socked feet back into her shoes. "When he's sitting, keep him out of that W-sit, and ask him to crawl instead of scoot. Always more tummy time—he needs that strength for everything. And then, like we talked about, when he's standing, moving him a little farther away from where he's trying to go so that he has to briefly let go."

"Ok, ok," I said, my voice, my arms, weightless.

What did I get—a few hours maybe? When he first crawled, and I sent out the video to my in-laws and Dale, who was at the park with Violet at the time, and then I probably had a beer because I thought we could finally rest, at least for a minute, before continuing the climb—what did all that add up to? Was it even one full breath?

I closed the door behind Jennifer and, instead of carrying Cody up to his room to change his diaper before school, slumped down to my knees and sat back on my heels, letting Cody slide off my lap. In the middle of our living room on a spring morning, our house felt cavernous. Ceiling unreachable, light streaming in through fifteen windows. What was usually exalting now felt swallowing.

I watched Cody fill up his school bus with wooden screws from his toolbox and thought, *I'm going to tell Dale about Jennifer's visit when he gets home from work tonight, and he won't know this sinking feeling I'm talking about.* He'll wrap his arms around me, say, *You're a great mama,* and I'll think but won't say, *But you're his dad. I feel all alone in this.*

And then: *You, his mother, are an asshole. Forcing him, making him cry. He is here. Just let him be.*

And: *If you don't help him develop, no one else will.*

And: *Remember how badly you wanted him?*

And I won't think, but I'll feel, somewhere deep within me: *You're not working full-time anymore. Shouldn't you be able to handle all this?*

Why can you not handle all this?

What the fuck is wrong with you?

And then, briefly, one urgent whisper of a thought: *Resources.*

Because this—all this—was still another life, not like the one we are taught to dream of, and yet I still didn't have permission to say *This is not what I asked for,* and *I could never have planned for this,* and *This is more than anyone could reasonably expect in life,* because here it was, all here, all the time, laying around me like scattered blocks, a giant fucking mess to pick up and carry because it was just *life,* on dry land, and I had done the one thing I could think of to make it better—leave my job—but that wasn't the thing, and the real thing was staring your worst nightmare right in the face and holding it and holding it and holding it through to the very end, where you come out on the other side feeling alive, and that's what it meant to get *through,* and I was just trying to get through, but nothing ever seemed to end, and I didn't know how to keep staring and holding and holding and holding, day in and day out, when all I had ever been was a bull.

I sat motionless, staring at the floor. Not seeing how I could still be spiraling so hard when I actually wanted this life. Or *a* life. Not seeing that this life was more than anyone could handle. This particular life—not its events or circumstances, but its body. That anyone in this body would be sinking.

•

I began to feel split. Life had been a rollercoaster for five years, but now the sine wave had gone from slow and languid to tightly coiled, the highs and lows exquisite, increasingly extreme.

I would exalt in the peace of a weekday afternoon spent writing on the deck, then burn with rage at Dale for leaving me alone with both kids for ten minutes, then sink into self-loathing for being so incapable of everything. And my one reprieve—Sienna on Sunday afternoons—had become a miracle at best, with neither of us willing to risk exposure when there was a sick kid, and between her one kid and our two, there was almost always a damn sick kid.

I still woke up at five a.m. every day to start my oatmeal and see the blue world, but by nine most mornings, I had a crushing headache. The best I could do was lie on the floor of my bedroom closet, lights off, and whisper to myself: *I can accept this life. I can accept this life. I can accept this life.*

33

know I had been seeing you for grief counseling," I said to Blair through the screen, my laptop sticking to my thighs. The lighting in my bedroom was bad, making my face look swollen and red, but I needed the thick cushions of the loveseat to hold me up. "But I was wondering if you do other kinds of therapy, too—like, outside of grief and loss."

She smiled. I longed to be back in the natural light of her office, coming in through the back patio over broad green leaves—a time that seemed so much simpler now, even for what it was—but the world hadn't yet gone back to normal, whatever that was. "Yes, it's totally normal, and actually quite typical, for my clients to want to explore therapy in other parts of their lives."

"Ok, cool. Because there are two main things I need help with: my mom and feeling overwhelmed. By parenting, I think. Or maybe just the craziness of our life."

"Definitely—we can work on those. Tell me how life has been."

I caught her up on everything since we last talked: Cody's birth and NICU stay; both kids' PICU stays and asthma diagnoses; leaving my job and pursuing writing; Cody's development and my parents' visit. At least some things stayed constant through all that: I still unwittingly only shared half-truths with her, focusing more on the events and less on myself. And not at all on the depth behind anything.

Turns out that wouldn't matter. The events themselves were enough; what I thought was just the surface was more than enough to drown in.

"Wow," she said, eyes wide. "You guys have been through a lot. That all sounds *really* hard. "

"Yeah. It's been a lot. But it's been almost four months since either of them has been in the hospital—and eight months for Violet—so that feels amazing."

"How do you and Dale do nowadays when one of them starts to get sick?"

"Better, now that we have the decision tree—the asthma protocol. But Dale still gets instantly stressed and kind of freaks out, and I just sort of... stop. I think, 'Oh no, not again.'" My shoulders slumped. "Especially if there's coughing—it's like that." I snapped my fingers.

Blair paused. "So, that's a trauma response you both are experiencing—his stress, your numbness."

I nodded, thinking she was talking about behavioral psychology—conditioned responses. Pavlov's dog salivating at the bell.

"How do you get through that initial response?"

"Just walk through the tree. It's kind of like when I was pregnant with Cody, and you told me to engage my prefrontal cortex when I felt anxious." I tapped my forehead. "Having a process to refer to—literally on paper—helps me keep going."

"Good, good. Bringing that thinking brain back online."

I agree that's what it sounded like—and, in large part, that's what it was. But what I didn't know was also worth mentioning was that, when I focused on process, the rest of me stayed shut down. And that the only vague sense I had of this going on was the overriding drive to survive, somehow, anyhow. Keep moving one foot after the other, to get out of it all.

"But it's wild, because even though they haven't been in the hospital, and everything is so much better..." I paused, somewhere between knowing whatever words I chose wouldn't be enough and worrying that they would be misunderstood. Not knowing if I should even finish the sentence. But Blair stayed silent, her eyes expectant. I exhaled. "Everything is still really hard. Or, not just hard—hard is not the right word. I can do harc—have been doing hard. It's just... too much. Like my head is being pushed in on all sides." I held my palms to the sides of my skull. "I don't know how else to describe it."

"Parenting is a lot," said Blair, letting the sentence hang in the air. "Especially with two little ones, and everything you have been through. It's ok that you're feeling it."

"That makes me think of something our HR director said to me just before I left my job. He had only been at the company a couple of months, so he didn't know anything about me. I was raving about the company, telling him how great it had been to me after Sloane died... but that, with all of the PICU hospitalizations, I always felt like I was taking some sort of advantage of the kindness. Even though I never let my work slip. Like, I was so grateful for everyone's support but couldn't trust it. Assumed compassion fatigue would set in. Anyway, he said 'It sounds like you're asking too much of yourself.' Like, that maybe I *didn't* need to be able to handle everything on my plate. Nobody had ever said anything like that to me before."

Blair mimed an epiphany, raising her eyebrows and leaning her head back, open-mouthed, as if to say, *A-haaaaa*. Instead, she said, "And what did you think of that?"

I swallowed hard, heat springing to the surface of my eyes, the depths of my belly. "I think he's probably right."

God, why did I sit in this room, I thought, seeing the little rectangular image of my camera view, the bright light over my head casting weird shadows on my reddening face. *I look like a fucking idiot.*

"If you're interested, I'd like to recommend a book."

"Always." She knew I was good at doing my homework.

"*Self-Compassion* by Kristin Neff. A lot, a lot of good stuff in there."

"I'm on it," I said from one half of my brain, the other half recalling a vague memory: I had taken a self-compassion assessment a year or two prior; I don't remember why. One of those online quizzes, but legitimate. Later, I would learn that the quiz, too, was by Dr. Neff. But the one thing I remembered about taking it: my score. 1 out of 5. Low self-compassion. Very low.

I wasn't alarmed—not even surprised. I didn't even know what self-compassion meant.

•

The Christmas before we moved to Albuquerque, my mom and one of my sisters unknowingly gave us the same book: a guide to hiking in New Mexico. It became our bible of sorts—one of those deeply personal gifts that stretches far beyond its physical dimensions. My sister was good at those, too.

It's a funny thing—hiking from a book. Most of the hikes are not actual trails, but more like parts of the wilderness that the author has explored and found something worthwhile in. Along with a crude map, a couple of grayscale photos, a snapshot of the stats—length, level of difficulty, amount of exposure, etc.—the directions for each hike are written out in paragraph form. The author educates the reader on the background of the area and the noteworthy features of the hike, casually inserting the actual steps into the narrative, as if he's walking alongside you, pointing out with an outstretched arm this sway of the land, that crumble of ruins.

The steps can be explicit or vague:

Walk two hundred meters through the arroyo until the slope becomes shallow enough to climb out.

Turn east at the cluster of hoodoos.

Walk through the meadow.

Sometimes we find our way; sometimes we don't. But that's the adventure: where we bring our unique selves into the story. Where we create something new.

It was on one of these hikes from the good book that Dale and I had found ourselves one Saturday morning in early November 2017. We had wanted something easy and close, to just get outside and stretch our legs, and we found that on the east side of the Sandias at the Golden Open Space. Throughout Albuquerque and the surrounding areas, open spaces are just that: preserved natural areas. In the 1960s, local citizens established this practice of keeping unique areas of the city's landscape free from development; each open space occupies thousands of undisturbed acres. Like a meditation for the land. Simply being. Open space.

I didn't know anything about meditation back then, but I had felt it: that when we stepped onto the trail, a month after my second miscarriage up in Santa Fe, everything before us opened and quieted. Golden autumn grass spread out in every direction; puffy white clouds poured over the mountains from the west and stretched into the blue ocean sky overhead. I had let Dale walk a few paces ahead, Leo already prancing in the distance, and I snapped a photo of the scene. They make up 5% of the shot, in the center foreground; the rest land and sky. And still when I look at this photo, in a wood and bone frame on my office shelf, I breathe easier.

As we walked—easily, lazily—through the open space, I felt willing to explore things unresolved.

"Is my sister just too busy with her kids to care?" I threw out into the stillness. "Does she not think this matters?"

They were questions that had tortured me for the ten months since my daughter had died and my sister hadn't asked me how I was doing. Out here, curving around the rim of a mesa, answers seemed more possible—and maybe, just slightly, less important.

"I don't think that's it," Dale said. "Maybe she just doesn't know how to go there with you. You guys are very different."

I suddenly wondered how we had even become sisters. Because when I said that word, back then—when she and I had gotten it tattooed on our forearms two years before—it meant something more than just parts of the same family. It meant we were the maids of honor in each other's weddings, that we had a secret language of nineties song lyrics and movie quotes. But maybe that was just it: that more often we communicated in jokes, in memories, than the directness of our lives. And that was the difference that Dale had noted: that I longed for that intimacy while she eluded it. I knew all of this, and yet, I still balked at how she hadn't been there for me in the most devastating experience of my life. That had become its own grief.

Dale and I dropped down into the arroyo seco below the mesa. The interwoven drainages created a choose-your-own-adventure phase to the hike—turn this way, then that, down, back up, around—that only seemed to lead nowhere if you were hell bent on getting somewhere. The book advised us to study the details of the overlook on the mesa, visualizing it from below so that we could find our way back when it was time.

I rewound the tape of the past ten months in my head and played it forward, rewound, played it forward, until I had enough. When we stopped for a drink of water, I said, "I need to just accept it. Accept her. Whatever the reason. I'm not going to change anyone."

Beneath the black bill of his hat, Dale looked at me with tenderness. He is so much better at forgiveness than I am.

"No, you're not," he said. "I'm sorry she hasn't been there for you like you need her."

It was those words that would stick with me, that would, in a few years, allow me to see that my sister had been a scapegoat for everything that I needed in grief and wasn't getting. Because what I needed most was permission to fall apart. To break into a thousand jagged pieces and not be lost, just held. A love so fierce that it would hold me together so that I, for once, didn't have to.

Dale, of course, had been holding me easily, tirelessly. But he wasn't the mother, the sister, the girlfriend that every other woman seemed to have, saving them over and over again. I needed someone in the lineage of womanhood—someone who knew what it was like to bleed, cramp, house a womb; to curve and swell beneath the weight of eyes, of oppression. A need that only deepened as my body fell further and further away from its own womanhood.

My mistake was in continuing to mine those same sources, for years and in new ways, still coming up dry.

In not seeing that we were all parts of the same family.

In forgetting that I was still waiting for permission to fall apart.

When we were ready to go home, the mesa wasn't hard to find again. All we had to do was look up and there it was, the rim stretching out directly before us.

The next time Blair and I met, three weeks later, I grabbed *Self-Compassion* from the corner of my desk and waved it before the camera.

"Got it," I said. "Haven't started it yet though."

"Oh, good, good," said Blair. "Tell me how things have been."

"Not too bad," I said, nodding. Flipping through a rolodex of mental images; skipping past the dark ones. "Getting a lot of writing done—I swear, I just want to do this forever. Going away—*by myself*—for the first time this weekend, up to the Santa Fe Literary Festival."

"Oooo," she crooned, one mom to another.

"I know. It's nuts. My in-laws are going to help watch the kids. And they're healthy at the moment, so that's good. Violet has been really getting into her three-nager phase—lots of big emotions, big needs. It's fun to see her develop in that way, but it's exhausting. And Cody is crawling more and starting to push his truck around. That's how Violet learned to walk, so fingers crossed. And I *finally* scheduled to get my tubes removed in August. So ready to just officially—*officially*—be done with this chapter of our lives."

Blair smiled. "Good for you."

"Thanks," I said, exhaling, dropping my shoulders. "I know we've talked about this, and you know how much it means to me. But some people just don't get it, and it blows my mind. I texted my mom, all excited, and she just wrote back with all these questions like, 'Is this what your doctor recommended? Why removed and not just tied?' and I'm just looking at my phone like, 'I am doing this for *me*. You know this—we've talked about it. *I need this.* Can't you just be happy for me?' So frustrating."

"Right? You've been pretty clear that this is something you want to do."

"It is." I lowered my eyes, sunk into my chest for a moment.

I hadn't opened the book yet, still didn't know what self-compassion meant, had no tools whatsoever, but I was unable to ignore the blazing isolation created by my own mother—which was to say, everyone in the entire world—and her inability to comprehend why I wanted to ensure that no further loss came from my womb.

Fuck that—not even comprehend. Just *care*.

It was just a moment. But it pulled me back.

"I am starting to feel like I can't talk to her about anything at all," I said, a new heat behind words I had never spoken. "After Violet's birthday party, I had decided, ok, no more hard stuff, nothing negative, because she's either going to ignore it or twist it around on me. But this

I was excited about—this was positive! So maybe just nothing that I really care about, which leaves… nothing at all. I have no interest in surface-level."

"It's good to learn what feels safe for you and what doesn't."

"Yeah, safe." My eyes drifted to my desk, its smooth, white surface. Glossy, reflecting things. "Geez, I can't even talk to my mom about meaningful stuff? How fucked up is that?"

"We don't all have the mom that we want, or that we need. But the good news is that the mother role doesn't have to be filled by your actual mother. It could be a teacher, a mentor, another relative. Even yourself."

"Oh," I said, a *whoosh* in my head pulling me up thirty-thousand feet. "Wow. Really?"

"One-hundred percent. Because those needs are real—they need to be met—but not necessarily by who you know as your mom."

I thought of the Thursday before. Dale was on a weeklong golf trip in Oregon with his dad and his brother; my mother-in-law had been helping me with the kids while he was gone. She had come over early that morning to watch Cody before his therapy session while I took Violet to school and then went for a run. Only I ended up just sitting in my car, parked at a trailhead, meditating to try to ease my throbbing head. Violet had been a disaster that morning, and I had lost it on her. Who can remember now what was said or done—there are only a thousand different versions of that scenario—but that morning, the entire situation had glommed itself onto my skull and wouldn't let go. Ten minutes before Jennifer was set to arrive, I walked back into my house with wet, red eyes.

"How was your run?" Theresa called out from the dining room. Cody was eating a snack: cubes of cheddar and round wheat crackers.

"Uhh, I didn't end up going." My voice shook. "I couldn't…"

She looked over her shoulder at me, then got up. As she walked toward where I had stopped in the kitchen, she said with a tenderness that broke me, "Oh, Alle, are you ok?"

She held out her arms, and I collapsed into them, sobbing.

"I'm trying so hard with Violet. It's so hard… so hard."

"Oh, I know, I know. She is a lot right now. But you're doin' great. You're a great mom, Alle."

She rubbed my back, and I sobbed harder, and I realized how long I had been waiting to just be held.

I told Blair about the containers—how Dr. Page and Dr. Jeffrey had felt like containers during my pregnancies. How Dale, and then later Rich, too, had been containers for my grief.

"That felt like love to me," I said. I spread my fingers, concaved my palms, and pulled my hands away from each other, as if I was stretching out the air. "Is that what it means to be a mother—to hold space for all of your child? To be bigger so that they feel safe, contained?"

Blair paused her shoulders and eyebrows at the top of a shrug. "I don't know. Is that what it means to you?"

It's a funny thing—developing self-compassion from a book. The content was part education, part implementation; part empirical research, part personal narrative; all heart and all gold.

The steps were simple, massive, and utterly foreign to me:

First recognize that you are suffering.
Then allow yourself to be moved by your own pain.
Then offer yourself warmth and sympathy.

Sitting at my desk every afternoon with a green highlighter in hand, I read and marked and occasionally looked up, across the room, and saw myself standing at the sliding door to the balcony, listening to the song of a siren, still not knowing that this was what I had been missing this whole time, but knowing that it's what cracked me open that day.

In the beginning, it all sounded so big and weird: give yourself these things you've never been given; talk to yourself in ways you've never been talked to. *How could it possibly help*, I wondered, and yet, its alienness was what drew me further into it. That and the clear and abundant truth that sat beneath the veil like a shimmering pearl: that my life as I had been living it was untenable, and this book offered me a new way of being that sounded... *good.*

Good like how it felt to be pregnant for the first time with Sloane. Good like how my body felt doing prenatal yoga with Violet. Good like the final moments I had alone with Cody in my belly. The quiet, simple, sweet goodness of caring for a being—which was inextricably part of your being, too—with all the love and tenderness they deserve.

So, I had been here before.

Children—they are a gift. Over and over and over again. If only we are willing to receive.

My angel, I called each of them now—and Leo, too—still not knowing why or what it meant, only that it felt right.

I didn't know why or what it meant that I had to force myself to do the exercises in the book, but they felt right, too. Like when I awkwardly crossed my arms over my chest and squeezed my biceps in a hug and felt myself soften into my mother's full chest. Or when I pulled three of my kids' colored chairs into a triangle in the middle of the great room and moved between them, having a conversation with different parts of myself: my inner critic in red, the one being criticized in blue, and my wise, compassionate self in yellow; eventually doubled-over in blue, unable to move, crying out into the empty room, "Why am I so hard to love?"

And on the day that *Roe v. Wade* was overturned in late June, forcing someone with a body like mine to go through all the risk and fear and intervention that a pregnancy requires, forcing kids like mine to go through all the risk and fear and intervention that survival requires, I wrote a letter to myself, as if it was from a compassionate friend, about part of me that, as the exercise prescribed, caused me to feel shame and insecurity: my body. This body that was now more mine than it was allowed to be.

Look at your face, I wrote. *I wish you could see how beautiful you are. The curiosity and love in your eyes, joy in your smile, empathy in every tiny facial muscle. Your body is nothing if not expressive.*

Look at your muscles, your bones; I wish you could see how strong you are. How the structure of your body has held grief and stress and fear—and held you up through it all. Your body is nothing if not resilient.

Look at your curves, inside and out; I wish you could see how rich you are. Milk from your breasts, a soothing sway in your hips; places for your husband's hands to lovingly hold. Your body is nothing if not life-giving.

Look at your belly, your womb; I wish you could see how powerful you are. They want control, and have at it, you say, in a fit of rage and disgust and violation; have it and everything that comes along with it: one dead infant, two miscarriages, two premature babies, six surgeries, one C-section scar, twelve weeks in the NICU, four PICU hospitalizations, four regular pediatric hospitalizations, five years of living at the edge of someone's death. Everything your body didn't choose but bore with grace. Your body is nothing if not transcendent.

So, look; really look. Soften your eyes 'till they are as tender as your own flesh. There is nothing here but love in human form.

And look I did. I pulled my face to within an inch of my bathroom mirror, stared into my own deep blue eyes, long, slow breaths fogging and fading, and for the first time, felt that I didn't need to look anywhere else.

But this was all practice—exercises from a book, on my own time. I never thought about the ability to get to this place of self-compassion in real life, in a moment, amidst everything else: monitoring illnesses, developing muscles, teaching skills, calming emotions, navigating conflict, cooking meals, cleaning messes, paying bills, bearing headaches, et cetera, et cetera. It seemed like this was separate, incompatible with and isolated from the chaos of our lives.

For all the openings that self-compassion had started to crack into my being, I never thought it could be the one thing big enough to save me. I never thought that I was doing the work so that I might know what it looked like from below. Never thought that one day, I could just look up, and there it would be, stretching out before me.

The way back.

34

The air outside had been hot and dusty for weeks, wildfires burning across northern New Mexico. In the afternoon, the heat pushed in through the windows, collected inside. Every day I fought to endure its weight for the sake of seeing the blue sky through all of my windows; every day my shoulders slumped as I pulled the shades closed in defeat. And still, during this time, everything seemed to sweat. Parenting pooled in all the uncomfortable places. My research work glistened but dried me out. Meals to viruses to meals to meltdowns, the days ran together. It was the last Saturday in July, when I was already cooked with exhaustion, that we got the text.

Violet raced her ride-on truck around the living room; Cody stood at the coffee table, moving farm animals in and out of his big plastic barn. He had just started coming down with something that morning, and every single intermittent cough split the air and tunneled right into my ear. From where I stood leaning against the back of the couch, gazing out at the haze blurring the horizon, the flash of my phone screen, forever on silent, caught my eye. No message, just a video—and I knew what it was immediately.

IknewitIknewitIknewit, I said inside, jaw tight. Long, steady exhale. I knew this day would come, and I tried to prepare for it—*I don't care, I'm happy for him*, which was, of course, true but not the whole truth—but it turned out there wasn't really anything that could ease the sting of seeing your thirteen-month-old full-term nephew walking for the first time while your twenty-one-month-old son was still holding on to the table.

Here's why: because the sting—the burn, the melt, the layers of skin peeling off—has absolutely nothing to do with the walking and everything to do with every moment that came before this one. Every moment of parenting a child that doesn't fit convention; every standard and guideline that doesn't apply; every second spent living on the fringe of normal life, gazing in at all you've lost and gazing out at the unknown territory that is yours to figure out.

"Ham is walking," I said to Dale, and for a beat, we just stared at each other.

His face—his beautiful face. I saw everything in his eyes— everything that I needed and everything that I couldn't allow myself. But also, a distance: the chasm that was Cody's development, growing ever wider between us. When I look back on that moment, and I imagine if Dale would have said something—anything—I think I might have crumpled to the floor right then and there. Instead, we dropped our eyes and hardened. We had kids to care for.

That afternoon, when the sky softened to gray and the air cooled to mild, we opened all the doors and headed onto the balcony. Earlier that summer, during monsoon season, the four of us had spent gray afternoons under the eaves, sticking our arms out into the pouring rain, letting it splatter our bare feet. I longed for more rain, felt the thirst of the earth below us, but settled for this—a small reprieve.

A drawn-out note.

Dale had the mind to bring out the bubble whale. He set the bright blue plastic fish down onto the bare slats, and uniform bubbles soon poured out of its open mouth. The kids, forever smitten with their ride-on trucks, pushed them up, down, and back around three sides of the house—Violet running at full speed, Cody tottering with care—and whenever the bubbles drifted into their driving lanes, they shrieked and giggled and tried to catch them on their fingers as they whizzed by. Leo lay down in the middle of everything, propped up on his elbows. I nearly counted the breaths when I could just sit and gaze, when no one needed me.

The sky.

The air.

A breeze blew—cool and good and cleansing, washing over my face and arms. I watched it move down the balcony—meaning I watched the bubbles and how it moved them, rushing them forward, those perfect, shimmering spheres—in smooth lines; no tumbling, no popping, no jerky moves or erratic paths. Just softly, simply: carried. And I felt it in my ears, how this was one of the most beautiful things I had seen in a long time.

How loving that force; how symbiotic that dance.

For weeks, I had been moderating online interviews for a major streaming service. It was my first time moderating since I left my full-time job, and it rushed back to me with a sweetness I had missed: hearing people's stories, guiding them to discover their truths, letting their sheer existence sink into my own; shape me, open me to the possibilities of life. Like with books, only these books I can ask questions of and they have to answer.

Which makes me wonder, if no one's asking us questions, are we ever really finding the answers of ourselves?

My last interview the day before was with a grad student in Portland, Oregon, studying social work with the aim of one day having his own movement-based outdoor therapy practice. Cool shit. I felt for him, pursuing a greater good despite being jaded by the reality that the world isn't willing to pay people like him enough to make a decent living. He found solace in listening to people play ultimate frisbee.

"It's something I wish I could be out there doing more," he said. "So, I sort of live vicariously through them instead. Sometimes I'll even put on a tournament I've already heard, just to hear the voices."

His voice, even through his microphone and out my speakers, had a quality of longing to it that told me it was going somewhere.

"What does that do for you," I asked, "to hear the voices?"

"Sometimes it distracts my busy mind—from schoolwork, from lesson plans I'm putting together—and other times it's just comforting. I can let the boring parts just play and then tune back in when I hear something exciting."

"Tell me about it being nice to have voices in the background."

He laughed. He had a strong jaw line, sharp nose. "That's kind of a deep question. I don't want to overshare."

"I'm here for it."

He settled in, pulling up from his chest, his belly. "Sometimes it can get lonely existing as a human. Thinking about life going on around you. My family lives far away and gone are the days when you just show up at someone's house and kick it. It's nice to just hear other people in the world, doing something they enjoy."

He wasn't the first in this set of interviews to speak about loneliness. But he was the most clear-eyed, the most non-sentimental. He reminded me of something I had just read in the book about one of the key components of self-compassion: mindfulness. That, if we focus only on the event itself, and not the pain caused by the event— that is, not seeing *everything* for what it is—we will overwhelm and exhaust ourselves trying to fix external problems without also tending to ourselves internally.

The rumble of truck wheels faded as my kids and husband disappeared around the far end of the balcony. Leo rolled onto his side, stretched out all four legs.

Maybe if I hadn't let that little ombre green book from Covington, Georgia just sit on my shelf all these years. Yes, meditation had become a solid daily practice—I had racked up 163 days in a row by that point—but it was still just a form of rest, of shutting off my dark head, letting my muscles melt, not exploring my internal landscape.

Afternoons like this—hell, not even whole afternoons, just mere moments when I could grab them—when no one was talking to me, crying on me, pulling at me for long enough for me to notice the magic of existence: this was the closest I got to mindfulness. And even then, I only held onto the good—the sweet fragility of the bubbles, the sheen of rainbow around their curves—and forsook the hard. The elephant sitting on my chest. My hollowed-out bones.

I thought this was enough—the best I could get.

Acceptance of this life.

Dale came back around the corner, his big dad hands clasped around Cody's chest, holding him upright, squishy legs dangling. Then he set our son down on the balcony, as if something was supposed to happen. Cody felt it, too: he stood there, frozen, legs wide and bent slightly at the knee, arms out for balance. A shit-eating grin on his face.

His face—his beautiful face.

Then he picked up one foot and stepped it forward.

The thrill that rushed through him was palpable; it dropped him to his hands and knees, still smiling. Looking at me the entire time.

He squawked, pushed his diapered butt up into the air, and stood back up, steadying himself with arms outstretched and fingers curled over the air. Smiling the whole damn time.

"Come on, buddy," I said, crawling slowly out of my chair, not wanting to throw him off. "You can do it, you can do it."

And he did. One step, then another, then two more before he collapsed onto his bottom, squealing with glee.

"You did it!" I rushed over to him, clapping my hands. "Cody, you're walking! Do you want to try again?"

And as he stood back up, and Dale and Violet swam into the picture, giving him their own congratulations, I didn't realize I was backing away until my hand caught the balcony railing. A swell hitched in my chest. And then something new happened: I felt myself push it back down, as if with the palm of my hand.

A conscious *No*.

And in that briefest of spaces—that simple awareness of the pain of the event, not just the event itself, and how I suppressed it—I felt another *No*.

No, I will not keep doing this to myself.

I dropped my shoulders, turned toward the open air beyond the railing, covered my face with my hands, and sobbed. Not because I was happy, like I told Violet when she asked, but because I was so fucking tired of life being so fucking hard for so fucking long.

It was a quick spiral, that tail-end of the thing that had been circling around me, ever-narrowing, for so long. I had fallen into its wide mouth—slowly, lazily—five years earlier, and now, having dragged me down and thinned me out, it whipped me around and around, faster and faster and faster.

I plummeted.

35

I saw a graphic recently on the internet that went something like this: a healthy person experiences something traumatic; worry and stress send them into emotional overload; former perfectly normal person, now under a pile of trauma, worry, stress, etc. etc. etc., stubs their toe, and suddenly, they are having a nervous breakdown.

Like the dog shit on my shoes in Atlanta swiftly unraveling me.

This is how experiences build, how they live on. This is how survival mode wrings you out, tells you it's done.

I knew about rock bottom. From all the research I had done on behavioral health conditions in the early days of the pandemic, I knew that it comes in a different form for everyone, and it is unknowable beforehand. For one young woman I interviewed, it was being alone in a motel room on her birthday, high on meth; for another, it was realizing she had lasting physical damage from her seventh suicide attempt. For still another, it was having a gun held to his head after a life on the streets, but only two months after his infant daughter died.

For me, it was sitting in my car, parked at a dead-end that led to a remote trailhead, two weeks after my son first walked.

It seemed as if one minute I was crying on the balcony, my face buried in my hands. And the next, five days later, I was dialing 911, apologizing to the operator because I was choking on my words—*He can't breathe, my son can't breathe*—and the next I was sitting in a hospital room, my eyes glued to my sons ribs—seeing them, really *seeing* them—

so that their rhythm started to bang back and forth inside my skull, and it was so loud, and then the next minute, it was the day before my tube removal and neither my mother nor my sisters had said one word to me about it, and I was sick with a bad cold, and no one in my house was giving me a fucking break for my fucking head that felt like it was collapsing in on itself, a black hole inside me, so I walked out the door, saying to Dale, *I need to go away for a little while*, and then the next minute—the last minute, the very last minute—I was sitting alone in my car, licking my lips, thinking past resources and that maybe I should call one of those numbers, thinking about Violet, about Cody, about Dale, about Sloane and what it was like in that hospital room with her and how so much was possible but where was any of it now—

And then, as if I was being pulled into the collapse, I suddenly felt an immense vacuous space expanding around me, stretching, stretching across my whole life, as tight and empty as my lungs in dry heat, and I burst into wracking sobs at this extreme loneliness that had been here all along but I was now hopelessly lost in.

Drowning, on dry land.

On another planet, in the twilight zone, in the middle of my very own life.

I watched myself pull out my phone and open my browser.

This is the time, I thought. *This is the time to call.*

But then louder, out of nowhere: *Dale—where was Dale?*

The first time Dale and I went down to the Gila, in June 2015, we set out to hike the Middle Fork of the Gila River. It was an eleven-mile loop that hugged the river on the out and then ascended above it on the way back. It was our first summer in New Mexico; we didn't even have Leo yet. We were carefree and in love, and we wanted adventure. Immersion. We wanted each other.

The hike started off easy, slow, the trail mostly clear with well-placed cairns and a few shallow river crossings. Tall grass tickled our shoulders for long idyllic stretches; cliffs soared above us on either side. We made a game of finding all the dark patches, the caves where things lived. The day before, we had gone to the Ancient Cliff Dwellings—

massive caves carved into the mountains where people had lived thousands of years ago. We had climbed around inside the gigantic maw, through rooms and doorways, primitive concepts of space and relations. Black soot scaled the walls to the domed ceilings. The life still there was palpable.

As we got deeper into Middle Fork, we began to blend with the surroundings. The trail only existed in patches now, the cairns few and far between. We backtracked, crossed in and out of the river, now up to our thighs, found our way over fallen trees, through dense grasses, into scratchy bushes. Ate half-melted cheese and sausage sliced with a pocketknife. Briefly got doused with rain.

At one point, I rounded a bush and nearly tripped over a dead horse, stumbling back a few steps, heart in my throat. Its head was cut off, in nearly a straight line midway down its neck, and completely missing, and yet the curves of its muscles were taut, and its golden-brown hair glistened, still so alive. For a few beats, I stood perfectly still, an unmistakable peace in the air.

The quiet of the wilderness, amidst all its bustling life, was breathtaking.

When I found Dale, we continued to move: together, apart, forward, backward, and every now and then, wondering aloud if we were truly lost, if we were even following any sort of trail, and if it was going to lead anywhere other than deeper into nowhere. Our doubt was visible, hanging beneath the chalky gray cloud cover, and yet… we kept moving. There was something else in the air, too—something more powerful. A trust, a bond. A knowing so solid it could move mountains so that we may keep finding our way.

Truthfully, I was surprised. We had been together for six years by that point, married for less than one, but still I was surprised at our partnership under the circumstances. At the ease and fluidity with which we made decisions together; the trust we had in each other when we both knew that neither of us totally knew what we were doing; our relentless commitment to do this together, or not at all. Not one flare of anger or frustration; not one cross word.

I didn't know it could be like this: love, partnership. Life. I didn't know this depth could exist. This was a dream I didn't know I had: to walk into the wilderness, hand in hand with another human being, and become one with everything. The trees, the grass, the dirt; the river, the cliffs, the sky. Each other.

When we finally landed on a solid trail, we were soaked to the bone, but nothing was crushed. If anything, we were ready for more. This whole life together.

I was sitting in my car, phone in hand, thinking of Dale and how he wouldn't tell me to lie down and rest while I was sick, when I realized I had always been pinning this vast desert of loneliness on him to fill. And he did it so well, so well—too well. But it was never his responsibility, and he was never going to be able to reach the edges, because even with the endless, unconditional love that he gave me, the love that had been missing was from myself.

I was devastatingly lonely for my own care.

My own tending. My own willingness to hold all of me.

Because, I realized, we must care about our own suffering.

My face leaky and sticky, I shoved my phone under my leg, pulled my notebook and a pencil from the bag I had thrown onto the passenger seat, and wrote, hand shaking:

I feel unwell.

It was a word I had never wanted to say because I knew I couldn't take it back, but there I was, saying what had needed to be said for years. I wrote without thinking, wrote with nothing to lose, wrote and wrote, until:

You are in pain, and you are suffering.

This is such a hard place to be.

I am so, so sorry.

You don't deserve this. You deserve light and joy and a beautiful life.

I didn't know where those words came from, but I let them sink in, down, down into my belly while breath returned to my lungs.

I do, I thought, eyes closed. *I do, I do.*

And then I pulled my phone back out from under my leg, opened my meditation app, and found that tender voice that knew everything that was going on inside of me at that moment:

I love you; I am listening, said Sarah Blondin.

When is the last time you closed your eyes and said these words to yourself? When is the last time you took the time to give to yourself what you endeavor to give to others?

...We realize we have been the one; we have always been the one...

...Let all searching outside of yourself stop here.

I wept and wept.

And the emptiness began to recede.

It sounds funny now—absurd, even, but I'm trying not to judge—that I never really knew the word *trauma* during all of this. Even when Blair said that Dale and I had trauma responses to our kids' coughing, it didn't mean anything special or extraordinary to me. This whole time I had just been calling it what I was taught: *life*.

When I told Taj this years later, he looked at me with wide eyes.

"What?" he said, his hair even grayer, now hanging beside his face, framed by the rectangular shape of his phone camera.

"Yeah," I said, "I was in a freeze state more or less the whole time. You know—fight, flight, freeze."

"Oh man. I just thought you were a badass. I always thought, 'I must be the weak one—she's over there just crushing it.'"

I thought of all those people in the days and months after Sloane died: *You're so strong. You're so amazing.*

"No, dude. I was totally numb. That's what my brain thought it had to do—to survive."

Later I would learn that this initial understanding wasn't entirely accurate—that I hadn't just been frozen but dissociated. Highly functioning in the face of trauma but emotionally absent—an adaptation from childhood that I would be unraveling for years to come. And truthfully, I still don't remember how I first came across the concept of trauma, or what made me eventually buy *The Body Keeps the Score* by Bessel van der Kolk and dive head first into trauma healing. All I know is that my newfound resource of self-compassion had created enough of a sense of safety within me for the false bottom to drop out and me to fall through.

Not to drown but to learn how to swim.

In the days and weeks that followed that afternoon in the car, after I had my fallopian tubes removed and Violet helped me recover— "You go in your potty, Mommy, and I'll go in mine, and I'll keep the door open to make sure you're ok."—I finally felt everything my protective mind hadn't allowed me to feel throughout this journey. Finally gave voice, like I did in the car, to everything that needed to be said. To myself, for myself.

And if I thought this story was no longer about grief, I was wrong. Because everything that comes out of trauma processing must be grieved. So, there I was, back in that twisty, knotted rollercoaster that I had drawn with my computer mouse for my co-workers five years prior, with all the confusing dots: sobs getting caught in my throat, hand clutching at my chest; sitting cross-legged on a couch on our deck, marveling at how beautiful the clouds were; collapsing on my bed in the middle of the afternoon, completely spent. And the chaos inside: red-hot anger at how much I could cut myself down; swells of sadness for the depths I had been brought to; rung after rung of guilt, shame, terror, and despair; and in brief moments, a new peace, like a flat silver sheet evening everything out, like forgiveness, like integration.

Grief doesn't end; it just changes.

But mostly, the process of trauma healing is a beautiful mess because it is both entirely mundane and perhaps the most profound undertaking a human could endeavor: to sit still, feel your insides, and let them breathe. Let the belly flood, let the heart split, let the throat tighten. And then listen:

What hurts?

What are you scared of?

What do you need?

All the questions I asked of people for over a decade in my job— the ones we often ask of our children, our friends, our loved ones every day—but rarely do we ever ask of ourselves.

I love you. I am listening.

As I started to write down everything that was coming up, sitting on the surface was the loss I was most conscious of but still pushed away every time I went to the grocery store or on Instagram: my lost dreams. The countdown to 40 weeks, parking in the "expecting mother" spot, maternity photos in the swaying grass of the foothills, the setting sun turning the Sandias behind us pink. Newborn photos, birth announcements, holding my wet and weighty baby to my bare chest beneath my hospital gown, sweaty locks of hair framing my face. But most of all: that full, round belly that undoubtedly my small frame would have struggled to handle but that, to me, was emblematic of motherhood.

I grieved everything that badge had always meant to me. Strength, love, the wonder of creation—since I was a little girl dreaming of my own child. And how I never got to wear it, never felt that I earned those accolades without it. Never felt like I truly *did it*—pregnancy—despite being pregnant five times.

And then, a layer deeper, was the shame I felt for not being mother enough, woman enough. Not built for this, capable of this, deserving of this role. A joke for trying to be something I wasn't.

Because even deeper, boiling in my stomach, I feared always being on the outside looking in. Forever different, forever apart—never folded into the loving arms of a circle of women, or even one.

I love you. I am listening.

Beneath those lost dreams lay the reality. Or, for me, the fact that reality had become something I no longer understood, could no longer find myself in: I grieved my lost footing. I knew this, had given it a name—the twilight zone—but I saw now that naming it, owning it, had only kept me from reckoning with it.

I grieved how impossible life felt after Sloane died. How it was up and down and around and in outer space and underground. How it was not only unfamiliar and unreliable, but how much of it had lost meaning, too—stories, statistics… even my own existence. And then how that impossible reality continued to devolve further down the rabbit hole with every impossible situation we were faced with, every impossible decision we had to make.

And then deeper was the shame I felt for being so lost. For not being more solid, more clear-eyed; not knowing how to handle this hard path.

Because even deeper, like a vacuum in my chest, I feared never being grounded again. Never landing on more than a fleeting sense of stability, sanity, security in this new world that couldn't be undone. Losing my grip on life—and *my* life—forever.

Suicidality was a unique pain all its own.

Then, there was a heaving: of shame, confusion, gratitude, for Violet's lips turning blue and giving me my first glimpse into how this unreal life could become real and rich and good if it was felt enough, seen enough, loved enough.

I love you. I am listening.

But I also saw how that alien life had protected me. My lost innocence after my first child dying also meant losing my ability to see what might look horrific in another life: miscarriage, high-risk pregnancy, premature birth. Because they are horrific, no matter what life you're living.

I grieved, plain and simple, just how awful it all was. The devastation of pregnancy loss, the terror of babies not yet ready for this world, and how I had taken that suffering for granted because it wasn't my dead child in my arms. But the truth was that all of it had still taken the breath from my lungs, trapped it somewhere deep: the blood, the tissue; the tubes, the incubators. All the tiny bodies that I loved with my whole being, struggling, hurting.

Then deeper was the shame of feeling like I didn't deserve support even in these better outcomes. That I had to be grateful, not hurt; capable, not needy.

Because even deeper, like a well in my gut, I feared no one caring. About me, my needs, my losses. That we all only get one tragedy, and I already had mine, so if I asked for more support, then I became the needy girl, and—*and*—I would get my needs rejected.

I love you. I am listening.

It became impossible to escape the truth of what actually happened. The things that, truly, only my body knew, and my mind had been wearing itself out trying to keep me from knowing: that I nearly lost all of my children. That the loss of life didn't just live in Sloane, but in Violet, in Cody, and as their mom, in me, too.

I grieved how close we had all been to death. How chaotic and violent Violet's birth was, being ripped from my womb; but what was also true: that had she stayed, with an abrupted placenta, she would have died. How paralyzing and fearful Cody's pregnancy was, being held together by a single thread; but what was also true: that had he come too soon, he would have died. And how that proximity to death, for so long, robbed me of so much.

Then deeper was the shame of opening so many lives to harm. Of believing the statistics and the procedures when maybe I shouldn't have; of trying my damnedest for them but still placing them in jeopardy. Of writing on sheets of paper torn out of a notebook and glued into Sloane's scrapbook: *I couldn't save you—I'm so sorry that I couldn't save you.*

Because even deeper, in the marrow of my bones, I still feared death breathing down my children's necks. Every 911 call, every hospitalization, the fear was there.

I listened to it, and I listened to it, but death still felt too tangled up with life for me to release it.

I love you. I am listening.

And through all of this—the journey, the losses upon losses—was the searing pain of isolation. I had Dale, and I had my in-laws, my doctors, and a handful of friends, but none of them was inside my body, experiencing what I was experiencing.

I wasn't even there—the deepest loneliness of all.

That grief would continue to sit on my chest like an elephant—big, gray, unable to forget—until, in time, I blew the doors off my whole life, from before all of this ever happened, and discovered how I became that way in the first place. But that is another book entirely.

"Let's see the incisions," said Dr. Page, standing over me. I was lying on my back on an exam table—my post-op appointment, somewhere in the blur that time had become in trauma recovery. I lifted my shirt, tucked it against my ribs.

She leaned in, pushed gently on my belly with her fingertips. The surgical tape had already fallen off two of the half-inch cuts, was still clinging to the third, at the belly button. Soon they would be a constellation of scars.

"Everything is looking great," she said. The corners of her eyes pinched in a smile, the rest of her face still behind a mask. "How has recovery been?"

"Great," I said. "Seriously such a huge relief, to finally be done with all this."

"I know there can be a lot of emotions after a procedure like this."

"Yes!" I knew we were probably talking about different things, but I wanted her in this, even if she didn't know it. "I can't believe it. The emotional release has been *wild*. Just so much—so much that I didn't realize I had been holding onto."

"Yeah, of course—you've been through so much."

I still fucking loved her with an ache.

She moved over to the counter, picked up a manila folder. "Do you want to see the pictures I took while I was in there?"

I straightened my shirt and sat up as she pulled out a stack of glossy paper, each page tiled with six images. My insides in red, pink, white; round organs and webbed veins. She walked me through each one.

"I removed as much scar tissue as I could," she said. "And see this tissue here?" Several images showed a thin, opaque matter stretching between pink masses. "This is where some organs had gotten stuck together a bit, so I cut that away."

"How does that happen?"

"Things can get moved around during a C-section. One of your tubes had been pushed up against this wall, and then there was some other bunching over here."

I looked at the photos, listened to the rest of her play-by-play. Gloriously stuck on the infinite wonder that was my body.

The bull, finally stopping to see the view.

36

Respiratory distress is like drowning," the attending physician explained to the student shadowing him.

He was chatty, this doctor in a bandana covered in cartoon characters. He had seen our kids before; I remembered him sitting down next to me on the built-in bench one day in June the year before, when Cody lay in a fog of oxygen, and when he asked how I was doing—sincerely, his tone dropping its overt garrulousness—all I wanted was for him to leave. Now, at the beginning of September 2022, watching an oxygen-tethered Cody sit on the floor of a pediatric room and stack wooden blocks, I found his presence comforting.

"If you were out in the middle of the ocean," he went on, "struggling to stay afloat, your body would be working really hard, just to get nowhere." He paddled his hands like a dog. "Over time, as you kept working that hard, your body would get tired. And then eventually, too tired to keep going. And it would start to shut down." He looked at Cody. "So, when a kiddo is in respiratory distress, when his lungs are working that hard just to breathe, we have to get him support before they get too tired and shut down."

I had read somewhere—maybe in *Self-Compassion*—that hearing your story played back to you, as if it were happening to someone else, can help you see it in a new way. Force you to witness the suffering you had refused to allow. Show you the precise level of your depth.

It is terrifying, and it is freeing.

I don't even remember what made Cody so upset later that afternoon, but whatever it was, it assuredly wasn't really that, but instead the combination of being stuck inside four walls, poked and prodded and stickered, pulling for breath, and generally, being almost two years old. That much I understood.

I had tried everything—held him, rocked him, talked to him, gave him different toys—and he had squirmed through it all, screaming, thrashing, yanking out his nasal cannula and smacking my hands when I put it back in.

"I don't know what he needs," I said, when a nurse came in. I sat on the floor with Cody jerking back and forth in my lap, nearly having to shout over his screams and through my mask. "He's been doing this for fifteen straight minutes already. This is so unlike him."

"Does he need a snack?" she asked. "I could get some graham crackers."

I looked up at the rolling tray table, an open cellophane wrapper sitting at the edge. Half a graham cracker still in there.

"I don't think so? He was eating them earlier, but then he didn't want anymore."

"Ok, I'll go and get some more just in case."

She left the room, and I laid Cody on the floor, folding a blanket beneath him so that he didn't hurt himself. I didn't feel good about it, but my arms needed a break; he was strong and wrangling him was exhausting. The nurse came back in and set a handful of individually-wrapped crackers on the table.

"You know, if it weren't for the size of his head," she said, "I wouldn't even know he was a preemie. How early was he?"

"29 weeks."

"Wow. He's doing amazing. You guys must be doing a really great job with him."

His pediatrician had told us something similar at his one-year check-up almost a year before: that we were—quote—awesome parents and that most really struggle with a child that premature, to do everything he needs. Now I could see that I hadn't really heard him at the time—that the constant tirade of grief, shame, and fear from my internal voices overrode everything.

"Thanks," I said, half-smirking and tilting my head toward a screaming Cody. "I'm trying."

And then, as she walked back out of the room, I suddenly knew what to do. I folded Cody's writhing body into my arms, muscled my way up to standing, and then slid him into a cradle hold so that I could get as much of my arms around him as possible, hugging him to my chest hard. Muscles flexed, joints locked. Firm containment, like the walls of the womb, our hands pressing down on his limbs in the incubator. Safety.

Within minutes, his cries calmed to whimpers. He was a wet mess—sweat soaking his hair, his splotchy face burrowed into my bicep—and heavy in my arms, and then heavier and wonderfully heavier still, as he fell asleep.

It sounds like just remembering something I learned long ago, but it was more than that. It was pulling a thread through a tiny hole, anchoring it with a solid knot, connecting a beginning to a present. It was acknowledging that the horrific circumstances of my children's births had prepared me for so much more than I had been willing to accept. It was, finally, gratitude for my own depth.

"I think you're on to something there," Jennifer said two weeks later, when she and Bea were in my living room for Cody's annual assessment, and I told her what had happened in the hospital. That extreme kind of meltdown had happened two more times since, and each time, I surprised myself with my patience and compassion in calming him down.

"It sounds like he is becoming so dysregulated that he needs a really intense form of care to cut through," she continued.

I get that, I thought.

"Well, he is doing amazing," said Bea, flipping the cover over her tablet and setting it in her lap. "Looking back on his scores from a year ago, I can't believe he is where he is."

Jennifer turned to me. "You have worked so hard."

It was almost too much. This white whale that I had been chasing for two years—needing to know that Cody would be ok—now coming ashore, landing at my feet. *It's too big, it's too big,* I wrote in my journal hours later, sitting at my desk, unable to do anything else. Cody had gotten a full pass: no notes, no follow-ups. And I couldn't seem to move on from it.

That's what you learn in trauma recovery—that the only arrival is again and again. In each new moment, each new sensation: what wants to speak now. Because we all live a thousand births and deaths, and if we're not there to witness every one, then we are nowhere at all.

I love you. I am listening.

I closed my eyes. Belly flopping like a fish. Chest swelling. And I felt nothing but love—the biggest love. It moved through me like one massive wave, rising, rising, filling out my kneecaps, my fingertips, but also lengthening, deepening, back and down, through space and time. It was glorious, the glow of something otherworldly, and just as it filled me to the crown of my head, my face broke into an open-mouthed smile, the muscles in my cheeks pulling back, back, and tears flowing down my cheeks.

This—this love, this peace, this joy.

This was how it felt when Sloane was born and died.

When that hit me, I opened my eyes and looked out the window, as if looking for her. Where my gaze landed—on a brush of white cloud, feathered like an angel's wing in the blue expanse—only made me weep harder, my heart squeezing inside.

And then suddenly, I felt brought to my knees at the foot of all this wreckage. I saw what the frozen state of trauma I had been in since first experiencing that feeling had resulted in: the loss of love.

I grieved everything I hadn't been able to give my living children. The space between us where intense love should have been. In my belly, in the NICU, in the PICU; on every normal day in-between. All those times that my mind rushed to protect me from heartache when it sensed a flash of that love—but all it really did was leave both me and my children wanting, wanting.

Deeper was the shame of not being the mother that Violet and Cody deserved in their most formative years—the years when that rupture between mother and child is felt deepest.

And still deeper, like a raw scrape the length of my torso, I feared that the damage I caused had left them with an unbearable inner loneliness.

I love you. I am listening.

When the heart of fall came, and all six of us—me, Dale, our kids, and my in-laws—piled into our car in the dark of five-thirty a.m. and drove to Balloon Fiesta, where Violet and Cody gleefully shoved foil-wrapped breakfast burritos in each other's faces, and we all turned our heads up to the sky dappled with white clouds and colorful balloons, I began to ease into a life crafted more out of love than fear.

This—isn't this always the dream.

It felt like stepping into one of those charming, oversized baskets: a container that would allow me to fly as I opened to the hardest phase of trauma recovery.

Forgiveness.

Laying bare all of the emotions that had been locked away inside me for so long had been overwhelming but almost… impartial. As if they existed separately from me, despite their wreaking havoc on my body during both their storage and their release. But forgiveness— forgiveness felt like extending a hand to all of this, folding it back in, allowing its footprints to remain. Acceptance. Integration.

I read somewhere once that truly accepting a situation meant no longer wishing it was different. Not necessarily liking or wanting the reality but not resisting any part of it either.

How could I not feel resistant to death?

It would take me until an afternoon in mid-January—Sloane's sixth birthday—to find out.

37

How are you doing?" I said quietly, folding Sienna, still our only babysitter, into a hug on the threshold between my kitchen and my dining room. She sniffled, and I held my belly taut.

"Okay, I guess," she said when we parted, looking over her shoulder where her son, now seven, was racing cars across the living room carpet. "I really scared everyone—including him."

When I had texted her the week before to see if she could watch the kids today—Sloane's birthday—I had asked how her holidays were.

Life's been very hard lately, she had written. *I spent the first days of the new year in the hospital for feeling suicidal. Now I'm just trying to love myself and be the best mom I can be.*

I had told her I could relate. Our stories were very different—the surface level that I knew of hers was that her husband had up and left around the start of the pandemic and was nowhere to be found, leaving her unable to serve him divorce papers and collect child support, so she had been single-parenting on nanny and babysitting jobs for going on three years—but we were both just everyday people trying to live with the heartache of life. And moms, no less.

"I'm so sorry you are going through this," I said.

She began to cry. "Everything has just been so hard for so long. I didn't feel like I could keep going."

"I know—you've had so much going on. And you're doing everything yourself. It's too much."

"I'm just thankful to be here." Her son, who had asked about his dad for the first six or seven months he was gone and then abruptly stopped, sidled up to her. She ruffled his thick, black hair and wiped her eyes.

When the paved street turned to wild trail, I heard the crunch of dry winter dirt under my boots. The section of the foothills around the corner from our house is a small, narrow canyon—by small and narrow, I mean straight up fourteen hundred feet over three miles, with the mouth spanning over six hundred feet—and tucked away from the more popular areas, so it often feels like my own private trail. I had been spending a lot of time there lately, the air of the cooler months refreshing and alive, the shape of the land like two cupped hands coming together, holding me.

Dale and I were supposed to be hiking together—with Leo, into the Sandias, for Sloane's birthday—but we somehow got on different pages: him wanting to take a longer nap, me wanting to do a longer hike. I left in a huff, feeling pulled toward the mountains, sleepy husband be damned. But before I did, I slipped *Self-Compassion* onto the coffee table next to the couch where Sienna sat while the kids napped.

"Just if you want," I said. "It really helped me."

By the time Leo and I got to the trail, I had cooled. The sky was covered in a thick pelt of gray, the air near freezing. And yet, I walked with an eagerness. The sound of my boots on the gravelly trail gave a rhythmic pulse to the dead yellow brush, the woody skeletons of the cholla, and before long, the heat coming off my skin made the whole canyon feel like one thrumming body.

Its beat: *Second chance. Second chance.*

The phrase kept drumming in my head, along with the events of the afternoon before. It was a Saturday, and I had been lying on my bed at midday, meditating while the kids napped. I had been steadfastly meditating daily, and more often with just a timer than a guided practice, and deep into a twenty-minute session, deliciously at peace, I saw something. It seemed like it appeared before my closed eyes: a girl, about the age of six, in a knit purple sweater and blue jeans, running across my field of vision.

Sloane.

And before I knew it, I had pushed my chest upward and heard myself say: *Come; come rest with me.*

That would have been enough—more than enough—the perfect bliss of whatever that was.

But then after the bell sounded and I rolled out of bed, I heard Cody cry out from his room. Both he and Violet were solid two-hour nappers; he had been asleep for less than one. When I went up to his room, he had a woozy insistence that I hold him, otherwise crying in a half-sleep delirium.

He had never done this before.

I brought him down to the living room, slouched down on the couch, and let him lay on me. Within minutes, he was sound asleep, his face stuck to my chest, his body sunk into mine. I inhaled deeply—the breath and skin and sweat of a living child, slightly sour but rich with life. And then I remembered what I had said.

Come; come rest with me.

Later, when I told Dale what happened, tears sprung to his eyes.

"What?" I asked.

"Just that," he said, shaking his head. "'Come rest with me.'"

There's a lot that I don't know. And what I had realized by then is that there's a lot that I don't need to know. But when it comes, I will take it.

Which is how I got to thinking, with my child sleeping on my chest: *This feels like a second chance.*

Which is how I got to realizing, at the top of the climb in the canyon, that I could accept all of this.

That even though death had felt like a closed door, lifting my resistance to it could open that door again, and wider than I had ever imagined. To whatever had happened the day before, which could only feel like the beginning of a beautiful new relationship with my first-born, and with life itself.

I sat down on a wide flat rock, soaking in the air. Leo sat watch at my feet. The cold on my cheeks was bliss; the silence in the canyon walls, the dead cholla, utter peace. My head was so quiet.

I took breath after breath, minute after minute, and saw Sloane's face in a rock, in the clouds, in the edges of the cliffs. And breath after breath, slowly at first, and then swiftly, and then with a mighty force, forgiveness coursed through my veins.

I forgave my anger for protecting my sadness; my sadness for protecting my shame; my shame for protecting my fear; and my fear for protecting me until I could find my own hand in the dark and learn to hold it all.

And then I wept, and it began to snow.

38

The new room was on the third floor and catty-corner to another wing of the hospital, so that the view out the window looked up a soaring tower. Its face was covered in seamless windows, the reflection of the solid sky and cotton-ball clouds nearly unbroken. Sun rays drifted in and out.

Violet slept soundly while I lay beside her in the bed. I had just read her a story from *Moonbeams*—my own copy from when I was a girl, familiar smears of nail polish on the cover, a drawing of two cats pointing up at a round moon, its beam shining back at them. I held the closed book against my hip, fingers curled around the edge. Legs stretched out long. Ankles crossed above my blue Vans.

Almost two years since she had last been here, and some parts were the same: the meaty scent of her sweaty head; the stickers on her round cheeks. But then also her soft, strong arms that could climb the monkey bars solo—forwards and backwards. Her nails that we had just started painting—*in a patter-in*, she would request, which meant alternating colors across her growing fingers. And her face, that looked more and more like her dad's, but when I paused for longer and watched the way her skin moved when she smiled, how her eyes gazed out from somewhere deeper, also felt like looking at myself.

I didn't know it yet, but that evening, Dale and Cody would carry a Dion's pizza—all pepperoni and half green chile—through the hospital, where visitors were no longer limited and nobody had to wear masks, and into this room. The bed would get the open pizza box while the four of us found other places to sit: Dale and Violet on the foldout sofa, me on the floor, Cody walking around, pushing the buttons on the bed, moving it up and down.

But what I knew right then was that this chapter of our lives was over. Because even though we were there, still, I was there for the very first time, writing new six-word sentences. *Grief doesn't end; it just changes*—that was still true. But bald and free and without all the heavy punctuation, so were:

We must care about our suffering.

Our resources must outweigh our pain.

And: *Life is meant to be witnessed.*

It is in the witnessing of our own lives, in their entirety, that we come alive. It is in the witnessing that we stay alive.

Lying next to my daughter in a hospital room, I closed my eyes. Listened to the plinking water. The soft purr of breath.

Epilogue

In the final days of penning this story, I vacillated between flying to the moon and crawling under a rock. I was on Violet about everything: getting dressed in the morning, eating the dinner I made her, the volume and tone of her voice. I also laughed until I ached as Cody sang "Let it Go" and threw himself onto his jade green beanbag chair over and over. And then, the morning after I wrote the final words, I woke up with a pool of grief in my chest.

I had known it was coming. But I didn't dread it. Instead, in the blue hour of morning, I sat in that pool, comforted by its presence.

Grief: my dear, old friend.

Because even our stories we must grieve and let go. Place them into a woven basket and let them rise on their own hot breath, so that when they fly free, we may see their true nature: one beautiful piece in an ever-shifting mosaic, receding into the sky.

Resources

The following is a list of specific resources that I have found helpful during the timeframe of this story and after in my ongoing recovery. May they open doors to your own resources and healing:

Trauma and Healing

The Body Keeps the Score: Brain, Mind, and Body in the Healing of Trauma
by Bessel van der Kolk, M.D.

No Bad Parts: Healing Trauma & Restoring Wholeness with the Internal Family Systems Model
By Richard C. Schwartz, Ph.D.

Trauma Alchemy: Transform Hardship, Stress, and Trauma into Your Best Life Through Yoga
by SaraBethYoga

Compassion, Love, and Acceptance

Self-Compassion: The Proven Power of Being Kind to Yourself
by Kristin Neff, Ph.D.

Radical Acceptance: Embracing Your Life with the Heart of a Buddha
by Tara Brach, Ph.D.

Needy: How to Advocate for Your Needs and Claim Your Sovereignty
by Mara Glatzel

Grief and Loss

Option B: Facing Adversity, Building Resilience, and Finding Joy
by Sheryl Sandberg and Adam Grant

Finding Meaning: The Sixth Stage of Grief
by David Kessler

The Unspeakable Loss: How Do You Live After a Child Dies?
by Nisha Zenoff, Ph.D.

Reproductive Trauma

Early: An Intimate History of Premature Birth and What it Teaches us About Being Human
by Sarah DiGregorio

I Had a Miscarriage: A Memoir, A Movement
by Jessica Zucker

Acknowledgements

First, thank you to everyone at the long-tail of this book thing: my mom for loving me enough when I was twelve to send my first manuscript, in multi-colored Comic Sans, by mail off to six publishing houses; Molly Templeton, who graciously responded to such a query with kindness and encouragement in a mailed letter; Steve van Dam, my high school freshman English teacher, who told me my writing would be sold at Borders (lol) one day; Patrick Kawahara, who had a melo like me and read and championed every word I wrote as an angsty teenager; and Monika Grzesiak, who recited my words by memory, in the kitchen of our Austrian dorm, just when I was at the edge and needed a lifeline. Writing saved my life; I am sure those stories will be in the next book.

And to those who were a lifeline on this reproductive thing: thank you to Dr. Page, Dr. Jeffrey, Ethan, Blair, and all of our doctors and nurses in triage, labor & delivery, the NICU, and the PICU, for showing me what it means to be seen on a journey like ours. To my dad, thank you for being there in the days before, the day of, and the days after Sloane died; you carried me in a way I didn't know I needed.

Now, I'm just gonna be real: I don't know if this book would have happened without The Book Incubator. For more reasons than I can even name, but mostly for its extreme amount of heart. Thank you to the entire TBI team for your enthusiastic support; to my early readers, Angela Yazbek, Cat Giste, and Ashley Strosnider, for your astute observations; and to Joselin Linder and Rufi Thorpe for your sage advice and willingness to be real. Thank you to Paloma Griffin Hebert,

Heidi Spinella, and the entire mastermind community for letting me experiment with sharing pieces of this story aloud and have it be received warmly. Thank you especially to my mentees who have been my biggest cheerleaders throughout the publication process; you know who you are, and it is the highest honor to be on your journey with you, and you on mine. To Sue Procko, thank you for your extreme generosity in getting this book to the right people. And above all, thank you to Mary Adkins for just about everything: your heart, your genius, your fire; your words, your courage, your trust. You are the wonder I've been hoping to run into all my life.

To Fletcher Cartwright, thank you for listening, reading, and making me into the person I needed to be in order to share this story; there is no gratitude big enough.

Thank you to my best friends: Carey Lefkowitz and Mike Farkas for always being my big brothers; Missi Lockwood and Jenevieve Hutchison, for twenty years of unbreakable friendship and your unwavering belief in me; and Jenny Bremer, for being absolutely everything that you are and carrying me through this story, while I was breaking and while I was putting myself back together.

To my in-laws, thank you for caring, listening, and supporting us tirelessly. You've loved me better than I could have ever imagined; there are no better parents or grandparents than the two of you.

To my kids, Sloane, Violet, and Cody, thank you for turning my world upside down in all the right ways—the ways that only each of you could because of your unique magic. As difficult as this story was to live through, I would do it again and again just to know each of you. I don't know how I got so lucky to be your mom, but I promise I will always admit my mistakes (there have been so many) and see you for the gold that you are.

And finally, to Dale—forever Dale. This story is for me and all the other women out there who get it, but really, it's for us—the fire that only we have walked through and been forged by, the white-water rapids that only we have had to navigate, time and again. If I had to live this life, I'm glad it was with you—scared to death, a couple of kids just tryna save each other; they should've seen us in color.